Her Majesty's Minister

by

William Le Queux

Her Majesty's Minister
by William Le Queux

ISBN: 978-93-59958-68-2

Published by

DOUBLE 9 BOOKS

2/13-B, Ansari Road
Daryaganj, New Delhi – 110002
info@double9books.com
www.double9books.com
Tel. 011-40042856

ABOUT THE AUTHOR

Anglo-French journalist and author William Tufnell Le Queux was born on July 2, 1864, and died on October 13, 1927. He was also a diplomat (honorary consul for San Marino), a traveler (in Europe, the Balkans, and North Africa), a fan of flying (he presided over the first British air meeting at Doncaster in 1909), and a wireless pioneer who played music on his own station long before radio was widely available. However, he often exaggerated his own skills and accomplishments. The Great War in England in 1897 (1894), a fantasy about an invasion by France and Russia, and The Invasion of 1910 (1906), a fantasy about an invasion by Germany, are his best-known works. Le Queux was born in the city. The man who raised him was English, and his father was French. He went to school in Europe and learned art in Paris from Ignazio (or Ignace) Spiridon. As a young man, he walked across Europe and then made a living by writing for French newspapers. He moved back to London in the late 1880s and managed the magazines Gossip and Piccadilly. In 1891, he became a parliamentary reporter for The Globe. He stopped working as a reporter in 1893 to focus on writing and traveling.

CONTENTS

Chapter One
His Excellency

"Then, plainly speaking, the whole thing remains a mystery?"

"Absolutely," I responded. "All my efforts have unfortunately failed."

"And you entertain no suspicion of anyone?"

"None whatever."

"Not of that woman Yolande—or whatever her name is?"

"Certainly not of her," I answered quickly. "She would assist us, if necessary."

"Why are you so sure of that? She has only been in Paris a week."

"Because I happen to know her."

"You know her!" exclaimed His Excellency, unclasping his thin white hands and leaning across his big writing-table—a habit of his when suddenly interested. "Is she a personal friend of yours?"

I hesitated for a moment; then replied in the affirmative.

"Where did you know her?" he inquired quickly, fixing me with that sharp pair of black eyes that shone behind the zone of soft light shed by the green-shaded reading-lamp upon the table. He was sitting in the shadow, his thin, refined face ashen grey, his hair almost white. The one spot of colour was the fine star of Knight Grand Cross of the Bath glittering on the breast of his braided diplomatic uniform. Lord Barmouth, British Ambassador to the French Republic, had just returned from the President's reception at the Elysée, and had summoned me for consultation.

"Well," I responded, "I knew her in Rome, among other places."

"H'm, I thought as much," he remarked in a dry, dubious tone. "I don't like her, Ingram—I don't like her;" and I knew by the impatient snap of the Ambassador's fingers that something had displeased him.

"You've seen her, then?"

"Yes," he answered in an ambiguous tone, taking up a quill and making what appeared to be geometrical designs upon his blotting-pad. "She's good-looking—uncommonly good-looking; but I mistrust her."

"It is part of our creed to mistrust a pretty woman," I remarked with a smile; for, as everyone knows, the fair sex plays a prominent part in the diplomacy of Europe. "But what cause have you for suspicion?"

He was silent for a moment; then he said:

"You were not at the ball at the Austrian Embassy the night before last, I believe?"

"No, I was not back from London in time," I replied. "Was she there?"

"Yes. She was dancing with Hartmann, and they were speaking of you. I was chatting with Olsoufieff, and distinctly overheard your name mentioned."

"With Hartmann!" I repeated. "That's curious. He is scarcely a friend of ours."

"I consider the circumstance suspicious, judged by the light of recent events," he said. "Remember that the cause of our piece of ill-fortune still remains a mystery, and the stroke of diplomacy that we intended to effect as a coup against our enemies has, by the dastardly betrayal of our secret, placed us in a very unenviable position. This untoward incident has entirely checkmated us."

"I fully realise our critical position," I said seriously, "and I have done my utmost to discover the truth. Kaye has been active night and day."

"Nevertheless, I fear that at Downing Street they will say hard things of us, Ingram;" and Her Majesty's representative sighed heavily, resting his weary head upon his hand.

The Ambassador's office was indeed a very thankless one, while my own position as second secretary of the Paris Embassy was a post not to be envied, even though it is popularly supposed to be one of the plums of the diplomatic service. With Paris full of spies endeavouring to discover our secrets and divine our instructions from Downing Street, and the cabinet noir ever at work upon our correspondence, it behoved us to be always on the alert, and to have resort to all manner of ingenious subterfuges in order to combat our persistent enemies.

The war-cloud hangs over Europe always. The mine is laid, and the slightest spark may fire it. The duty of the diplomatist is to intrigue so as to prevent that spark. It is the intrigue that is difficult, for counter-plots are met with everywhere. The power of England is feared; hence her isolation.

Those who live at home at ease think little of the small band of Englishmen in each of the capitals who, living ever upon the edge of a volcano, are straining every nerve to preserve the peace of Europe. How often the stability of empires trembles in the balance the British public little dreams. "The European Situation" is a stock heading in the London newspapers, but fortunately the journalists never know the secrets of our embassies, otherwise the world would very often be scared. Many a time in my own diplomatic career in Rome, in Brussels, and in Vienna, had I remained awake at night, fearing on the morrow a declaration of war; yet the chiefs under whom I have worked—those honest, upright, valiant servants of Queen and country—had skilfully evaded the threatened danger, and Europe remained in ignorance of how terribly near it had been to the clash of arms.

That night, as I sat with the chief, a trusted servant of Her Majesty, in his handsome private room in the Embassy, I knew that war was in the air. The responsibility resting upon him was of a sort to involve the prestige of the Queen's Empire and the lives of thousands of her valiant sons. An ill-advised despatch, a hasty word, or an injudicious attitude would inevitably mean the disastrous explosion so long feared—the great European war that prophets have been predicting ever since the downfall of the French Empire.

Paris that July night was stifling. To us the tension of the day had been terrible. The catastrophe so long feared seemed now upon us. There was a breathless calm in the air outside, foreboding a storm.

"Has Kaye absolutely nothing to report?" asked His Excellency, at last breaking the silence.

"He returned from Madrid at nine o'clock to-night. His journey there was futile."

"Ah!" exclaimed His Excellency, whose thin lips closed tightly again.

Through the years that I had served under him in Rome and afterwards in Paris I had never before seen him outwardly betray the slightest apprehension. So skilled was he as a diplomatist that his sangfroid was always perfect. His motto—one that he had often impressed upon me—was that the British lion should always remain fearless of his enemies. But now, for the first time, he was plainly agitated, dreading that war might result.

"Get me out the special cipher-book," he said hoarsely at last. "I must telephone to Downing Street."

In obedience I rose, opened with the key upon my chain the big safe, and took out the small morocco-bound volume containing the secret cipher by means of which His Excellency could communicate with Her Majesty's

Secretary of State for Foreign Affairs—a book supplied only to ambassadors themselves; and, because it is kept locked, its contents are never seen even by the staff of an embassy.

His Excellency unlocked it with his own key, took up his quill, and after searching here and there through the pages, commenced writing a bewildering row of letters and numerals intermingled, while in the meantime I had gone to the telephone instrument at the opposite end of the room and "rung up" London, until there came an answering voice from one of the night staff of the Foreign Office.

"Hulloa! I'm Ingram, of the Paris Embassy. Who are you?" I asked.

In response came a password by which I knew I was actually speaking with Downing Street.

"Is the Marquess in London, or at Alderhurst, to-night?"

"Alderhurst. He left town this afternoon."

"Then put me on there for an important despatch."

"All right," was the response; and some five minutes later the tiny bell rang, with an inquiry from the private secretary of the great statesman as to what I wanted.

I answered; then, His Excellency having risen and handed me the slip of official paper on which he had printed the cipher figures heavily with his quill, I prefaced the message by the usual formal announcement:

"From Lord Barmouth, Paris, to the Most Noble the Marquess of Malvern, London. July 12th, 1:30 a.m."

Then in continuation I read slowly and distinctly each letter and numeral, the secretary at Alderhurst afterwards repeating the whole message, so that there should be no possibility of mistake.

Nearly a quarter of an hour elapsed, during which time His Excellency, with his hands behind his back, paced feverishly up and down the room. Of the nature of that despatch I was in utter ignorance, but from his manner it was evident that the problem was one vital to the interests of the British Empire. By night, as well as by day, those responsible for the maintenance of the prestige of England as the first Empire of the world are always active. How little the public knows of the stealthy, treacherous ways of modern diplomacy, of the armies of spies seeking always to plot and counter-plot, of the base subterfuges employed by certain noted foreign diplomatists, or of the steady perseverance of the Queen's representatives at the Courts of Europe! And how little, I fear, they care!

To most people the diplomatic career is synonymous with an easy occupation in which the wearing of a uniform and the attendance at brilliant functions are the greatest inconveniences. The newspapers flippantly criticise our actions in leading articles, and declare that our diplomacy is utterly worthless beside that of Germany, Russia, or France. Those who write, as well as those who read, never reflect that our chief duty is to foil the provocations offered to us by the Powers who are anxious for war. Every British Ambassador at a foreign Court had been told from the lips of his beloved Sovereign—now, alas! deceased—that he must prevent war. That instruction was to him as sacred as a religion.

"The President talked for twenty minutes to-night with de Wolkenstein," observed His Excellency, halting suddenly and facing me. "I wonder if they know anything in Vienna?"

"I think not," I replied. "I met Count Berchtold in the Grand Café purposely this evening, and he made no mention of anything to lead me to believe that the secret was out in that direction."

"If it is out, then it has been circulated by our friends in the Rue de Lille," he said, meaning the German Embassy.

"Perhaps," I responded. "But I hardly think that Count de Hindenburg would care to imperil his position by so doing. He would rather endeavour to assist us in this affair, because the interests of England and Germany are entirely mutual in this matter."

"I tell you, Ingram," he cried angrily—"I tell you that this dastardly piece of trickery is some woman's work!"

As he spoke, the door suddenly opened, and there burst into the room a tall girlish figure in a pretty toilette of turquoise chiffon, wearing an open cape of handsome brocade about her shoulders.

"O father!" she cried merrily, "we've had such an awfully good time at the Baroness's!" Then, next instant, astonished by his words, she drew back in quick surprise.

"What trickery is a woman's work?" she asked, glancing inquiringly at me.

"Nothing, my dear," His Excellency hastened to reply, placing his thin hand tenderly upon her shoulder—"nothing, at least, that concerns you."

"But you are not well!" she cried in alarm. Then, turning to me, said: "Look, Mr Ingram, how pale he is!"

"Your father is rather overburdened by important business," I replied.

Her face assumed a puzzled expression. Sibyl, the pretty, dark-haired daughter of Lord Barmouth, was acknowledged on all sides to be more than usually beautiful, and was the pet of diplomatic Paris. With her mother she went everywhere in that dazzling vortex of gaiety, in which the diplomatist accredited to France is bound to move. Ah! that glare and glitter, that constant whirl, that never-ceasing music! How weary I was of it all, and how it jarred upon me!

And why? Well, to speak the truth, I myself had an affair of the heart, and my thoughts were always far from those brilliant spectacles in which I was merely an official in a braided uniform.

"What has occurred, Mr Ingram?" asked the Ambassador's daughter anxiously. "Father is certainly not himself to-night."

"Another political complication," I responded; "that is all."

"Sibyl, my dear," exclaimed her father, gently taking her hand, "you know that I forbid any inquiries to be made into matters which must be secret, even from you."

"I came to tell you all about the ball," she said, pouting. "I was introduced to a most pleasant man named Wolf, and danced with him several times."

"Wolf!" I cried quickly. "Rodolphe Wolf?"

"That was his name. He was dark, about forty, with a small pointed black beard. Do you know him?"

"Wolf!" I repeated; then, suddenly recovering from the surprise she had caused me by uttering that name, I answered carelessly: "Perhaps it may be the same man I knew slightly some years ago."

"We had awfully good fun. He is so amusing, but seems quite a stranger in Paris."

I smiled inwardly. Rodolphe Wolf a stranger in Paris! The thought was amusing.

"And what was your conversation about?" I inquired of her, smiling pleasantly the while.

"You want to know whether he flirted with me, Mr Ingram?" she laughed mischievously. "I know you of old. It really isn't fair."

"He said nothing to you about your father, or about the composition of his staff?" I inquired eagerly.

"Nothing."

"And you did not mention my name?" I asked anxiously.

"No. Why? You talk as though you don't want him to know you are in Paris."

"You have exactly guessed my desire," I replied. "If you meet him again, kindly oblige me by saying nothing."

"Do not utter a word regarding matters here at the Embassy, Sibyl," added her father seriously. "You understand?"

"Of course not. I'm a diplomat's daughter, and can keep a secret when necessary. But tell me, father," she added, "who is the woman of whom you were speaking when I came in?"

"It is our affair, my dear—entirely our affair," he said in a hard voice. "It is nothing you need trouble your head over. I'm glad you've enjoyed the ball. Say good-night, and leave us."

"But you look quite ill," she said with concern in her voice, stroking his heated forehead with her hand. "Cannot I get you something?"

"Nothing, dear."

She was a charming type of English girl, smart, accomplished, and utterly devoted to her father. That she delighted in mild flirtations here and there in the cosmopolitan circle in which she moved I was well aware, and we were such old friends that I often chaffed her about her fickleness. But that night she had met Rodolphe Wolf, of all men. The fact was strange, to say the least.

"Shall I send Harding to you?" she asked, standing there in the shadow, the diamond star in her well-dressed hair alone catching the light and gleaming with a thousand fires. The star was a parting gift to her by Queen Margherita of Italy, with whom she had been an especial favourite while her father was Ambassador in Rome.

"No," answered His Excellency. "Please say good-night, dear, and leave us."

Then he bent, kissed her tenderly on the brow, and dismissed her.

"Well," she laughed poutingly, "if I am ordered off, I suppose I must go. I'm a striking example of the obedient daughter. Good-night, Mr Ingram."

And as I held open the door for her to pass out, she added mischievously:

"I'll leave you to talk together over the shortcomings of my sex;" and laughing gaily she disappeared down the corridor.

Chapter Two
Two Enigmas

"Who is this Wolf?" the Ambassador inquired quickly, as soon as I had closed the door. "I don't seem to recollect the name."

"I have a suspicion," I responded. "When it is established I will explain."

"An alias—eh?"

"I think so," I said. "Your daughter should be warned against him. They had better not meet."

"I will see to that," he said, and the next instant the telephone-bell rang loudly, announcing the response from Alderhurst.

In a moment we were both at the instrument. Then with the receiver at my car I inquired who was there.

"Durnford, Alderhurst," was the response. "Are you Ingram?"

I replied in the affirmative, adding the word without the receipt of which no cipher despatch is ever sent by telephone, lest some trickery should be attempted.

"Take down, then," came the secretary's voice from the other side of the Channel. "From the Marquess of Malvern, to His Excellency, Lord Barmouth, Paris. July 12th, 2:10 a.m.;" and then followed a long row of ciphers, each of which I carefully wrote down upon the paper before me, reading it through aloud, in order that he might compare it with his copy.

Then, when the voice from Alderhurst gave the word "End," I hung up the receiver and gave the paper into His Excellency's eager hands.

Those puzzling lines of letters and numerals were secret instructions from the ruler of England's destiny, who had been called from his bed to decide one of the most critical problems of statesmanship. Truly the position of the British Minister for Foreign Affairs is no enviable one. The responsibility is the heaviest weighing upon any one man in the whole world.

His Excellency seated himself quickly at his table, and with the aid of a second book which I handed him from the safe proceeded to decipher the Chief's despatch. With his pen he placed the equivalent beneath each cipher, and as he did so I saw that his countenance fell. He went pale as death.

"Ah!" he gasped, when he had finished the arrangement and had read the deciphered message through. "It is exactly as I feared. Never in the course of my career as Ambassador has such a serious complication arisen—never!"

I was silent. What, indeed, could I say? I well knew that he was not the man to betray the slightest emotion without good reason.

For a moment he sat there, resting his brow upon his hand, staring blankly at the paper I had given him. The nature of his secret instructions I knew not. His utter despair was sufficient to convince me, however, that a catastrophe was inevitable. Only the low ticking of the clock upon the high mantelshelf broke the painful silence. The representative of Her Majesty—one of England's most skilled and trusted diplomats—sighed heavily, for he knew too well how black was the outlook at that moment—how, indeed, because of our mysterious betrayal, our enemies had triumphed, and how, at the other embassies, that very night the downfall of England's power was being discussed.

"All this is a woman's doing, I tell you!" he cried, striking the table fiercely, rising and pacing the room. "We must discover the truth—we must, you hear?"

"I am making every possible effort," I answered; adding, "I think I have hitherto shown myself worthy of your confidence?"

"Certainly, Ingram," he hastened to assure me. "Without you here I should not dare to act as I have done. I know that nothing escapes you. Your shrewdness is equal to that of old Sterk, the Chief of Police in Vienna."

"You are too complimentary," I said; "I have merely done my duty."

"But if we could only get at the truth in this affair!"

"At present it is an absolute mystery. Only two persons were aware of the secret. You knew it, and I also knew it. And yet it is out—indeed, the very terms of the agreement are known!"

Suddenly halting, he pushed open the window, and looked out upon the hot, overcast night. Paris was still bright with her myriad electric lights, and the glaring cafés on the boulevards were still as busy as during the hour of the absinthe. The City of Pleasure never sleeps.

He leaned over the balcony, gasping for air; but in an instant I was behind him, saying:

"Someone may be watching outside. Is it really wise for you to be seen?"

"No," he answered. "You're right, Ingram;" and he turned back and closed the long windows opening upon the balcony. "A bold front must be maintained through all." He walked to his table, took up the despatch, and, striking a vesta, ignited it, holding it until it was completely consumed. Then he cast the blackened tinder into the grate, growing in a single instant calm again. "You are right, Ingram," he repeated rather hoarsely. "Our enemies must not obtain any inkling that we know the truth, if we are to effect a successful counter-plot. In this affair I detect the hand of a woman. Is not that your opinion?"

"I must admit that it is," I responded. "I believe there is a female spy somewhere."

"But who is she?" he cried anxiously.

"Ah!" I said, "we have yet to discover her name."

"It is not Yolande?" he asked dubiously.

"No. Of that I feel quite certain."

"But you are certain of nothing else?"

"All the rest is, I regret, an absolute mystery."

There was no disguising the fact that the information which by very mysterious means had leaked out from the Embassy had created the most intense excitement in certain other foreign embassies in Paris. Kaye, the chief of our secret service in the French capital—a shrewd fellow, whose capacity for learning which way the diplomatic wind was blowing was little short of marvellous—had come to me at midnight to report that the Spanish Ambassador was exchanging frequent despatches with Madrid. That statement was sufficient to show the enemy's hand.

For fully six months France had been scheming to obtain a naval station in the Mediterranean, and the point she coveted was Ceuta, on the Moorish coast, opposite Gibraltar. Knowledge of this caused us to exercise the most delicate diplomacy in order to thwart the conspiracy to aim a blow against England's naval power in the Mediterranean. A week ago I had been in London, and the Marquess of Malvern himself had given me a crossed despatch to convey to my chief in Paris. This had contained certain instructions in cipher, which, on my return, I had helped to translate into English. Then the despatch was burnt by His Excellency, and we alone knew its contents. From the moment I received it in the Marquess's private room at the Foreign Office, until the moment when I handed it over to Lord Barmouth in Paris with its five great seals intact, it had never left the pouch of chamois-leather which, when travelling with despatches, I always wore around my waist, next my skin. For spies to have obtained a copy of it was impossible. I had seen it written, and had likewise seen it destroyed. It was not likely either that the British Ambassador had himself exposed his secret instructions in a matter of such delicacy, where the greatest finesse and the most skilful diplomacy were necessary; and equally certain was it that I myself had not uttered a single word.

The secret instructions showed marvellous foresight, as did all the actions of the great statesman in whose hands rested the prestige of England among the Powers. They were briefly to show with great delicacy to the Spanish Ambassador that his Government, having regard to existing relations, had no right to sell Ceuta to any Power, and that if any attempt were made by any other Government to establish a naval station there, England would oppose it to the utmost, even to the extent of hostilities. Yet somehow, by means that formed a most puzzling enigma, these secret instructions had become instantly known to France; and even before Lord Barmouth could obtain an interview with the Marquis Leon y Castillo, the French Minister of Foreign Affairs had called at the Embassy in the Boulevard de Courcelles, and had apparently arranged a line of action. Thus England had been checkmated, and in all probability the sale of that most important strategic point in the Mediterranean had already been effected.

Kaye had been to Madrid, and his inquiries in the Spanish capital tended to confirm this theory.

Truly we were in evil case. So decisive had been His Excellency's instructions that if he did not now vigorously protest and threaten a cessation of diplomatic negotiations it would exhibit such weakness as the British Government must never show. That motto of Lord Malvern's, "To be strong is to avert war; to be weak is to invite it," is ever foremost in the mind of each representative of Her Majesty at a foreign Court. Yet Lord Barmouth's dilemma was, indeed, a serious one. He had declared the exposure of our secret due to some woman's scheming, and suspected one person—the pretty Yolande de Foville. His suspicion of her caused me a good deal of reflection; and as I walked along the boulevard to my bachelor apartment au troisième, I pondered seriously. What, I wondered, had caused him to think ill of her? If she had danced with Hartmann, this action was surely not enough to condemn her. Yet why, I wondered, had she mentioned myself? And why, indeed, was Rodolphe Wolf, of all men, in Paris?

No, I did not like the aspect of things in the least. The night was absolutely breathless, and the asphalt of the boulevard seemed to reflect back into one's face the heat of the sun that had blazed upon it during the day. I removed my hat, and walked with it in my hand, my brain awhirl. The spies of France had effected a coup against us, and within twenty-four hours Europe might, I knew, be convulsed by a declaration of war.

Here and there the cafés were still open, but few customers were inside. A pair of drunken roysterers staggered past me singing that catchy song of the less fashionable boulevards:

"Dansons la ronde
Des marmites de Paris,
Ohé! les souris!
Les rongeuses de monde!
Faisons sauter avec nous
Nos michets et nos marlous.
Dansons la ronde!
Paris est à nous!"

With that single exception all was silent. From half-past three till four in the morning is the quietest period that the City of Pleasure experiences. She is dormant only one half-hour in the whole twenty-four.

Yolande was suspected of being a spy! The thought seemed absolutely absurd. She was Belgian, it was true, and there is somehow always a prejudice against Belgian women in Paris, due perhaps to the fact that although they speak French with an accent, they are often perfect linguists. But for Yolande to be actually a spy—why, the thing was ridiculous!

Arrived at my own rooms, I found Mackenzie, my old Scotch manservant, awaiting me.

"Mr Kaye called, sir, half an hour ago," he said. "He could not wait, for he was leaving Paris."

"Leaving Paris?" I echoed, for the ubiquitous chief of the secret service had only come back from Madrid a few hours before.

"Yes, sir. He left you a note;" and my well-trained man drew a letter from his pocket. He always kept my letters upon his person, in order that any callers might not pry into them during my absence.

I tore open the note eagerly, and read the few scribbled lines. Next instant the paper almost fell from my fingers. I held my breath, scarcely believing my own eyes. Yet the writing was plain enough, and was as follows:

"Within the past hour I have ascertained that your friend Yolande de Foville is a secret agent. Keep strict watch upon her. I have left instructions that if she leaves Paris she is to be followed. I go to Berlin at once to make inquiries, and am leaving by the 4:30 train this morning. I have the address you gave, and the particulars concerning her. Shall return as soon as possible.

"K."

I crushed the note in my hand, and, walking on into my sitting-room, gulped down some brandy. Everything had conspired against me. When I had given Kaye those details concerning my charming little friend three years ago, I had never dreamed that he would register them and afterwards use them in an endeavour to fasten upon her a charge of being a spy. Yet he was actually on his way to Berlin, and any attempt upon my part to hinder him would only be misconstrued into a treasonable endeavour to shield her.

Upon the table before me stood her photograph in a silver frame, looking out at me. I took it up. Those eyes were so innocent that I could not bring myself to believe that any evil lurked in them. Surely she would not attempt to harm me? Such an action was absolutely contrary to any woman's nature.

Yolande! The sound of that name brought back to me a sweet, tender memory of the past. I sighed as the recollection of that bygone day arose within me, and flung myself down into an easy-chair to smoke and to think. In the blue ascending rings from my cigarette her face seemed to smile at me with those red parted lips and merry eyes, clear and azure as a child's. How charming and chic she had once appeared to me in those days when we had first met—in those days before I had known Edith Austin, my absent well-beloved! Her portrait, too, was there—the picture of a woman, sweet, tender, grave-faced, of similar age perhaps, but whose peerless beauty was typically English and devoid of any artificiality. I took it up and touched it reverently with my lips. I loved the original of that photograph with all the strength of my being, hoping always that some day ere long I might ask her to become my wife.

Some there are who hold the theory that to all diplomatists, ambassadors excepted, wives are an unnecessary encumbrance. I admit that there is much to be said in favour of the celibate state as the ideal existence for the secretary or attaché, who is bound, more or less, to make himself agreeable to the many cosmopolitan ladies who make up the diplomatic circle, and sometimes even to flirt with them, when occasion requires. Yet after fifteen years or so beneath the shadows of the various thrones of Europe, a man tires of the life, and longs for the one sweet woman whom he can trust and love. In this I was no exception. I loved Edith Austin with all my heart and all my soul; and she, I felt assured, reciprocated my affection.

It is part of the diplomatist's creed to be on good terms with all and sundry of the feminine butterflies who hover about the embassies, no matter what their age or nationality. Hence it was that five years ago, while stationed at Brussels, I had become attracted by Yolande de Foville. Once, long before I met Edith, I fancied myself in love with her. Her father, Count de Foville, was aide-de-camp to King Leopold, and with her mother she moved in the best society in Paris and Brussels. On several occasions I had been invited for the boar hunting at the great gloomy old château at Houffalize, in the Ardennes forest, where the powerful de Fovilles had been seigneurs through five centuries.

It was a dull, snowbound, dreary place in winter, bare and chill, furnished in ancient style, and situated thirty miles from the nearest railway, in the midst of a flat forest country. It was, therefore, not surprising that on the death of the Count, Yolande and her mother should prefer to leave Belgium and travel in England and Italy, spending the winter at Rome or at Monte Carlo, the spring in Paris, and summer in one or other of the fashionable French watering-places. During three years we had been excellent friends, and after I had been promoted from Brussels to the Embassy in Rome, she came with her mother and spent the spring in the Eternal City, with the result that our firm friendship became even firmer. I am fain to admit that our flirtation was of the kind called desperate, and that it had ended in love.

And a week ago she had suddenly arrived in Paris at the smart little flat in the Rue de Courcelles, which her mother had possessed for years, but now so seldom occupied. Her arrival was unexpected, and I had only known of it from Giraud, the military attaché at the Belgian Legation, a friend of my Brussels days, whom I met in the Café de Paris one evening after the opera, and who had said suddenly:

"Do you, my dear Ingram, know that a little friend of yours has arrived in Paris?"

"Who?" I inquired eagerly.

"Yolande," was the response. "You used to be her cavalier in Brussels in the old days. Have you forgotten her?"

His announcement surprised me. Since my friendship with Edith had grown to be a grand passion, I had exchanged no correspondence with Yolande. Indeed, the last I had heard of her was that she and the Countess were at Cairo spending the winter.

To tell the truth I was rather glad that she had not sought me out, for I had no wish to renew her acquaintance, now that I had found a woman in England whom I meant to try to win for my wife. Yet as I looked back at the past through the haze of my cigarette-smoke I was compelled to admit that I had spent some charming hours by her side, dancing at those brilliant balls in Brussels or driving in that pretty wood so beloved of the Bruxellois, the Bois de la Cambre. Many were the incidents that came back to me as I sat there pondering. Nevertheless, in the storehouse of memory I found nothing half sweet enough to tempt me from my love for Edith.

The denunciation of the pretty Yolande as a spy staggered belief; yet the Chief himself, as well as Kaye, was convinced, and the latter was already on his way to the north to prosecute inquiries.

What, I wondered, had really aroused their suspicions? As His Excellency had not seen Kaye since his return from Madrid, they could not have exchanged views. It seemed my duty to call and see her, to renew the acquaintance that I so strongly desired to end, and, indeed, to continue the flirtation of bygone days with a view to discovering the truth. Was it fair? Was it just? I hesitated to call upon her, half fearful lest her charm and natural chic should again attract me towards her. Nevertheless, it was my duty, as servant of my Sovereign, to attempt to discover England's secret enemies.

Chapter Three
Yolande

The remainder of that night I spent in restless agitation, and at the Embassy early next morning showed His Excellency the note that Kaye had left for me.

"You must see her, Ingram," he said briefly. "You must obtain her secret from her."

"But I cannot believe that she is a secret agent!" I declared. "We were friends, and she surely would not seek to injure me?"

"Trust nobody, my dear Ingram," answered the grave-eyed old man. "You know how unreliable women are where diplomacy is concerned. Remember the incident of the Princess Ghelarducci in Rome."

My lips compressed themselves. He referred to a matter which, for me, was anything but a pleasant recollection. The Princess, after learning our intentions regarding Abyssinia, had openly betrayed us; and I had very foolishly thought her my friend.

"I shall call on her this afternoon," I answered briefly. "The worst of it is that my action will lead her to think that I desire to renew the acquaintance."

"H'm, I see," observed His Excellency quickly, for his shrewdness had detected the truth. "You were once in love with her—eh?"

I nodded.

"Then don't allow her to think that your love has cooled," he urged. "Act diplomatically in this matter, and strive to get at the truth."

"And deceive her?"

"Deception is permissible if she is a spy."

"But she is not a spy," I declared quickly.

"That remains to be seen!" he snapped. He then turned on his heel and passed into an adjoining room.

At three o'clock I presented my card at the flat in the Rue de Courcelles, and was admitted to a cosy little salon, where the persiennes were closed to keep out the blazing July sun, and the subdued light was welcome after the glare of the streets. Scarcely, however, had my eyes become accustomed to the semi-darkness, when the door suddenly opened, and I found myself face to face with the woman I had loved a few years ago.

"Gerald! You!" she cried in English, with that pretty accent which had always struck me as so charming.

Our hands clasped. I looked into her face and saw that in the two years which had elapsed she had grown even more beautiful. In a cool white dress of soft, clinging muslin, which, although simply made, bore the unmistakable stamp of a couturière of the first order, she stood before me, my hand in hers, in silence.

"So you have come to me?" she said in a strained voice. "You have come, at last?"

"You did not let me know you were in Paris," I protested.

"Giraud told you four days ago," she responded, "and you could not spare a single half-hour for me until to-day!" she added in a tone of reproach. "Besides, I wrote to you from Cairo, and you never replied."

"Forgive me," I urged—"forgive me, Yolande. It is really my fault."

"Because you have forgotten me," she said huskily. "Here, in Paris, you have so many distractions that memories of our old days in Brussels and at Houffalize have all been swept away. Come, admit that what I say is the truth."

"I shall admit nothing of the kind, Yolande," I answered, with diplomatic caution. "I only admit my surprise at finding you here in July. Why, there is nobody here except our unfortunate selves at the embassies. The boulevards are given over to the perspiring British tourist in knickerbockers and the usual week-end trippers who 'do' the city in a char-à-banc."

She laughed for the first time, and seated herself upon a large settee covered with yellow silk, motioning me to a chair near her.

"It is true," she said. "Paris is not at all pleasant just now. We are only here for frocks. In a week we go to Marienbad. And you—how are you?" and she surveyed me with her head held slightly aside in that piquante manner I knew so well.

"The same," I laughed—"ever the same."

"Not the same to me," she hastened to protest.

"I might make a similar charge against yourself," I said. "Remember, you did not tell me you were in Paris."

"Because I thought you would know it quickly enough. I wanted, if possible, to meet you accidentally and surprise you. I went to the ball at the German Embassy, but you were not there."

"I was in London," I explained briefly, my thoughts reverting to the allegation against her and the unhesitating action of the wary Kaye in travelling direct to Berlin.

If there was any man in Europe who could clear up a mystery it was the indefatigable chief of the British secret service. He lived in Paris ostensibly as an English lawyer, with offices in the Boulevard des Italiens, next the Café Américain. Hence his sudden journeys hither and thither were believed to be undertaken in the interests of various clients. But although he had an Irish solicitor, O'Brien by name, to attend to the inquiries of any chance clients, the amount of legal business carried on in those offices was really nil. The place was, in fact, the headquarters of the British secret service on the Continent.

"I, too, was in England a year ago," she said. "We were invited to a house-party up in Scotland. Mother was bored, but I had great fun. An English home seems somehow so much jollier than the houses where one visits in any other country. You know how I love the English!"

"Is that meant as a compliment?" I laughed.

"Of course," she answered. "But English diplomatists are just as grave as those of any other nation. Your people are always full of all sorts of horrid secrets and things."

She referred to the old days in Brussels, for she knew well the difficulties under which our diplomacy had been conducted there, owing to the eternal questions involving Egypt and the Congo.

But I laughed lightly. I did not intend that she should suspect the real motive of my call. Evidently she knew nothing of my love for Edith Austin, or she would have referred to it. Fortunately I had been able to keep it a secret from all.

"And you are actually leaving us in a week?"

I observed, for want of something else to say. "I hear that Marienbad is crowded this season."

"We are going to visit my uncle, Prince Stolberg, who has a villa there."

Then I asked her of our mutual friends in Brussels, and she in return retailed to me all the latest gossip concerning them. As she sat there in the subdued light, her white dress, relieved by a touch of turquoise at the wrists and waist, she presented a picture graceful, delicate, and altogether charming. I reasoned with myself as she went on chattering. No; it was not surprising that I had once fallen in love with her. She was more French than Belgian, for the days of her girlhood had been passed mostly in France; her Christian name was French, and in manner she possessed all that smartness and chic peculiar to the Parisienne. Mentally I compared her with Edith, but next instant laughed within myself. Such comparison was impossible. Their styles were as different as were their nationalities. Beside Edith, my well-beloved, the beauty of this fair-haired, gesticulating girl paled entirely, and became insipid. The Englishwoman who held me beneath the spell of her soft and truthful eyes was without a peer.

Still, Yolande amused me with her chatter. The reader will forgive me this admission, for in calling there I was only acting a part. I was endeavouring in the interests of my country to find out whether there was any truth in the allegation recently made against her by my friend. Of a sudden a thought crossed my mind, and I asked:

"Have you met many acquaintances since you've been in Paris?"

"Only Hartmann and some of the people at the Legation," she responded. "We are just going to five o'clock with the Princess Olsoufieff this afternoon."

"There is an old friend of yours just arrived," I said. "Have you met him?"

"An old friend?" she echoed in surprise. "Man or woman?"

"A man," I answered. "Rodolphe Wolf."

"Rodolphe Wolf!" she gasped, starting up, the colour dying from her lips in an instant. "Rodolphe Wolf in Paris—impossible!"

"He was at the Baroness de Chalencon's last night," I said quite calmly, watching her face the while.

Her sudden fear and surprise made plain a fact of which I had not before been aware—namely, that there was something more than a casual link between them. Years ago, when in Brussels, I had suspected Wolf of being a secret agent, and the fact that she was closely acquainted with him appeared to prove that my Chief's suspicion was not unfounded.

She had risen. Her hands were trembling, and although she strove desperately to betray to me no outward sign of agitation, she was compelled to support herself by clutching the small table at her side. Her countenance was blanched to the lips. She presented the appearance of one haunted by some terrible dread.

"Wolf!" she gasped again, as though speaking to herself. Then, turning to me, she stretched forth both her hands, and, looking earnestly into my eyes, cried in wild desperation: "Gerald, save me! For the sake of our love of the old days, save me!"

"From what?" I cried, jumping up and catching her by both hands. "Tell me, Yolande. If I can assist you I certainly will. Why are you so distressed?"

She was silent, with one trembling hand pressed upon her heart, as though to stay its wild, tumultuous beating.

"No," she said in a hoarse whisper, "it is useless—all useless."

"But if you are in distress I can surely help you," I said.

"Alas! you cannot," she answered in despair. "You do not know—you cannot understand."

"Why not tell me? Confide in me," I urged.

"No," she replied. "I am very foolish—forgive me;" and she tried to smile.

"The news that Wolf is here has upset you," I said. "Why?"

"He has escaped."

"From where?"

"From prison."

I was silent. I knew not what to say. This declaration of hers was strange. It was startling news to me that Rodolphe Wolf had been in prison.

"You have asked me to save you," I said, reverting to her wild supplication. "I will do so willingly if you only tell me how."

"It is impossible," she said in a broken voice, shaking her head mournfully. "By what you have told me I am forewarned."

A deep sigh escaped her, and I saw that her fingers worked restlessly in the palms of her hands. She was desperate.

"Can I do absolutely nothing?" I asked in a tone of sympathy, placing my hand tenderly upon her shoulder.

"Nothing," she answered in a hoarse whisper. "I am not fit to talk further. Let us say good-bye."

"Then you prefer that I should leave you?"

"Yes," she said, holding out her hand. "Forgive me for this, but I want to go to my own room to think. What you have told me has upset me."

"Tell me plainly—you fear that man?"

She nodded in the affirmative.

"And you will not allow me either to advise or to assist you?"

"No," she said hoarsely. "Go, Gerald. Leave me! When we meet again I shall be calmer than I am now."

Her face was deathly pale; her eyes had a distinct look of terror in them.

"Very well," I answered when again she had urged me to leave her; "if you insist, I will go. But remember that if I can be of service, Yolande, I am ready at once to render you assistance. Good-bye," and I pressed her hand in sympathy.

She burst into tears.

"Farewell," she faltered.

Then I turned, and, bowing, went forth into the glaring sunshine of the boulevard.

She had virtually admitted a close acquaintance with a man upon whom distinct suspicion rested, and her actions had been those of a guilty woman. My thoughts were full of that interview and its painful ending as I walked back towards the Embassy.

Chapter Four
A Curious Story

There was war in the air. At the Embassy we could not conceal from ourselves the seriousness of the situation. From hour to hour we were living in dread lest diplomatic negotiations should be broken off with the French Republic. We had discovered what seemed very much like a conspiracy against England, and as an energetic protest it appeared quite possible that the Marquess of Malvern might order my Chief to leave Paris. This would mean a rupture of diplomatic relations, and in all probability war.

Never in the history of modern Europe had there been a day so critical as that blazing, well-remembered one in mid-July. There were ugly rumours of complications in the Transvaal. The fate of certain nations trembled in the balance. In every capital diplomatists were active, some striving to force war, others endeavouring to prevent it. A diplomatist's life is assuredly no sinecure. The British public, as I have said before, little dreams of the constant anxiety and terrible tension which are parts of the daily life of its faithful servants abroad.

On my return to the Embassy I found that some important despatches had been brought from London by Anderson, the foreign service messenger.

He was sitting in my room smoking a cigarette, and awaiting me in order to obtain the receipt for his despatch-box. A tall, round-faced, merry man of middle age, he was an especial favourite in all the embassies as far as Teheran. A thorough cosmopolitan and man of the world, he had resigned his commission in the Scots Greys to become one of that half-dozen of the greyhounds of Europe known as Queen's messengers.

"Well, Anderson," I exclaimed, shaking his hand on entering, "what's the news from Downing Street?"

"Oh, nothing very fresh," he laughed, sinking back in his chair again, and passing me over the receipt for signature. "Old Tuite, of the Treaty Department, has retired on his pension this week. That's about all that's new. The Chief, however, seems busy. I'm loaded with despatches."

"Where for?"

"Vienna and Constantinople. I leave by the Orient express in an hour's time," he answered, with a glance at his watch.

"Then you're getting over a little ground just now?" I laughed.

"A little ground!" he echoed. "Well, I've been two trips to Petersburg this month, twice here to Paris, and once to Vienna. I've only slept one night in London since the 1st."

"You're a bit sick of it, I should think," I observed, looking at the round face lit up by its pair of merry grey eyes. He was an easy-going fellow; his good-humour never seemed ruffled.

"Oh, it agrees with me," he laughed lightly. "I don't care as long as I get the monthly run to Teheran now and then. That's a bit of a change, you know, after these everlasting railways, with their stuffy sleeping-cars and abominable arrangements for giving a man indigestion."

I examined the box to see that the seals affixed in Downing Street were intact, then signed the receipt and handed it back to him.

Of the corps of Queen's messengers—nicknamed "the greyhounds" because of the badge which each wears suspended round his neck and concealed beneath his cravat, a silver greyhound surmounted by the Royal arms—Captain Jack Anderson was the most popular. A welcome guest at every embassy or legation, he was on friendly terms with the whole staff, from the Ambassador himself down to the hall-porter, and he carried the gossip of the embassies to and fro across Europe. From him we all gathered news of our old colleagues in other capitals—of their joys and their sorrows, their difficulties and their junketings. His baggage being by international courtesy free from Customs' examination, he oft-times carried with him a new frock for an ambassador's wife or daughter—a service which always put him high in the good graces of the feminine portion of the diplomatic circle.

"Kaye seems bobbing about pretty much," he observed, handing me his cigarette-case. Anderson's cigarettes were well known for their excellence, for he purchased them at a shop in Petersburg, and often distributed a box in one or other of the embassies. "I met him a week ago on board the Calais boat, and two days later I came across him in the buffet down at Bâle. He was, however, as close as an oyster."

"Of course. It isn't likely that he'd talk very much," I remarked. "His profession is to know everything, and at the same time to affect ignorance. He went to Berlin last night."

"We had breakfast together in the early morning at Bâle, and he questioned me closely about a friend of yours."

"Who?"

"A lady—Mademoiselle de Foville. You remember her in Brussels, don't you?"

"Mademoiselle de Foville!" I echoed. The denunciation of her as a secret agent instantly flashed through my mind.

"Yes, you were extremely friendly with her in Brussels," he went on. "Don't you recollect that you introduced me to her one evening at an alfresco concert in the Vauxhall Gardens, where we sat together for quite a long time chatting?"

"I remember distinctly," I responded. Every detail of that balmy summer night in those gaily illuminated gardens came back to me in that moment. I loved Yolande in those long-past days. "And what did Kaye want to know regarding her?"

"He asked me whether I had ever met her, and I told him that you had once introduced us."

"Well?"

"Oh, nothing much else. He remarked how very charming she was—a verdict in which we both agreed. Have you seen her lately?"

I hesitated for a moment.

"Yes, she's here, in Paris."

He bent forward quickly, regarding me curiously.

"That's strange. How long has she been here?" he inquired with a rather puzzled look.

"Only a few days. I did not know that she was here till yesterday," I replied with affected carelessness.

"Ah, I thought she could not have been here long."

"Why?"

"Because only a week ago she travelled in the same compartment as myself between Berlin and Cologne."

"And did you claim acquaintance with her?" I inquired quickly.

"No. She had a companion with her—a pimply-faced, ugly Johnnie, whom I took to be a German. They spoke in German all the time."

Could it be, I wondered, that Yolande and her companion had travelled with Anderson with some evil intent?

"Didn't you speak to them?"

"The man tried to open a conversation with me, but I pretended to be Italian, without any knowledge of German or English, so he didn't get very far. To affect Italian is generally a sure game, for so few people speak it in comparison with those who know other Continental languages."

"You wanted to overhear their conversation—eh?"

"I wanted to ascertain what their game was," answered the Queen's messenger. "They eyed my despatch-box very curiously; and it was to me an extremely suspicious circumstance that although they joined the train at Berlin they did not enter my compartment until an hour later, when the express stopped to change engines."

"You were alone?"

"Yes, and it was at night," he answered, adding: "To me it was also a curious circumstance that only three days afterwards Kaye should become so deeply interested in her. I had never seen her from that night in Brussels until we had met in the train, but I've a good memory for faces. I can swear I was not mistaken."

"You speak as though you suspected her," I said, looking straight into his ruddy countenance, which had grown unusually serious while we had been speaking.

"Well, to tell the truth, I did suspect her," he responded. "I didn't half like the look of the man. He was well-dressed, but as you know I've always a sharp eye where my fellow-travellers are concerned, and I felt certain that there was something shady about him. They shifted about all night, and were constantly watching to see whether I had gone to sleep. But all their watching was without reward. Jack Anderson never sleeps while he has a crossed despatch upon him;" and he blew a cloud of smoke upward from his lips.

"But surely you don't think that their intention was to steal your despatches?" I cried.

"They were welcome to the whole collection in the box," he laughed. "They were only consular reports and necessary evils of that sort. What they wanted was the crossed despatch from Berlin that I had in my belt next my skin."

"They made no attempt to get at it?"

"Yes, they did. That's just where my suspicion was proved."

"How?" I asked breathlessly, bending eagerly towards him.

"Well, as you know, I always carry among my wraps a little cushion covered with black satin. Experience has taught me that that cushion has saved me many an aching head and stiff neck when on long journeys. So I placed it behind my head, and through the night read a novel by the dim, uncertain light. About two o'clock in the morning we ran into Hanover, and I got out to get a drink. When I returned, however, and placed the cushion behind my head, I felt a slight dampness upon it. In an instant suspicion seized me. Some liquid had been sprinkled upon it in my absence. My two fellow-travellers, wrapped in their rugs, were apparently sleeping. At once I resolved to act with caution, and, turning my cheek towards the pillow, smelt it. There was a curious odour, sweet and subtle, like some new perfume. I had suspected chloroform, but it was certainly not that. Yet almost the instant after I had inhaled it a curious and unaccountable drowsiness seized me. Then I knew the truth. They had plotted to render me insensible and afterwards steal the despatch! I struggled against this feeling of weariness, and, rising to my feet, buttoned my overcoat as though I were chilly. This action allowed the cushion to fall away from my head, and, again re-seating myself, I made a feint of being interested in my book; but in reality my head was awhirl, and in the pocket of my ulster I had my hand upon my revolver, ready to use it should that pimply-faced ruffian attempt violence. The pair commenced to shift about uneasily in their seats, and I could see that their failure had considerably disconcerted them."

"You gave them no idea that you had discovered their intentions?"

"None whatever. I was anxious to see how they would act after being foiled."

"Well, what did they do?"

"They exchanged glances of annoyance, but spoke no word. They were silent for over an hour, during which time it occurred to me to move the cushion farther from me, in case the evaporation of the mysterious liquid should cause insensibility. I was determined that your pretty little friend's companion should be the first to be thus affected. The feeling of drowsiness, however, wore off, and at Cologne the pair, after chatting in German regarding the train to Venlo, bustled about hastily and descended. They had no baggage, and went into the buffet to breakfast."

"You, of course, continued your journey?"

"Yes, to Ostend and London."

"It seems as though you had rather a narrow escape," I observed thoughtfully.

"It was a daring attempt to get at that despatch," he remarked with some warmth. "Depend upon it, my dear Ingram, that woman is a spy. I know she's a friend of yours, but I can't help saying just what I think."

"But I can't believe it!" I declared. "Indeed, I won't believe it!" I added vehemently.

"As you like," he said coldly, with a slight shrug of his broad shoulders. "I've told you the plain truth as to what occurred."

"She's wealthy, and of one of the best families in Belgium. There is no necessity whatever for her to be in the pay of any foreign Government," I protested.

"We have nothing to do with her reasons," he said. "All we know is that she and her companion tried to drug me in order to get at the despatch."

"You have no idea, I suppose, of the contents of the despatch in question?" I inquired.

"None, except that when I gave it into the Chief's own hands in his private room at Downing Street, he appeared to be very much surprised by its contents, and at once wrote a reply, with which I posted back to Berlin by the same night's mail from Charing Cross."

"Then it was upon a matter of importance?"

"I judged it to be of extreme importance. Yolande de Foville was evidently well aware that I had the despatch in my belt."

"You had never before seen this man who accompanied her?"

"Never. But now he has made one attempt it is quite probable he may make another. I'm on the look-out for him again."

"And the cushion? Have you discovered what they placed upon it?"

"I left it in London with Dr Bond, the analyst, at Somerset House. He's trying to discover the liquid used. I hope he will be successful, for the stuff was so potent that I have no desire for it again to be sprinkled upon my belongings."

"They were at least ingenious," I exclaimed, amazed at this extraordinary story, which seemed to prove so conclusively the truth of Kaye's denunciation.

Yet I could not believe that Yolande, my charming little friend, in whom I had in the old days reposed so many confidences, and by whose side I had lingered through many idle hours in the Bois or in that almost endless forest around her feudal home, was actually a spy. The suggestion seemed too absurd. Nevertheless, Kaye was not a man to make unfounded charges, nor was Anderson given to relating that which was untrue. Truth to tell, this story of his held me absolutely dumbfounded. I recollected my conversation with her an hour ago, and the strange effect my announcement that Wolf was in Paris had made upon her. She had implored me to save her. Why?

A silence fell between us. I was preoccupied by my own thoughts. But a few moments later the Queen's messenger again glanced at his watch, and, rising, said:

"I must be off, or I shan't catch the Orient. Any message for them down at Constantinople?"

"No," I responded, gripping his strong hand in farewell. "Take care of yourself, and don't let any of those confounded spies get at you again."

"Trust me, my dear fellow," he laughed, and lighting another cigarette he went forth on his long journey to the East as airily as though he were strolling down to get a cocktail at Henry's.

When he had gone I sat for a long time thinking. A remembrance of the mad love of those days that had gone came back to me, sweet, charming memories of that half-forgotten time when Yolande was my ideal, and when her lips met mine in tender, passionate caresses. Ah! how fondly I had loved her in those days! But with an effort I at last arose, and, casting all those reflections behind me with a sigh, broke the seals of the despatch-box, and, seating myself at the big writing-table, commenced to examine them with a view to ascertaining their contents.

There-were several important papers, and very soon I became absorbed in them. Nearly an hour later there came a sudden rap at the door, and one of the English footmen entered, saying:

"There is a man below, sir, who wishes to see you at once on important business. He says he is valet-de-chambre of the Countess de Foville."

"Of the Countess de Foville!" I echoed, much surprised.

I at once ordered him to be shown upstairs, and a few moments later a tall, thin-faced, clean-shaven Frenchman entered.

"M'sieur Ingram?" he inquired breathlessly in French, evidently in a state of great agitation.

"Yes," I said. "What is your message?"

"I have been sent by Madame la Comtesse to ask you to be good enough to come to her at once. A most distressing incident has occurred."

"What has occurred?" I demanded quickly.

"Ah, m'sieur, it is terrible!" he cried with much Gallic gesticulation. "Poor Mademoiselle Yolande! She is asking to see you. She says she must speak with you, m'sieur."

"With me?"

"Yes, m'sieur. Do not let us lose a single instant, or it may be too late. Ah! my poor young mistress! Poor mademoiselle! it is terrible—terrible!"

Chapter Five
La Comtesse

The Countess, a handsome, well-preserved woman of middle age, slightly inclined to embonpoint, met me on the threshold, and in silence grasped my hand. From the window she had apparently watched me alight from the fiacre, and had rushed forth to meet me.

That something unusual had occurred was plain from the paleness of her countenance and the look of despair in her eyes. We had been excellent friends in Brussels in bygone days, for she had favoured my suit and had constantly invited me to her pretty home in the Boulevard de Waterloo or to the great old château in the Ardennes. A glance was sufficient to show me that she had grown considerably older, and that her face, although it still bore distinct traces of a faded beauty, was now worn and haggard. She was essentially a grande dame of the old régime, now fast disappearing from our ken, but at no time could she be considered a great hostess. She was somewhat intransigent, a woman of strong prejudices, usually well justified, and incapable of pretence or shams. But the law of kindliness was ever on her tongue, and she contented herself with giving those of whom she disapproved a wide berth. She was dressed plainly in black, with a single wisp of lace at the throat—a costume unusual for her. In Brussels her handsome toilettes, obtained from Paris, had always been admired. Although matronly, like the majority of Belgian women, she was extremely chic, with an almost girlish waist, and at whatever hour one called one always found her dressed with extreme taste and elegance. I must, however, admit that her appearance surprised me. Her hair had grown greyer, and she seemed as though utterly negligent of her personal appearance.

"Madame!" I exclaimed in alarm as our hands met, "tell me what has occurred."

"Ah, m'sieur," she cried in French, "I am in despair, and have sent for you! You can help me—if you will."

"In what manner?" I inquired breathlessly.

"Yolande!" she gasped, in a choking voice.

"Yolande!" I echoed. "What has happened to her? Your man will tell me nothing."

"He has orders to say nothing," she explained, leading the way into the elegant salon. "Now tell me," she said, looking at me very earnestly, "I am in sheer desperation, as you may see, or I would not presume to question you. Will you forgive me if I do?"

"Most certainly," I responded.

"Then before we go further I will put my question to you," she said in a strange voice. "Do you love Yolande?"

Such direct inquiry certainly took me by complete surprise. I stood looking at her for a few seconds absolutely open-mouthed.

"Why ask me that?" I inquired, puzzled. "Tell me what has happened to her."

"I can tell you nothing until you have answered my question," she replied quite calmly. I saw from her countenance that she was desperate.

"I think, madame, that when we were together in Brussels my actions must have betrayed to you—a woman—the state of my heart towards your daughter," I said. "I do not seek to deny that at that time I loved her more fondly than I could ever love again, and—"

"Then you do not love her still?" she cried, interrupting me.

"Allow me to conclude," I went on, speaking quite calmly, for I saw in this curious question of hers some mysterious motive. "I loved her while in Brussels, and for two years hoped to make her my wife."

"And then you grew tired of her?" the Countess asked, in a tone that was almost a sneer in itself. "It is always the same with you diplomatists. The women of every capital amuse you, but on your promotion you bow your adieux and seek fresh fields to conquer."

"I think you misjudge me," I protested, rather annoyed at her words. "I loved Yolande. When I admit this, I also admit that, like other men whose calling it is to lounge in the principal salons of Europe, I had not escaped the fascination exercised by other eyes than hers. But to me she was all the world. Surely, madame, you remember the days at Houffalize? You cannot disguise from yourself that I really loved her then?"

"But all that is of the past," she said seriously, her white hands clasped before her. "Briefly, you no longer entertain any love for her. Is not that so?"

I hesitated. My position was a difficult one. I was a diplomatist, and could speak untruths artistically when occasion required, but she had cornered me.

"Madame has guessed the truth," I answered at last.

"Ah!" she cried hoarsely, "I thought as much. You have found some other woman whom you prefer?"

I nodded assent. It was useless to lead her to believe what was not the truth. Yolande was of course charming in many ways; but when I thought of Edith I saw that comparison was impossible.

"And you have no further thought of her?" she asked.

"As far as marriage is concerned, no," I responded. "Nevertheless, I still regard her as an intimate friend. I was here only two or three hours ago chatting with her."

"You!" she cried, glaring at me strangely. "You were here—to-day?"

"Yes," I replied. "I thought she would certainly tell you of my visit."

"She told me nothing. I was quite unaware of it. I was out, and the servants told me that a gentlemen had called in my absence."

"I gave a card," I replied. "It is no doubt in the hall."

"No, it is not. It has been destroyed."

"Why?" I asked.

"For some mysterious reason known to Yolande." Then, turning quickly again to me, she placed her hand upon my arm in deep earnestness, saying: "Tell me, is your love for her absolutely and entirely dead—so dead that you would not care to perform her a service?"

Anderson's strange and startling story flashed through my mind. I made no reply.

"Remember the affection you once bore her," she urged. "I am a woman, m'sieur, and I presume to remind you of it."

I needed no reminder. The recollection of those sweet idyllic days was still fresh as ever in my memory. Ah! in those brief sunny hours I had fondly believed that our love would last always. It is ever the same. Youth is ever foolish.

"I should have loved her now," I answered at last, "were it not for one fact."

There was a mystery which had ended our love, and I saw now an opportunity of clearing it up. "To what fact do you refer?"

"To the reason of our parting."

"The reason!" echoed the Countess. "I have no idea whatever of the reason. What was it?"

I held my breath. Would it be just to tell her the truth? I wondered. I reflected for a moment, then in a calm voice answered:

"Because I discovered that her heart was not wholly mine."

She regarded me with undisguised amazement.

"Do you mean that Yolande had another lover?"

"No!" I cried with sudden resolve. "This conversation is not fair to her. It is all finished. She has forgotten, and we are both happy."

"Happy!" cried the Countess hoarsely. "You are, alas! mistaken. Poor Yolande has been the most unhappy girl in all the world. She has never ceased to think of you."

"Then I regret, madame," I responded.

"If you really regret," she answered, "then your love for her is not altogether dead."

She spoke the truth. At this point I may as well confide to you, my reader, the fact that I still regarded my charming little friend of those careless days of buoyant youth with a feeling very nearly akin to love. I recollected the painful circumstances which led to our parting. My memory drifted back to that well-remembered, breathless summer's evening when, while walking with her along the white highway near her home, I charged her with friendliness towards a man whose reputation in Brussels was none of the best; of her tearful protests, of my all-consuming jealousy, of her subsequent dignity, and of our parting. After that I had applied to the Foreign Office to be transferred, and a month later found myself in Rome.

Perhaps, after all, my jealousy might have been utterly unfounded. Sometimes I had thought I had treated her harshly, for, truth to tell, I had never obtained absolute proof that this man was more than a mere acquaintance. Indeed, I think it was this fact, or just a slight twinge of conscience, that caused a suspicion of the old love I once bore her to remain within me. It was not just to Edith—that I knew; yet notwithstanding the denunciations of both Kaye and Anderson, I could not altogether crush her from my heart. To wholly forget the woman for whom one has entertained the grand passion is often most difficult, sometimes, indeed, impossible of accomplishment. Visions of some sweet face with its pouting and ready lips will arise, constantly keeping the past ever present, and recalling a day one would fain forget. Thus it was with me—just as it has been with thousands of others.

"No," I admitted truthfully and honestly at last, "my love for Yolande is perhaps not altogether dead."

"Then you will render me a service?" she cried quickly. "Say that you will—for her sake!—for the sake of the great love you once bore her!"

"Of what nature is this service you desire?" I asked, determined to act with caution, for the startling stories I had heard had aroused within me considerable suspicion.

"I desire your silence regarding an absolute secret," she answered in a hoarse half-whisper.

"What secret?"

"A secret concerning Yolande," she responded. "Will you, for her sake, render us assistance, and at the same time preserve absolute secrecy as to what you may see or learn here to-day?"

"I will promise if you wish, madame, that no word shall pass my lips," I said. "But as to assistance, I cannot promise until I am aware of the nature of the service demanded of me."

"Of course," she exclaimed, with a faint attempt at a smile. My words had apparently reassured her, for she instantly became calmer, as though relying upon me for help. "Then as you give me your promise upon your honour to say nothing, you shall know the truth. Come with me."

She led the way down the long corridor, and turning to the left suddenly opened the door of a large and handsome bed-chamber, the wooden sun-blinds of which were closed to keep out the crimson glow of the sunset. The room was a fine one with big crystal mirrors and a shining toilette-service in silver, but upon the bed with its yellow silk hangings lay a female form fully dressed, but white-faced and motionless. In the dim half-light I could just distinguish the features as those of Yolande.

"What has occurred?" I cried in a hoarse whisper, dashing towards the bedside and bending down to look upon the face that had once held me in fascination.

"We do not know," answered the trembling woman at my side. "It is all a mystery."

I stretched forth my hand and touched her cheek. It was icy cold.

In those few moments my eyes had become accustomed to the dim light of the darkened room, and I detected the change that had taken place in the girl's countenance. Her eyes were closed, her lips blanched, her fair hair, escaped from its pins, fell in a sheen of gold upon the lace-edged pillow.

I held my breath. The awful truth was distinctly apparent. I placed my hand upon her heart, the bodice of her dress being already unloosened. Then a few seconds later I drew back, standing rigid and aghast.

"Why, she's dead!" I gasped.

"Yes," the Countess said, covering her face with her hands and bursting into tears. "My poor Yolande! she is dead—*dead*!"

The discovery appalled me. Only a couple of hours before we had chatted together, and she seemed in the best of health and spirits, just as in the old days, until I had made the announcement of Wolf's presence in Paris. The effect of that statement upon her had apparently been electrical. Why, I knew not. Had she not implored me to save her? This in itself was sufficient to show that she held him in deadly fear.

Again I bent in order to make further examination, but saw the unmistakable mark of death upon her countenance. The lower jaw had dropped, the checks were cold, and the silver hand-mirror which I had snatched from the table and held at her mouth was unclouded. There was no movement—no life. Yolande, my well-beloved of those long-past days, was dead.

I stood there at the bedside like a man in a dream. So swiftly had she been struck down that the terrible truth seemed impossible of realisation.

The Countess, standing beside me, sobbed bitterly. Truly the scene in that darkened chamber was a strange and impressive one. Never before in my whole life had I been in the presence of the dead.

"Yolande—Yolande!" I called, touching her cheek in an effort to awaken her, for I could not believe that she was actually dead.

But there was no response. Those blanched lips and the coldness of those cheeks told their own tale. She had passed to that land which lies beyond the range of human vision.

How long I stood there I cannot tell. My thoughts were inexpressibly sad ones, and the discovery had utterly upset me, so that I scarcely knew what I said or did. The blow of thus finding her lifeless crushed me. The affair was mysterious, to say the least of it. Of a sudden, however, the sobs of the grief-stricken Countess aroused me to a sense of my responsibility, and taking her hand I led her from the bedside into an adjoining room.

"How has this terrible catastrophe occurred?" I demanded of her breathlessly. "Only two hours ago she was well and happy."

"You mean when you saw her?" she said. "What was the object of your call?"

"To see her," I responded.

"And yet you parted ill friends in Brussels?" she observed in a tone of distinct suspicion. "You had some motive in calling. What was it?"

I hesitated. I could not tell her that I suspected her daughter to be a spy.

"In order to assure her of my continued good friendship."

She smiled, rather superciliously I thought.

"But how did the terrible affair occur?"

"We have no idea," answered the Countess brokenly. "She was found lying upon the floor of the salon within a quarter of an hour of the departure of her visitor, who proved to be yourself. Jean, the valet-de-chambre, on entering, discovered her lying there, quite dead."

"Astounding!" I gasped. "She was in perfect health when I left her."

She shook her head sorrowfully, and her voice, choking with grief, declared:

"My child has been killed—murdered!"

"Murdered! Impossible!" I cried.

"But she has," she declared. "I am absolutely positive of it!"

Chapter Six
A Piece of Plain Paper

"What medical examination has been made?" I demanded.

"None," responded the Countess. "My poor child is dead, and no doctor can render her assistance. Medical aid is unavailing."

"But do you mean to say that on making this discovery you did not think it necessary to send for a doctor?" I cried incredulously.

"I did not send for one—I sent for you," was her response.

"But we must call a doctor at once," I urged. "If you have suspicion of foul play we should surely know if there is any wound, or any injury to account for death."

"I did not consider it necessary. No doctor can return her to me," she wailed. "I sent for you because I believed that you would render me assistance in this terrible affair."

"Most certainly I will," I replied. "But in our own interests we must send for a medical man, and if it is found to be actually a case of foul play, for the police. I'll send a line to Doctor Deane, an Englishman whom I know, who is generally called in to see anybody at the Embassy who chances to be ill. He is a good fellow, and his discretion may be relied upon."

So saying, I scribbled a line on the back of a card, and told the man to take a cab down to the Rue du Havre, where the doctor occupied rooms over a hosier's shop a stone's throw from the bustling Gare St. Lazare.

A very curious mystery was evidently connected with this startling discovery, and I was anxious that my friend, Dick Deane, one of my old chums of Rugby days, should assist me in clearing it up.

The Countess de Foville, whose calmness had been so remarkable while speaking with me before we entered the death-chamber, had now given way to a flood of emotion. She sank back into her chair, and, burying her face in her hands, cried bitterly.

I tried to obtain some further information from her, but all that escaped her was:

"My poor Yolande! My poor daughter!" Finding that my endeavours to console her were futile, I went forth and made inquiries of the three frightened maidservants regarding what had occurred.

One of them, a dark-eyed Frenchwoman in frilled cap, whom I had seen on my previous visit, said, in answer to my questions:

"Jean discovered the poor mademoiselle in the petit salon about a quarter of an hour after m'sieur had left. She was lying upon her face near the window, quite rigid. He shouted; we all rushed in, and on examining her found that she was already dead."

"But was there no sign of a struggle?" I inquired, leading the way to the room indicated.

"The room was just as m'sieur sees it now," she answered, with a wave of her hand.

I glanced around, but as far as I could distinguish it was exactly as I had left it.

"There was no mark of violence—nothing to show that mademoiselle had been the victim of foul play?"

"Nothing, m'sieur."

Could it have been a case of suicide? I wondered. Yolande's words before I had taken leave of her were desponding, and almost led me to believe that she had taken her life rather than face the man Wolf who had so suddenly arrived in Paris—the man who exercised upon her some mysterious influence, the nature of which I could not guess.

"It was not more than fifteen minutes after I had left, you say?" I inquired.

"No, m'sieur, not more."

"Mademoiselle had no other visitor?"

"No, m'sieur. Of that we are all certain."

"And the Countess, where was she during the time I was here?"

"She was out driving. She did not return till about five minutes after we had made the terrible discovery."

"And how did madame act?"

"She ordered us to carry poor mademoiselle to her room. Poor madame! She bore the blow with wonderful fortitude."

That remark caused me to prick up my ears.

"I don't quite understand," I said. "Did she not give way to tears?"

"No, m'sieur; she shed no tears, but sat erect, motionless as a statue. She appeared unable to realise that poor mademoiselle was actually dead. At last she rang, and sent Jean to you."

"You are absolutely certain that mademoiselle had no visit or after I left?"

"Absolutely."

"It would, moreover, not be possible for anyone to enter or leave without your knowledge?" I suggested.

"M'sieur understands me perfectly. Mademoiselle must have fallen to the floor lifeless immediately after I had let you out. She made no sound, and had Jean not entered with her letters, which the concierge had brought, my poor young mistress might be lying there now."

The average Frenchwoman of the lower class is always dramatic wherever a domestic calamity is concerned, and this worthy bonne was no exception. She punctuated all her remarks with references to the sacred personages of the Roman Catholic religion.

"You haven't searched the room, I suppose?"

"No, m'sieur. Madame gave orders that nothing was to be touched."

This reply was eminently satisfactory. I glanced again around the place, now dim in the falling twilight, and ordered her to throw back the sun-shutters.

The woman went to the window and opened them, admitting a flood of mellow light, the last crimson of the glorious afterglow. Up from the boulevard came the dull roar of the traffic, mingling with the sound of distant bells ringing the Ave Maria. The bonne—an Alsatian, from her accent—crossed herself from force of habit, and retreated towards the door.

"You may go," I said. "I will remain here until the doctor arrives."

"Bien, m'sieur," answered the woman, disappearing and closing the door after her.

My object in dismissing her was to make a thorough search of the apartment, in order to discover whether any of Yolande's private possessions were there. She had been denounced by Kaye and Anderson as a spy, and it occurred to me that I might possibly discover the truth. But she was dead. The painful fact seemed absolutely incredible.

The room was not a large one, but well furnished, with considerable taste and elegance. There was the broad, silk-covered couch, upon which

Yolande had sat in the full possession of health and spirits only a couple of hours before; the skin rug, upon which her tiny foot had been stretched so coquettishly; the small table, by which she had stood supporting herself after I had made the fatal announcement that Wolf was in Paris.

As I stood there the whole of that strangely dramatic scene occurred to me. Yet she was dead—dead! She had died with her secret in her heart.

At any moment Dick Deane might arrive, but I desired to be the first to make an examination of the room, and with that object crossed to the little escritoire of inlaid olive-wood, one of those rather gimcrack pieces of furniture manufactured along the Ligurian coast for unsuspecting winter visitors. It was the only piece of incongruous furniture in the room, all the rest being genuine Louis Quatorze.

One or two letters bearing conspicuous coats-of-arms were lying there, but all were notes of a private nature from one or other of her friends. One was an invitation to Vichy from the Baronne Deland, wife of the great Paris financier; another, signed "Rose," spoke of the gaiety of Cairo and the dances at Shepheard's during the past winter; while a third, also in French, and bearing no signature, made an appointment to meet her in the English tea-shop in the Rue Royale on the following day at five o'clock.

That note, written upon plain paper of business appearance, had apparently been left by hand. Who, I wondered, was the person who had made that appointment? To me the writing seemed disguised, and probably, owing to the thickness of the up-strokes, had been penned by a male hand. There was a mistake in the orthography, too, the word "plaisir" being written "plasir." This showed plainly that no Frenchman had written it.

I placed the letter in my pocket, and, encouraged by it, continued my investigations.

In the tiny letter-rack was a note which the unfortunate girl had written immediately before being struck down. It was addressed to "Baronne Maillac, Château des Grands Sablons, Seine et Marne." The little escritoire contained four small drawers; the contents of each I carefully scrutinised. They were, however, mostly private letters of a social character—some from persons whom I knew well in Society. Suddenly, from the bottom of one of the smaller drawers, I drew forth several sheets of plain octavo paper of a pale yellow shade. There were, perhaps, half-a-dozen sheets, carefully wrapped in a sheet of plain blue foolscap. I opened them, and, holding one up to the light, examined the water-mark.

Next instant the truth was plain. That paper was the official paper used in French Government offices for written reports. How came it in her possession, if the accusation against her were untrue?

I held it in my hand, glaring at it in bewilderment. Sheet by sheet I examined it, but there was no writing upon it. Apparently it was her reserve store of paper, to be used as wanted. In the French Ministry of Foreign Affairs everything is methodical, especially the preparation of the dossiers. A certain dossier had once fallen into Kaye's hands, and it contained sheets of exactly similar paper to that which I held in my hand.

Eagerly I continued my search, striving to discover some writing which might lead me to a knowledge of the truth, but I found nothing. I had completed an examination of the whole of the contents of the drawers, when it occurred to me that there might be some other drawer concealed there. Years ago I had been offered an escritoire of this pattern in Genoa, and the sun-tanned fellow who endeavoured to induce me to purchase it had shown behind the centre drawer in the table a cunningly contrived cavity where private correspondence might be concealed.

Therefore I drew out the drawer, sounded the interior at the back, and, finding it hollow, searched about for the spring by which it might be opened. At last I found it, and next moment drew forth a bundle of letters. They were bound with a blue ribbon that time had faded. I glanced at the superscription of the uppermost, and a thrill of sympathy went through me.

Those carefully preserved letters were my own—letters full of love and tenderness, which I had written in the days that were dead. I stood holding them in my hand, my heart full of the past.

In this narrative, my reader, it is my intention to conceal nothing, but to relate to you the whole, undisguised truth, even though this chapter of England's secret history presents a seemingly improbable combination of strange facts and circumstances. Therefore I will not hide from you the truth that in those moments, as I drew forth one of the letters I had written long ago and read it through, sweet and tender memories crowded upon me, and in my eyes stood blinding tears. I may be forgiven for this, I think, when it is remembered how fondly I had once loved Yolande, before that fatal day when jealousy had consumed me, and I had turned my back upon her as a woman false and worthless.

Letter after letter I read, each bringing back to me sad memories of those days, when in the calm sunset hour we had wandered by the riverside hand in hand like children, each supremely content in each other's love, fondly believing that our mad passion would last always. In all the world she had been, to me, incomparable. The centre of admiration at those brilliant balls at the Royal Palace at Brussels, the most admired of all the trim and comely girls who rode at morning in the Bois, the merriest of those who picnicked in the forest round about the ancient château, the sweetest, the most tender, and the most pure of all the women I knew—Yolande in those days had been mine. There, in my hand, I held the letter which I had written from Scotland when on leave for the shooting, asking if she loved me sufficiently to become my wife. To that letter I well remembered her reply—indeed, I knew it verbatim; a tender letter, full of honest love and straightforward admission—a letter such as only a pure and good woman could have penned. Yes, she wrote that she loved me dearly, and would be my wife.

And yet it was all of the past. All had ended.

I sighed bitterly—how bitterly, mere words cannot describe. You, reader, be you man or woman, can you fully realise how deeply I felt at that moment, how utterly desolate the world then seemed to me?

Those letters I slowly replaced in the cavity and closed it. Then, as I turned away, my eyes fell upon the photographs standing upon a small whatnot close by the escritoire. They were of persons whom I did not know—all strangers, save one. This was a cabinet portrait in a heavy silver frame, and as I took it up to scrutinise it more closely a cry involuntarily escaped my lips.

The picture was a three-quarter length representation of a black-bearded, keen-eyed man, standing with his hands thrust idly in his pockets, and smoking a cigarette. There was no mistaking those features. It was the photograph of the man the discovery of whose presence in Paris had produced such an extraordinary effect upon her—Rodolphe Wolf.

Chapter Seven
By a Thread

I was still standing by the window, holding the photograph in my hand, and gazing upon it in wonder, when Dick Deane was shown in.

"What's the matter, old chap? Are you the man in possession here?" he asked breezily, gripping me by the hand.

He was a fair, merry-faced fellow of thirty-five, rather good-looking, smartly dressed in black frock-coat of professional cut, and wearing a pair of gold-rimmed pince-nez. He had been born in Paris, and had spent the greater part of his life there, except during the years when he was at school with me before going to Edinburgh, where he took his degree. Then he had returned to Paris, taken his French degree, and had soon risen to be one of the fashionable doctors in the French capital. He was an especial favourite in the salons, and, like every good-looking doctor, a favourite with the ladies.

"I'm not in possession," I answered. "A very serious affair has happened here, and we want your assistance."

In an instant he became grave, for I suppose my tone showed him that I was in no humour for joking.

"What's the nature of the affair?" he asked.

"Death," I replied seriously. "A lady here—a friend of mine—has died mysteriously."

"A mystery—eh?" he exclaimed, instantly interested. "Tell me about it."

"This place," I replied, "belongs to the Countess de Foville, a lady whom I knew well when I was at the Brussels Embassy, and it is her daughter Yolande who has been found dead in this room this evening."

"Yolande de Foville!" he repeated, with knit brows. "She was a friend of yours once, if I mistake not?" he added, looking me straight in the face.

"Yes, Dick, she was," I responded. "I told you of her long ago."

"You loved her once?"

"Yes," I answered with difficulty, "I loved her once."

"And how did the unfortunate affair occur?" he asked, folding his arms and leaning back against a chair. "Tell me the whole story."

"I called here this afternoon, and spent half an hour or so with her," I said. "Then I left and returned straight to the Embassy—"

"You left her here?" he inquired, interrupting. "Yes, in this very room. But it seems that a quarter of an hour later one of the servants entered and discovered her lying upon the door, dead."

"Curious!" he ejaculated. "Has a medical man seen her?"

"No. The Countess sent for me as being one of her daughter's most intimate friends, and I, in turn, sent for you."

"Where is the poor young lady?"

"In her room at the end of the corridor," I answered hoarsely.

"Is there any suspicion of murder?"

"Apparently none whatever. She had no visitor after I left."

"And no suspicion of suicide?" he asked, with a sharp look. "Did you part friends?"

"Perfectly so," I responded. "As to suicide, she had no reason, as far as anyone knows, to make an attempt upon her life."

He gave vent to an expression which sounded to me much like a grunt of dissatisfaction.

"Now, be perfectly frank with me, Gerald," he said, suddenly turning to me and placing his hand upon my shoulder. "You loved her very dearly once—was that not so?"

I nodded.

"I well remember it," he went on. "I quite recollect how, on one occasion, you came over to London, and while dining together at Jimmy's you told me of your infatuation, and showed me her photograph. Do you remember the night when you told me of your engagement to her?"

"Perfectly."

"And as time went on you suddenly dropped her—for what reason I know not. We are pals, but I have never attempted to pry into your affairs. If she really loved you, it must have been a hard blow for her when she heard that you had forsaken her for Edith Austin."

"You reproach me," I said. "But you do not know the whole truth, my dear fellow. I discovered that Yolande possessed a second lover."

He nodded slowly, with pursed lips.

"And that was the reason of your parting?"

"Yes."

"The sole reason?"

"The sole reason."

"And you have no suspicion that she may have committed suicide because of her love for you? Such things are not uncommon, remember, with girls of a certain temperament."

"If she has committed suicide, it is not on my account," I responded in a hard voice.

"I did not express that opinion," he hastened to protest. "Before we discuss the matter further it will be best for me to see her. Death may have been due to natural causes, for aught we know."

I stood motionless. His suggestion that my sweetheart of the old days had committed suicide because I had forsaken her was a startling one. Surely that could not be so?

"Come," my friend said, "let us lose no time. Which is the room?"

I led him along the corridor, and opened the door of the chamber in which she was lying so cold and still. The light of the afterglow fell full upon her, tipping her auburn hair with crimson and illuminating her face with a warm radiance that gave her back the appearance of life. But it was only for a few moments. The slanting ray was lost, and the pallor of that beautiful countenance became marked against the gold of her wondrous hair.

In silence I stood at the foot of the bed watching my friend, who was now busy with his examination. He opened her eyes and closed them again, felt her heart, raised her arms, and examined her mouth, uttering no word. His serious face wore a look as though he were infinitely puzzled.

One after the other he examined the palms of her hands long and carefully, then, bending until his eyes were close to her face, he examined her lips, brow, and the whole surface of her cheeks. Upon her neck, below the left ear, was a mark to which he returned time after time, as though not satisfied as to its cause. Upon her lower lip, too, was a slight yellow discoloration, which he examined several times, comparing it with the mark upon the neck. He was unable to account for either.

"Curious!" he ejaculated. "Very curious indeed!"

"What is curious?" I inquired eagerly.

"Those marks," he answered, indicating them with his finger. "They are very puzzling. I've never seen such marks before."

"Do they point to foul play?" I inquired, feeling suspicious that she had by some mysterious means fallen the victim of an assassin.

"Well, no," he responded, after some hesitation; "that is not my opinion."

"Then what is your opinion?"

"At present I have none. I can have none until I make a thorough examination. There are certainly no outward marks of violence."

"We need not inform the police, I suppose?"

"Not at present," he replied, his eyes still fixed upon the blanched face of the woman who had once been all the world to me.

I raised her dead hand, and upon it imprinted a last fervent kiss. It was cold and clammy to my lips. In that hour all my old love for her had returned, and my heart had become filled with an intense bitterness and desolation. I had thought that all my love for her was dead, and that Edith Austin, the calm, sweet woman far away in an English county, who wrote to me daily from her quiet home deep in the woodlands, had taken her place. But our meeting and its tragic sequel had, I admit, aroused within me a deep sympathy, which had, within an hour, developed into that great and tender love of old. With men this return to the old love is of no infrequent occurrence, but with women it seldom happens. Perhaps this is because man is more fickle and more easily influenced by woman's voice, woman's glances, and woman's tears.

The reader will probably accuse me of injustice and of fickleness of heart. Well, I cannot deny it; indeed, I seek to deny nothing in this narrative of strange facts and diplomatic wiles, but would only ask of those who read to withhold their verdict until they have ascertained the truth yet to be revealed, and have read to the conclusion, this strange chapter of the secret history of a nation.

My friend the doctor was holding one hand, while I imprinted a last kiss upon the other. A lump was in my throat, my eyes were filled with tears, my thoughts were all of the past, my anguish of heart unspeakable. That small chill hand with the cold, glittering ring—one that I had given her in Brussels long ago—seemed to be the only reality in all that hideous phantasmagoria of events.

"Do not despair," murmured the kind voice of my old friend, standing opposite me on the other side of the bed. "You loved her once, but it is all over—surely it is!"

"No, Dick!" I answered brokenly. "I thought I did not love her. I have held her from me these three years—until now."

"Ah!" he sighed, "I understand. Man always longs for the unattainable."

"Yes, always," I responded.

In that moment the memory of the day when we had parted arose gaunt and ghost-like. I had wronged her; I felt confident that I had. All came back to me now—that cruel, scandalous denunciation I had uttered in the heat of my mad jealousy—the false tale which had struck her dumb by its circumstantial accuracy. Ah! how bitter it all was, now that punishment was upon me! I remembered how, in the hour of my worldly triumph and of her highest hope—at the very moment when she had spoken words of greater affection to me than she had ever used before—I had made the charge against her, and she had fallen back with her young heart crushed within her. My ring was there, still glittering mockingly upon her dead hand. By the unfounded charge I had made against her I had sinned. My sin at that moment arose from its grave, and barred the way for ever to all hope—to all happiness.

The summer twilight was stealing on apace, and in the silence of the room there sounded the roar of life from the boulevard below. Men were crying Le Soir with strident voices, and all Paris was on its way to dine, and afterwards to enjoy itself in idleness upon the terraces of the cafés or at those al-fresco variety performances in the Avenue des Champs Elysées, where the entrance-fee includes a consommation.

Deane still held my old love's hand, bending in the dim light until his eyes were close to it, watching intently. But I took no notice, for my eyes were fixed upon that face that had held me in such fascination, and had been so admired at those brilliant receptions given by King Leopold and the Countess of Flanders. The doctor stretched forth his hand, and of a sudden switched on the electric light. The next instant I was startled by his loud ejaculation of surprise.

"Thank God!" he cried. "She's not dead, after all!"

"Not dead!" I gasped, unable fully to realise his meaning.

"No," he answered breathlessly. "But we must not lose a single instant." And I saw that with a lancet he had made an incision in her delicate wrist, and there was blood there. "She is in a state of catalepsy, and we must do all in our power to bring her round."

"But do you think you can?" I cried.

"I hope so."

"Do your best, Dick," I implored. "Save her, for my sake."

"Rely upon me," he answered calmly, adding: "Run along to Number 18 in the boulevard—the corner house on the right—and bring Doctor Trépard at once. He lives au troisième. Tell him that I sent you, and that the matter is one of life or death." He scribbled some words on a card, and, giving it me, added: "Tell him to bring this. Meanwhile, I will commence artificial respiration. Go!"

"But do you think she will really recover?" I demanded.

"I can't tell. We have already lost so much time. I had no idea of the truth. It has surprised me just as it has surprised you. This moment is not one for words, but for actions. Don't lose an instant."

Thus urged, I snatched up my hat and tore along the boulevard like a madman. Without difficulty I found Trépard's appartement, and on being admitted found him a grave-faced, rather stout old Frenchman, who, on the instant I mentioned Dick's name and gave him the card with the words upon it, naming some drugs he required, went into an adjoining room, and fetched a phial of tiny red pillules, which he held up to the light. Then he put on his hat, and descended with me to the street. A fiacre was passing, which we took, and five minutes later we were standing together in the room where Yolande was lying.

"This is a most curious case, my dear Trépard," began Dick, speaking in French—"a case of coma, which I have mistaken for death;" and, continuing, he briefly explained how the patient had been found in a state so closely resembling death that he himself had been deceived.

The old Frenchman placed his hand upon her heart, and, withdrawing it, said:

"She's breathing now."

"Breathing!" I echoed. "Then she is recovering!"

"Yes, old fellow," Dick replied, "she is recovering—at least we hope we shall save her." Then, turning to his colleague, he raised her hand and pointed to the finger-nails, asking: "Do you notice anything there?"

The other, adjusting his pince-nez, bent and examined, them one by one.

"Yes," he answered at last. "A slight purple discoloration at the base of the nails."

"And upon the lower lip does anything strike you as peculiar?"

"A yellow mark," he answered, after carefully inspecting the spot indicated.

"And there?" Deane asked, touching the mark upon the neck.

"Very strange!" ejaculated the elder man. "It is a most unusual case."

"Yes. Have you brought the hydrated peroxide of iron?"

For answer the Frenchman produced the tiny tube, saying:

"Then you suspect poison?"

"Most certainly," he replied; and, taking a glass, he placed a single pillule in it, dissolving it in water, which he afterwards forced between the grey lips of my unconscious love. Afterwards he glanced at his watch, observing: "We must give another in fifteen minutes."

Then, drawing a chair to the bedside, he seated himself, holding her wrist and watching her countenance for any change that might take place there.

"Have you no idea of the nature of the poison?" I inquired eagerly.

"None," he responded. "Ask me no questions now. When we have brought her round will be time enough. It should be sufficient for you to know that she is not dead. Why not leave us for the present? Go and break the good news to the Countess."

"You wish to be alone?"

"Yes. This is a serious matter. Leave us undisturbed, and on no pretext allow her mother to enter here."

Thus urged, and feeling reassured by their statement that she still lived and that the pulsations of her heart were already quite perceptible, I left the room, noiselessly closing the door after me, and sought the Countess in the small blue boudoir to which she had returned plunged in grief and dark despair.

She was seated in a chair, motionless and statuesque, staring straight before her. The blow had utterly crushed her, for she was entirely devoted to her only daughter now that her husband was dead. I well knew how deep was her affection for Yolande, and how tender was her maternal love.

The room was in semi-darkness, for she had not risen to turn on the light. As I entered I did so with her permission, saying quietly:

"Madame, I come to you with a message."

"From whom?" she asked in a hard mechanical voice.

"From my friend Deane, the English doctor whom I have summoned. Yolande still lives!"

"She lives!" she cried, springing to her feet in an instant. "You are deceiving me!"

"I am not, madame," I reassured her, smiling. "Your daughter is still breathing, and is increasing in strength perceptibly. The doctors say that she will probably recover."

"Thank God!" she gasped, her thin white hands clasped before her. "I pray that He may give her back to me. I will go to her."

But I held her back, explaining that both the medical men had expressed a wish to remain there alone.

"But what caused that appearance so akin to death?" she asked quickly.

"At present they cannot tell," I responded. "Some deleterious substance is suspected, but until she has returned to consciousness and can give us some details of her sudden attack we can determine nothing."

"But she will recover, m'sieur?" the Countess asked. "Are you certain?"

"The chances are in her favour, the doctors say. They have given her a drug to counteract the effect of the poison."

"Poison! Was she poisoned?" gasped the Countess.

"Poison is suspected," I answered quietly. "But calm yourself, madame. The truth will be discovered in due course."

"I care nothing so long as Yolande is given back to me!" the distressed woman cried. "Was it your English friend who discovered the truth?"

"Yes," I replied. "He is one of the cleverest men in Paris."

"And to him my poor Yolande will owe her life?"

"Yes, to him."

"And to you also, m'sieur? You have done your utmost for us, and I thank you warmly for it all."

"Madame," I said earnestly, "I have done only what a man should do. You sought my assistance, and I have given it, because—"

"Because of what?" she inquired sharply the instant I paused.

"Because I once loved her," I responded with perfect frankness.

A sigh escaped her, and her hand sought my arm.

"I was young once, m'sieur," she said in that calm, refined voice which had long ago always sounded so much to me like that of my own dead mother. "I understand your feeling—I understand perfectly. It is only my poor daughter who does not understand. She knows that you have forsaken her—that is all."

It was upon my tongue to lay bare to her the secret of my heart's longings, yet I hesitated. I remembered that calm, serious, sweet-faced woman on the other side of the English Channel, far from the glare and glitter of life as I knew it—the fevered life which the diplomat in Paris is forced to lead. I remembered my troth to Edith, and my conscience pricked me.

"Could it be possible," I reflected, "that Yolande was really in the pay of a Government hostile to England?" Kaye was already nearing Berlin with the intention of searching out her actions and exposing her as a spy, while Anderson had already denounced her as having been a party to an attempt to secure the secret which he had carried from Berlin to Downing Street.

With a mother's solicitude the Countess could for some time only speak of Yolande's mysterious attack; but at last, in order to prosecute my inquiries further, I observed, during a lull in the conversation:

"At the Baroness de Chalencon's last night a friend of yours inquired about you, madame."

"A friend? Who?"

"A man named Wolf—Rodolphe Wolf."

The next instant I saw that the mention of that name affected the mother no less markedly than it had affected the daughter. Her face blanched; her eyes opened wide in fear, and her glance became in a moment suspicious. With marvellous self-possession she, however, pretended ignorance.

"Wolf?" she repeated. "I do not remember the name. Possibly he is some person we have met while travelling."

"Yolande knew him, I believe, in Brussels," I remarked. "He appeared to be acquainted with you."

"My daughter's friends are not always mine," she remarked coldly, with that cleverness which only a woman of the world can possess, and at once returned to the discussion of Yolande and the probability of her recovery.

This puzzled me. I felt somehow convinced that she knew the truth. She had some distinct object in endeavouring to seal my lips. What it was, however, I could not determine.

She was expressing a fervent hope that her daughter would recover, and pacing the room, impatient to go to her bedside, when, of a sudden, Dick opened the door, and, putting his head inside, addressed me, saying:

"Can I speak with you a moment, Ingram?" She dashed to the door in eagerness, but after a word of introduction from myself, he informed her that Yolande had not sufficiently recovered to be disturbed.

"Perfect quiet is absolutely necessary, madame," he urged. "Your daughter, I am pleased to tell you, will live; but she must be kept absolutely quiet. I cannot allow you to approach her on any pretext whatsoever."

"She will not die, will she?" the woman implored distractedly.

"No," he replied, in a voice somewhat strained, I thought, "she will not die. Of that you may rest assured."

Then turning to me, he beckoned, and I followed him out of the room.

Chapter Eight
The Old Love

"I don't like that woman, old fellow," were the first words Dick uttered when we were alone in the room in which Yolande had been found.

"Why not?" I asked, rather surprised. "The Countess de Foville is always charming."

He shrugged his shoulders, saying:

"One sometimes has strange and unaccountable prejudices, you know. This is one of mine."

"And Yolande," I asked, "what of her?"

"She's better. But it was fortunate I made the discovery just when I did, or she would no doubt have passed away. I never saw an appearance so closely resembling death in all my experience; in fact, I'd have staked my professional reputation that there was no spark of life."

"But what was the cause of it all?" I demanded. "You surely know the reason?"

"No, we cannot yet tell," he answered. "The marks puzzle us. That mark on her lower lip is the most peculiar and unaccountable. At present we can say nothing."

"Then why did you call me out?"

"Because I want to consult you," he replied. "The fact is, that in this affair there is a strong element of mystery which I don't like at all. And, moreover, the few seconds during which I've seen the Countess have plainly impressed upon me the belief that either she has had something to do with it, or else that she knows the truth."

I nodded. This was exactly my own theory. "Do you think Yolande has been the victim of foul play?" I inquired a moment later.

"That's my suspicion," he responded. "But only she herself can tell us the truth."

"You really think, then, that a dastardly attempt has been made upon her life?" I cried incredulously.

"Personally, I think there can be no doubt."

"But by whom? No one called here after my departure."

"It is that mystery which we must elucidate," he said. "All I fear is, however, that she may render us no assistance."

"Why?"

"Because it is a mystery, and in all probability she will endeavour to preserve the secret. She must not see the Countess before we question her."

"Is she yet conscious?" I asked in eagerness.

"Yes; but at present we must put no question to her."

"Thank Heaven!" I gasped. Then I added, fervently grasping my friend's hand: "You cannot realise, Dick, what great consolation this is to me!"

"I know, my dear fellow—I know," he answered sympathetically. "But may I speak to you as a friend? You won't be offended at anything I am about to say, will you?"

"Offended?—certainly not. Our friendship is too firm for that, Dick. What is it you wish to say?"

I saw that he was uneasy, and was surprised at his sudden gravity.

"Well," he said, after a moment's hesitation, "you'll forgive me for saying so, but I don't think that in this affair you've told me exactly the truth."

"What do you mean?" I inquired quickly.

"I mean that when you parted from her this afternoon you were not altogether good friends."

"You are mistaken," I assured him. "We were as good friends as ever before."

"No high words passed between you?"

"None."

"And nothing that you told her caused her any sudden grief? Are you quite certain of this?" he asked, looking at me very fixedly through his glasses.

"I made one observation which certainly caused her surprise," I admitted. "Nothing else."

"Was it only surprise?" he asked very calmly.

"Surprise mingled with fear."

"Ah!" he ejaculated, as though obtaining some intelligence by this admission of mine. "And may I not know the nature of the information you gave her?"

"No, Dick," I responded. "It is a secret—her secret."

He was silent.

"You refuse to tell me?" he said disappointedly.

"I am unable," I replied.

"And if I judge rightly, it is this secret which has parted you?"

"No, it is not," I answered. "That's the most curious part of the whole affair. The very existence of the secret has brought us together again."

"You mean that you have forsaken Edith and returned to her?" he observed, raising his brows slightly in surprise.

"No; don't put it in that way," I implored. "I have not yet forsaken Edith."

He smiled, just a trifle superciliously, I thought.

"And the Countess is also in possession of this mysterious secret—eh?"

"Of that I am not at all certain," I replied.

He sniffed in distinct suspicion that what I had told him was not the truth. At the same instant, however, the Countess entered and demanded to know the condition of her child.

"She is much better, madame," he answered. "Perfect quiet is, however, necessary, and constant observation of the temperature. To-morrow, or the day after, you may, I think, see her."

"Not till then!" she cried. "I cannot wait so long."

"But it is necessary. Your daughter's life hangs upon a single thread."

She was silenced, for she saw that argument was useless.

A few minutes later Jean entered with a message from Trépard asking Dick and myself to consult with him. We therefore left the Countess again, and passed along the corridor to the room in which my love of long ago was lying. As we entered she lifted her hand slowly to me in sign of recognition, and in an instant I was at her side.

"Yolande!" I cried, taking her hand, so different now that death had been defeated by life. "Yolande! my darling," I burst forth involuntarily, "you have come back to me!"

A sweet, glad smile spread over her beautiful face, leaving an expression of calm and perfect contentment, as in a low, uncertain voice, as though of one speaking afar off, she asked:

"Gerald, is it actually you?"

"Yes," I said, "of course it is. These two gentlemen are doctors," I added. "This is my old friend Deane; and the other is Doctor Trépard, of whom I daresay you have heard."

She nodded to them both in acknowledgment of their kind expressions; then in a few low words inquired what had happened to her. She seemed in utter ignorance of it all.

"You were found lying on the floor of the little salon soon after I left, and they thought you were dead," I explained. "Cannot you tell us how it occurred?"

A puzzled expression settled upon her face, as though she were trying to remember.

"I recollect nothing," she declared.

"But you surely remember how you were attacked?" I urged.

"Attacked!" she echoed in surprise. "No one attacked me."

"I did not mean that," I answered, rather puzzled at her quick protest. "I meant that you were probably aware of the symptoms which preceded your unconsciousness."

"I felt a strange dizziness and a curious tightness in the throat and chest. That is all I remember. All became blank until I opened my eyes again and found myself lying here, with these two gentlemen standing at my side. The duration of my unconsciousness did not appear to me longer than a few minutes."

"Then mademoiselle has no idea of the cause of her strange illness?" inquired Deane in French. "None whatever, m'sieur."

"Tell us one fact," he urged. "During the time which elapsed between your parting with M'sieur Ingram and your sudden unconsciousness, did anyone enter the room?"

"No one; of that I am absolutely certain."

"How were you occupied during that time?"

"I was writing a letter."

"And before you rose did you feel the curious giddiness?"

"No, not until after I stood up. I tried to shout and attract help, but could not. Then I reached to press the bell, but stumbled forward, and the next instant I was lost in what seemed to be a dense fog."

"Curious!" ejaculated Trépard, who stood by with folded arms, eagerly listening to every word — "very curious!"

"Did you feel any strange sensation on the left side of your neck beneath the ear, or upon your lower lip?" inquired Deane earnestly.

She reflected for a moment, then said:

"Now that I remember, there was a curious numbness of my lip."

"Followed immediately by unconsciousness?"

"Yes, almost immediately."

The doctors exchanged glances, which showed that the mark upon the lip was the chief enigma of the situation.

Trépard glanced at his watch, dissolved yet another pillule of hydrated peroxide of iron, and handed her the draught to swallow. The antidote had acted almost like magic.

"You are absolutely certain that no person entered the room after Ingram had left?" repeated Deane, as though not yet satisfied.

"Absolutely."

Dick Deane turned his eyes full upon me, and I divined his thoughts. He was reflecting upon the conversation held between us before we entered that room. He was endeavouring to worm from her some clue to her secret.

"My mother knows that I am recovering?" she went on. "If she does not, please tell her. She has been so distressed of late that this must have been the crowning blow to her."

"I have told madame your mother everything," I said. "Do not be uneasy on her account."

"Ah," she sighed, "how I regret that we came to Paris! I regret it all, Gerald, save that you and I have met again;" and she stretched out her hand until it came into contact with my coat-button, with which she toyed like a child.

"And this meeting has really given you satisfaction?" I whispered to her, heedless of the presence of the others.

"Not only satisfaction," she answered, so softly that I alone could catch her words, and looking into my face with that expression of passionate affection which can never be simulated; "it has given back to me a desire for happiness, for life, for love."

There were tears in those wonderful blue eyes, and her small hand trembled within my grasp. My heart at that moment was too full for mere words. True, I loved her with a mad fondness that I had never before entertained for any woman; yet, nevertheless, a hideous shadow arose between us, shutting her off from me for ever—the shadow of her secret— the secret that she, my well-beloved, was actually a spy.

Chapter Nine
At the Elysée

Having reassured myself of Yolande's recovery, I was compelled to rush off, slip into uniform, and attend a dinner at the Elysée. The function was a brilliant affair, as are all the official junketings of the French President. At the right of the head of the Republic, who was distinguishable by his crimson sash, sat the Countess Tornelli, with the wife of the United States Ambassador on his left. The President's wife—who wore a superb gown of corn-coloured miroir velvet, richly embroidered and inlaid with Venetian lace, a veritable triumph of the Rue de la Paix—had on her right the Papal Nuncio, Monsignor Lerenzelli, the doyen of the Diplomatic Corps, while on her left was my Chief, Lord Barmouth.

The seat next me was allotted to his daughter Sibyl, who looked charming in rose chiffon. During dinner she chatted merrily, describing a charity bazaar which she had attended that afternoon accompanied by her mother. On the other side of her sat Count Berchtold, the secretary of the Austrian Embassy, who was, I shrewdly suspected, one of her most devoted admirers. She was charming—a typical, smart English girl; and I think that I was proved to be an exception among men by reason of the fact that I did not flirt with her. Indeed, we were excellent friends, and my long acquaintance with her gave me a prescriptive right to a kind of brotherly solicitude for her welfare. Times without number I had chaffed her about her little affairs of the heart, and as many times she had turned my criticisms against myself by her witty repartee. She could be exceedingly sarcastic when occasion required; but there had always been a perfect understanding between us, and no remark was ever distorted into an insult.

Dinner was followed by a brilliant reception. The great Salon des Fêtes, which only a year before was hung with funeral wreaths, owing to the death of the previous President, resounded with that peculiar hum made up of all the intonations of conversation and discreet laughter rolled together against the sustained buzzing of the orchestra a short distance away. The scene was one of glittering magnificence. Everyone knew everyone else. Through the crowd of uniforms—which always give an official reception at the Elysée the appearance of a bal travesti—I passed Monsieur Casimir

Perrier, former President of the Republic; Monsieur Paul Deschanel, the lion of the hour; Monsieur Benjamin-Constant, always a prominent figure; Prince Roland Bonaparte, smiling and bowing; the Duchess d'Auerstadt, with her magnificent jewels; and Damat, the dapper Grand Chancellor of the Legion of Honour. All diplomatic Paris was there, chattering, laughing, whispering, and plotting. Around me sounded a veritable babel of tongues, but no part of the function interested me.

From time to time I saluted a man I knew, or bent over a woman's hand; but my thoughts were of the one woman who had so suddenly and so forcibly returned into my life. The representatives of the Powers of Europe were all present, and as they passed me by, each in his bright uniform, his orders flashing on his breast and a woman on his arm, I asked myself which of them was actually the employer of my well-beloved.

The startling events of the day had upset me. Had it been possible I would have left and returned to my rooms for a quiet smoke and for calm reflection. But my duty required my presence there; hence I remained, strolling slowly around the great crowded salon with its myriad lights and profuse floral decorations, until I suddenly encountered the wizen-faced, toothless old Baronne de Chalencon, whose salon was one of the most popular in Paris, and with whom I was on excellent terms.

"Ah! my dear M'sieur Ingram!" she cried, holding forth her thin, bony hand laden with jewels. "You look tired. Why? No one here to-night who interests you—eh?"

"No one save yourself, Baronne," I responded, bending over her hand.

"Flatterer!" she laughed. "If I were forty years younger I might accept that as a compliment. But at my age—well, it is really cruel of you."

"Intelligence is more interesting to a diplomat than a pretty face," I responded quickly. "And there is certainly no more intelligent woman in all Paris than the Baronne de Chalencon."

She bowed stiffly, and her wrinkled face, which bore visible traces of poudre orchidée and touches of the hare's-foot, puckered up into a simpering smile.

"Well, and what else?" she asked. "These speeches you have apparently prepared for some pretty woman you expected to meet here to-night, but, since she has not kept the appointment, you are practising them upon me."

"No," I said, "I really protest against that, Baronne. A woman is never too old for a man to pay her compliments."

We had strolled into a cool ante-room, and were sitting together upon one of the many seats placed beneath clumps of palms and flowers, the only light being from a hundred tiny electric lamps hung overhead in the trees. The perfect arrangement of those ante-rooms of the Salle des Fêtes on the nights of the official receptions is always noteworthy, and after the heat, music, and babel of tongues in the grand salon it was cool, quiet, and refreshing there.

By holding her regular salon, where everybody who was anybody made it a point to be seen, the Baronne had acquired in Paris a unique position. Her fine house in the Avenue des Champs Elysées was the centre of a smart and fashionable set, and she herself made a point of being versed in all the latest gossip and scandal of the French capital. She scandalised nobody, nor did she seek to throw mud at her enemies. She merely repeated what was whispered to her; hence a chat with her was always interesting to one who, like myself, was paid to keep his ears open and report from time to time the direction of the political wind.

Tournier, the French Minister of Foreign Affairs, and his wife were her most intimate friends; hence she was frequently aware of facts which were of considerable importance to us. Indeed, once or twice her friendliness for myself had caused her to drop hints which had been of the greatest use to Lord Barmouth in the conduct of his difficult diplomacy at that time when the boulevard journals were screaming against England and the filthy prints were caricaturing Her Majesty, with intent to insult. Even the *Figaro*—the moderate organ of the French Foreign Office—had lost its self-control in the storm of abuse following the Fashoda incident, and had libelled and maligned "les English." I therefore seized the opportunity for a chat with the wizen-faced old lady, who seemed in a particularly good-humour, and deftly turned the conversation into the political channel.

"Now, tell me, Baronne," I said, after we had been chatting some little time, and I had learnt more than one important fact regarding the intentions of Tournier, "what is your opinion regarding the occupation of Ceuta?"

She glanced at me quickly, as though surprised that I should be aware of what she had believed to be an entire secret.

"Of Ceuta?" she echoed. "And what do you at your Embassy know regarding it?"

"We've heard a good deal," I laughed.

"No doubt you've heard a good deal that is untrue," the clever old lady replied, her powdered face again puckering into a smile. "Do you want to know my honest opinion?" she added.

"Yes, I do."

"Well," she went on, "I attach very little importance to the rumours of a projected sale or lease of Ceuta to us. I might tell you in confidence," she went on, dropping her voice, "that from some words I overheard at the garden-party at de Wolkenstein's I have come to a firm conclusion that, although during the next few years important changes will be made upon the map of the world, Ceuta will remain Spanish. My country will never menace yours in the Mediterranean at that point. A Ministry might be found in Madrid to consider the question of its disposal, but the Spanish people would rise in revolution before they would consent. Spain is very poor, but very proud. Having lost so many of her foreign possessions, she will hold more strongly than ever to Ceuta. There you have the whole situation in a nutshell."

"Then the report that it is actually sold to France is untrue?" I asked eagerly.

"A mere report I believe it to be."

"But Spain's financial indebtedness to France might prove an element of danger when Europe justifies Lord Beaconsfield's prediction and rushes into war over Morocco?"

"Ah, my dear M'sieur Ingram, I do not agree with the prediction of your great statesman," the old lady said vehemently. "It is not in that direction in which lies the danger of war, but at the other end of the Mediterranean."

Somehow I suspected her of a deliberate intention to mislead me in this matter. She was a shrewd woman, who only disclosed her secrets when it was to her own interests or the interests of her friends at the Ministry of Foreign Affairs to do so. In Paris there is a vast network of French intrigue, and it behoves the diplomatist always to be wary lest he should fall into the pitfalls so cunningly prepared for him. The dividing line between truth and untruth is always so very difficult to define in modern diplomacy. It is when the European situation seems most secure that the match is sufficiently near to fire the mine. Fortunate it is that the public, quick to accept anything that appears in the daily journals, can be placed in a sense of false security by articles inspired by one or other of the embassies interested. If it were not so, European panics would certainly be of frequent occurrence.

My Chief sauntered by, chatting with his close personal friend, Prince Olsoufieff, the Russian Ambassador, who looked a truly striking figure in his white uniform, with the Cross of St. Andrew glittering at his throat. The latter, as he passed, exclaimed confidentially in Russian to my Chief, who understood that language, having been first Secretary of Embassy in Petersburg earlier in his career:

"Da, ya po-ni-mai-ù. Ya sam napishu." ("Yes, I understand. I will write for you myself.")

Keen antagonists in diplomacy though they very often were, yet in private life a firm friendship existed between the pair—a friendship dating from the days when the one had been British Attaché in Petersburg and the other had occupied a position in the Russian Ministry of Foreign Affairs—that large grey building facing the Winter Palace.

"The lion and the bear strolling together," laughed the toothless old Baronne, after they had passed. "Olsoufieff is a charming man, but he never accepts my invitations. I cannot tell why. I don't fancy he considers me his friend."

"Sibyl was at your reception the other evening," I remarked suddenly. "She told me she met a man who was a stranger in Paris. His name, I think she said, was Wolf—Rodolphe Wolf. Who is he?"

"He was introduced by de Wolkenstein, the Austrian Ambassador," she replied quickly. "I did not know him."

"Have you never met him before?" I asked, looking sharply into her eyes.

"Once, I think, but I am not certain," she said, with a palpable effort to evade my question.

I smiled.

"Come, madame," I said good-humouredly, "you know Rodolphe Wolf quite as well as I do. When you last met, his name was not Wolf. Is not that so?"

"Well," she answered, "now that you put it in that manner I may as well admit that your suggestion is correct."

"And what is the object of his sudden visit to Paris?"

"I cannot make out," she replied in a more confidential tone. "As I tell you, de Wolkenstein introduced him, but, as m'sieur knows, I am very quick to detect a face that I have once seen, and I recognised him in an instant."

"Sibyl told me that he had a long chat with her, and she described him as a most charming fellow."

"Ah, no doubt! I suspected him and watched. It was evident that he came to my salon in order to meet her."

"To meet Sibyl! Why?"

"That I cannot tell."

"But I think, Baronne, we may be both agreed upon one point."

"And that is?"

"That the man who now calls himself Rodolphe Wolf is here in Paris with some secret motive."

"I am entirely in accord, m'sieur—quite. Some steps must at once be taken to ascertain that man's motives."

"It seems curious that he should have been introduced for the purpose of meeting Sibyl. What information did he want from her?"

"How can we tell? You know better than myself whether she ever knows any secrets of the Embassy."

"She knows nothing,—of that I am absolutely convinced," I responded. "Her father is devoted to her; but, nevertheless, he is one of those strict diplomatists who do not believe in trusting women with secrets."

"Yet Wolf had a distinct object in making a good impression upon her," she said reflectively.

"No doubt. As soon as she returned she began to talk of him."

And next instant I recollected the strange effect the news of his arrival in Paris had had upon Yolande, and the curiously tragic event which had subsequently occurred. All was puzzling—all inscrutable.

A silence fell between us. I was revolving in my mind whether I should ask this wizen-faced old leader of Society a further question. With sudden resolve I turned to her again and asked:

"O Baronne, I had quite forgotten. Do you chance to know the Countess de Foville, of Brussels? They have a château down in the Ardennes, and move in the best set in Belgium?"

"De Foville? De Foville?" she repeated. "What, do you mean the mother of that little witch Yolande?"

"Yes. But why do you call her a witch?" I demanded, with feigned laughter.

"Why?" cried the old woman, the expression of her face growing dark with displeasure. "Well, I do not know whether she is a friend of yours, but all I can tell you is that should she be, the best course for you to pursue is to cut her acquaintance."

"What do you mean?" I gasped.

"I mean exactly what I have said."

"But I don't understand," I cried. "Be more frank with me," I implored.

"No," she answered in that hard voice, by which I knew that mention of Yolande's name had displeased her. "Remember that we are friends, and that sometimes we have interests in common. Therefore, take this piece of advice from an old woman who knows."

"Knows what?"

"Knows that your friendship with the pretty Yolande is dangerous—extremely dangerous."

Chapter Ten
Confession

Next day, when the manservant asked me into the tiny boudoir in the Rue de Courcelles, I found Yolande, in a pretty tea-gown of cream silk adorned with lace and ribbons, seated in an armchair in an attitude of weariness. The sun-shutters were closed, as on the previous day, for the heat in Paris that July was insufferable, and in the dim light her wan figure looked very fair and fragile. The qualities which imparted to her a distinct individuality were the beautiful combination of the pastoral with the elegant—of simplicity with elevation—of spirit with sweetness.

She gave vent to a cry of gladness as I entered, rose, and stretching out her hands in welcome, drew a seat for me close to her. I looked at her standing before me in her warm, breathing, human loveliness.

"You are better, Yolande? Ah! how glad I am!" I commenced. "Last night I believed that you were dead."

"And if I had died would it really have mattered so very much to you?" she asked in a low, intense voice. "You have forgotten me for three whole years until now."

"I know—I know!" I cried. "Forgive me."

"I have already forgiven," she said, allowing her hand still to remain in mine. "But I have been thinking to-day—thinking ever so much."

Her voice was weak and faltering, and I saw that she was not herself.

"Thinking of what?"

"Of you. I have been wondering whether, if I had died, you would have sometimes remembered me?"

"Remembered you?" I said earnestly. "Why, of course, dearest. Why do you speak in such a melancholy tone?"

"Because—well, because I am unhappy, Gerald!" she cried, bursting into sudden tears. "Ah! you do not know how I suffer—you can never know!"

I bent and stroked her hair, that beautiful red-gold hair that I had so often heard admired in the great salons in Brussels. It had been bound but lightly by her maid, and was secured by a blue ribbon. She had apologised for receiving me thus, but declared that her head ached, and it was easier so. Doctor Deane had called twice that morning, and had pronounced her entirely out of danger.

"But why are you suffering?" I asked, caressing her and striving to charm away her tears. "Cannot you confide in me?"

She shook her head in despair, and her body was shaken by a convulsive sob.

"Surely there is confidence between us?" I urged. "Do you not remember that day long ago when we walked one evening in the sunset hand-in-hand, as was our wont, along the river-path towards La Roche? Do you not remember how you told me that in future you would have no single secret from me?"

"Yes," she answered hoarsely, with an effort, "I recollect."

"Then you intend to break your promise to me?" I whispered earnestly. "Surely you will not do this, Yolande? You will not hide from me the cause of all this bitterness of yours?" She was silent. Her breast, beneath its lace, rose quickly and fell again. Her tear-filled eyes were fixed upon the carpet.

"I would not break my promise," she said at last, clasping my hand convulsively and lifting her eyes to mine; "but, alas! it is now imperative."

"Why imperative?"

"I must suffer alone," she responded gloomily, shaking her head. Her countenance was as pale as her gown, and she shivered as though she were cold, although the noonday heat was suffocating.

"Because you refuse to tell me anything or allow me to assist you?" I said. "This is not in accordance with the promise made and sealed by your lips on that evening long ago."

"Nor have your actions been in accordance with your own promise," she said slowly and distinctly.

"To what do you refer?"

"You told me that you loved me, Gerald," she said in a deep voice, suddenly grown calm. "You swore by all you held most sacred that I was all the world to you, and that no one should come between us. Yet past events have shown that you have forgotten those words of yours on the day when we idled in the Bois beneath the trees. You, too, remember that day, do you not—the day when our lips met for the first time, and we both believed our path would in future be strewn with flowers? Ah!" she sighed, "and what an awakening life has been to me since then!"

"We parted because of your refusal to satisfy me as to the real state of your feelings towards the man who was my enemy," I said rather warmly.

"But was it justifiable?" she asked in a tone of deep reproach and mingled sweetness. Her blue eyes looked full upon me—those eyes that had held me in such fascination in the golden days of youth. "Has any single fact which you have since discovered verified your suspicions? Tell me truthfully;" and she leaned towards me in an attitude of deepest earnestness.

"No," I answered honestly, "I cannot say that my suspicions have ever been verified."

"And because of that you have returned to me when it is too late."

"Too late!" I cried. "What do you mean?"

"Exactly what I have said. You have come back to me when it is too late."

"You speak in enigmas, Yolande. Why not be more explicit?"

Her pale lips trembled, her eyes were brimming with tears, her chilly hand quivered in mine. She did not speak for some moments, but at last said in a low, tremulous voice half choked by emotion:

"Once you loved me, Gerald,—of that I feel confident; and I reciprocated your affection, God knows! Our love was, perhaps, curious, inasmuch as you were English and I was of a different creed and held different ideas from those which you considered right. It is always the same with a man and woman of different nationality—there must be a give-and-take principle between them. Between us, however, there was perfect confidence until, by a strange combination of circumstances—by a stroke of the sword of Fate—that incident occurred which led to our estrangement."

She paused, her blanched lips shut tight. "Well?" I asked, "I am all attention. Why is it too late now for me to make reparation for the past?"

I loved her with all my soul. I was heedless of those words of the old Baronne, of Anderson's suspicions, and Kaye's denunciation. Even if she were a spy, I adored her. The fire of that old love had swept upon me, and I could not hold back, even though her touch might be as that of a leper and her lips venomous.

"Reparation is impossible," she answered hoarsely. "Is not that sufficient?"

"No, it is not sufficient," I answered clearly. "I will not be put off by such an answer."

"It were better," she cried—"better that I had died yesterday than suffer like this. You rescued me from death only to torture me."

Her words aroused within me a distinct suspicion that her strange illness had been brought to pass because, using some mysterious means, she had made an attempt against her own life. I believed that she had suffered, and was still suffering, from the effects of some poison, the exact nature of which neither Deane nor Trépard could as yet determine.

"I do not seek to torture you, dearest," I protested. "Far from it. I merely want to know the truth, in order that I may share your unhappiness, as your betrothed ought to do."

"But you are not my betrothed."

"I was once."

"But not now. You taunt me with breaking that promise which I made three years ago, yet you yourself it was who played me false—who left me for your prim, strait-laced English miss!"

In an instant the truth was plain. She was aware that I had transferred my affections to Edith! Someone had told her—no doubt with a good many embellishments, or perhaps some scandalous story. In the salons through which we of the diplomatic circle are compelled to move, women's tongues are ever at work match-making and mischief-making. On the Continent love and politics run always hand-in-hand. That is the reason why the most notorious of the demi-monde in Paris, in Vienna, and in Berlin are the secret agents of their respective Governments; and many are the honest men innocently denounced through jealousy and kindred causes. A false declaration of one or other of these unscrupulous spies has before now caused the downfall of a Ministry or the disgrace of a noble and patriotic politician.

"I know to whom you refer," I said, with bowed head, after a moment's pause. "It is currently reported that I love her. I have loved her. I do not seek to deny it. When a man sustains such a blow as I sustained before we parted, he often rushes to another woman for consolation. The influence of that second woman often prevents him from going to the bad altogether. It has been so in my case."

"And you love her now?" she cried, the fire of fierce jealousy in her eyes. "You cannot deny it!"

"I do deny it," I cried. "True, until yesterday I held her in esteem, even in affection; but it is not so now. All my love for you, Yolande, has returned to me. Our parting has rendered you dearer and sweeter to me than ever."

"I cannot believe it," she exclaimed falteringly.

"I swear that it is so. In all my life, although am compelled to treat women with courtesy and sometimes to affect flirtation, because of my profession as a diplomatist, I have loved only one woman—yourself;" and I raised her chilly hand to my lips, kissing it fervently.

Mine was no mere caprice at that moment. With an all-consuming passion I loved her, and was prepared on her account to make any sacrifice she demanded. Let the reader remember what had already been told me, and reflect that, like many another man, I loved madly, and was heedless of any consequences that might follow. In this particular I was not alone. Thousands before me had been allured to their ruin by a woman's eyes, just as thousands of brave women's hearts have been broken and their lives wrecked by men's false oaths of fidelity. I have heard wiseacres say that the woman only suffers in such cases; the man never. Whether that rule proves always true will be shown in this strange story of my own love.

She drew her hand away slowly, but forcibly, saying:

"You cannot love two women. Already you have shown a preference for a wife of your own people."

"It is all over between us," I protested. "Mine was a mere passing fancy, engendered, I think, by the loneliness I suffered when I lost you."

"Ah," (she smiled sadly), "that is all very well! A woman, when once played false by the man she loves and trusts, is never the same—*never!*"

"Then am I to understand, Yolande, that you refuse to pardon me, or to accept my affection?"

"I have already pardoned you," she faltered; "but to accept the love you once withdrew from me without just reason is, I regret to say, impossible."

"You speak coldly, as though you were refusing a mere invitation to dinner, or something of no greater importance," I protested. "I offer you my whole heart, my love—nay, my life;" and I held her hand again, looking straight into those wonderful eyes, now so calm, so serious, that my gaze wavered before them.

Slowly she shook her head, and her trembling breast rose and fell again.

"Ours was a foolish infatuation," she answered with an effort. "It is best that we should both of us forget."

"Forget!" I cried. "But I can never forget you, Yolande. You are my love. You are all the world to me."

Her eyes were grave, and I saw that tears stood in them.

"No," she protested quietly; "do not say that. I cannot be any more to you than other women whom you meet daily. Besides, I know well that in the diplomatic service marriage is a serious drawback to any save an ambassador."

"When a man is in love as I am with you, dearest, he throws all thoughts of his career to the winds; personal interests are naught where true love is concerned."

"You must not—nay, you shall not—wreck your future on my account," she declared in a low, intense voice. "It is not just either to yourself or to the Englishwoman who loves you."

"Why do you taunt me with that, Yolande?" I asked reproachfully. "I do not love her. I have never truly loved her. I was lonely after you had gone out of my life, and she was amusing,—that was all."

"And now you find me equally amusing—eh?" she remarked, with just a touch of bitter sarcasm.

"Why should you be jealous of her?" I asked. "You might just as well be jealous of Sibyl, Lord Barmouth's daughter."

"With the latter you are certainly on terms of most intimate friendship," she answered with a smile. "I really wonder that I did not object to her in the days long ago."

"Ah!" I laughed, "you certainly had no cause. It is true that we have been good friends ever since the day when she arrived home from the convent-school at Bruges, a prim young miss with her hair tied up with ribbon. Thrown constantly together, as we were, I became her male confidant and intimate friend; hence my licence to give her counsel in many matters and sometimes to criticise those actions of which I don't approve."

"Then if that is so, you care a little for her—just a little? Now admit it."

"I don't admit anything of the kind," I answered frankly. "For five years we have been constantly together; and times without number, at Lady Barmouth's request, I have acted as her escort here and there, until she looks upon me as a kind of necessary appendage who has a right to chaff her about her flirtations and annoy her by judicious sarcasm. I don't entertain one single spark of love for her. In brief, she has developed into an essentially smart girl, in the true sense of the word, and by reason of our constant companionship knows that to attempt a flirtation with me would result in a most dismal failure. I accused her once, not long ago, of having designs upon my heart, whereupon she replied that to accomplish such a thing would be about as easy as to win the affection of the bronze Neptune in the garden-fountain of the Embassy."

"You have been seen together a great deal of late?"

"Who told you so?"

"A friend who knows you both." Then she added: "From my information I hear that last season you danced so much with her and were so constantly at her side that people were talking of a match between you."

"Ridiculous!" I exclaimed. "Of course gossips are always too ready to jump to ill-formed conclusions. As one of the staff of the Embassy, and her most intimate male friend, it was only courtesy to take her beneath my care. When she had no other partner and wanted to dance, then she sometimes asked me. I think she did it to annoy me, for she knew that I was never fond of dancing."

"Do you remember the Countess of Flanders' balls at Brussels—how we danced together?" she remarked.

"Remember them!" I echoed. "They were in the golden days when everything seemed to our eyes couleur de rose—the days when our love was perfect."

She sighed again, but no word escaped her. She was, I knew, reflecting upon those blissful days and nights when we met here and there at all hours and at all the best houses in Brussels, dining, lunching, dancing, and gossiping—together always.

"Will you not resolve to forget the past, Yolande?" I asked fervently, taking her hand in mine again. "Come, tell me that you will—that you will not hold me aloof like this? I cannot bear it—indeed I can't, for I love you;" and I bent until my lips touched her finger-tips.

"I cannot!" she cried at last, with an effort rising and firmly withdrawing her hand from my grasp.

"You cannot? Why?" I demanded, taken somewhat aback by her sudden attitude of determination.

"I will not allow you to ruin yourself, Gerald, on my account," she declared in a very low but calm voice.

"But why should my love for you prove my ruin?" I cried madly. "The truth is that you do not love me. Why not admit it at once?"

"You are in error," she hastened to protest. "I do love you. I love you to-day with the same fond affection as I entertained for you until that day — fatal to me — when you turned your back upon me and left me. But, alas! we can never now be the same to one another as we were then." She paused for a moment to regain breath; then, pale-faced, with eyes filled with tears, she gripped my arm frantically, crying: "Gerald, my love, hear me! These are my last words, but I pronounce them — I make confession — so that you may understand the barrier that now lies between us."

"Well," I said, "speak — tell me!"

"Ah!" she cried hoarsely, covering her face with her hands, "you wring this confession from me. I am the most unhappy girl in all the world. Would that I were dead that it was all ended! If I did not love you, Gerald, I should deceive you, and leave you to discover the truth after our marriage. But I cannot — I cannot! Even though we shall part to-day for ever, I have resolved to be frank with you because I still have one single spark of honesty left within my heart!"

"I don't understand," I exclaimed. "Tell me."

"Then listen," she said in a hard, unnatural voice, after a few moments of hesitation. "When we were lovers in the old days I was, as you know, a pure, honest, upright woman, with thoughts only for my God and for yourself. But I am that no longer. I am unworthy your love, Gerald. I am unfit to be your wife, and can never be — never!" and she threw herself upon the couch near by and burst into a flood of tears, while I stood there rigid as a statue.

Chapter Eleven
Deane Speaks his Mind

An hour later I was seated in my room at the Embassy staring blankly at the blotting-pad before me, utterly perplexed and bewildered. I loved Yolande—nay, she was my idol; nevertheless she had firmly refused to allow me to resume my place at her side. At one moment it seemed to me as though she had actually made a sacrifice for my sake; yet at another I could not help regarding both her and her mother with distinct suspicion. My love's strange words were in themselves a sufficient self-condemnation. Her service as a political agent had been secured by one or other of the Powers—France, I suspected; and, to put it plainly, she was a spy!

This knowledge had come upon me like a thunderbolt. Of all the women I had known and least suspected of endeavouring to learn the secrets of our diplomacy, Yolande was certainly the chief. The events which had culminated in her accepting this odious office were veiled in mystery. Why had she done this? Who had tempted her or forced her to it?

Those tears of hers, when she had made confession, were the tears of a woman in the depths of despair and degradation, and I, loving her so fondly, could not but allow my heart to go forth in sympathy. There was an affinity between us that I knew might some day prove fatal.

But we had parted. She had announced her intention of leaving Paris, accompanied by her mother, on the morrow, and had begged and implored that I would never seek her again.

"I shall take care to evade you," she had said. "To-day we meet for the last time. We must each go our own way and strive our hardest to forget."

Ah! to forget would, I knew, be impossible. When a man has loved as ardently and intensely as I loved Yolande, memories cling to him and are carried to the grave. You, reader, have loved in those half-forgotten days of long ago, and even now, with age creeping on, and, perchance, with grey hairs showing, sometimes give a passing thought to that fair one who in youth's golden days was your all in all. The sound of a song, the momentary perfume from a woman's chiffons as she passes, the sight of some long-forgotten scene, stirs the memory and recalls those hours of love and laziness when the world was so very pleasant and seemed to have been made for you alone. You recollect her sweet smile, her calm, womanly influence, her full red lips, and the fervency of her kisses. The tender memory to-day is sweet, even though it be tinged with bitterness, for you wonder whom she has married, and how she has fared; you wonder, too, if you will ever meet again, or whether she is already dead. The most charming reflection permitted to man is the memory of a half-forgotten love.

I had been a fool. This bitter truth was forced upon me as I sat there ruminating. I had cast aside that patience and discretion which I, as a diplomatist, had carefully cultivated, and had actually contemplated marriage with a woman who had been denounced by Kaye as a secret agent. My own peril had been a grave one indeed, and as I reflected I began to wonder how it was that I should have so completely lost my self-control. True, indeed, it is that love is blind.

I drew forth a sheet of note-paper and penned her a long, fervent letter, expressing a hope that some day we might meet again, and declaring that my affection for her would last for ever. What mad words I wrote I almost forget. All I know is that even then I could not hold back, so deep and intense was my love for her, so completely did she hold me beneath the spell of her beauty. I tried to put the letter aside for calmer reflection, but could not. My pen ran on, recording the eloquence of my heart. Then, scaling it, I addressed it, rang for the messenger of the Embassy, and gave him instructions to take it to her.

"There is no answer, m'sieur?" the man inquired.

"None," I answered.

Then the door closed again, and I was alone.

Yes, I saw now how great and all-consuming was my love for this woman who was a spy, and who had actually confessed herself worthless. Fate had indeed played me a sorry trick at this, the greatest crisis of my life.

Some ten minutes later Harding entered, saying: "Doctor Deane has called, and wishes to see you, sir."

I at once gave orders for his admission, and in a few moments he came across the thick pile carpet with hand outstretched.

"Hulloa, Ingram, old chap!" he cried, glancing at me in quick surprise, "what's the matter? You don't look yourself."

"Oh, nothing," I answered with ill-feigned carelessness. "A bit worried, that's all."

"Worried over mademoiselle—eh?" he asked, fixing me with his keen eyes.

I nodded in the affirmative.

"Ah, I guessed as much," he replied, with a sigh, placing his hat on the table and flinging himself into a chair. "Mind if I smoke? I've been busy all day, and am dying for a weed."

"Smoke? Why, of course," I answered, pushing my cigars and some matches before him.

I took one also, thinking that it might soothe my nerves, and when we had lit up he leaned back in his chair, and, looking at me curiously through the smoke, asked at last:

"What has occurred between you? Mademoiselle is leaving Paris to-morrow."

"How did you know?"

"I called half an hour ago, and found both her and the Countess making preparations for a hasty departure. Have you quarrelled again?"

"No, there is no quarrel between us," I answered gravely. "On the contrary, there is a perfect understanding."

An incredulous smile crossed his features. "Well," he said, "I don't know, after all, what right I have to interfere in your private affairs at all, old chap, but if I might be allowed to make an observation I should say that there is some very extraordinary mystery surrounding both the Countess and her daughter."

"You don't like the Countess?"

"No, I don't. I conceived a violent prejudice against her on the first occasion that I saw her. That prejudice has already ripened into—well, I was about to say hatred."

"Why?"

"Well, I called upon them this afternoon with an object, and found the Countess determined to place impediments in my way."

"What was your object?"

"I wished to satisfy myself of a certain fact."

"Of what fact?" I inquired with quick suspicion. "Of the cause of her daughter's sudden attack last night."

"And what did you find?" I asked eagerly.

"I discovered a rather curious circumstance," he said. "You will remember telling me that when you searched the room you found she had written a letter almost immediately before her mysterious attack. Well, when I had a look round that room later I saw the letter sealed in its envelope and addressed to the Baroness Maillac, at Grands Sablons, lying in the little letter-rack, and took possession of it, in the faint hope that it might direct me to some clue as to the cause of her curious condition. You will remember, too, the curious, unaccountable mark upon her lip. I wished to see that mark again. I examined it, but against the wish of the Countess, who appeared to regard me with considerable animosity."

"What was in the letter? You opened it, of course?"

"Yes, I opened it, but the note inside was of no interest whatever. Nevertheless, I had my suspicions, and have proved them to be well grounded."

"What have you proved?"

"Briefly this: the mark upon mademoiselle's lip caused me to suspect poisoning; yet it was apparent that she had not attempted suicide, but that the poison, whatever its nature, had entered the tiny crack in the lip by accident. I therefore came to the conclusion that her lip had come into contact with some baneful substance immediately prior to her attack, and when you mentioned the writing of the letter it appeared to me that the gum upon the envelope might be the channel by which the poison was conveyed to the mouth. The greater part of the night I spent in dissolving the gum and making experiments with the solutions thus obtained."

"And what did you discover?"

"I discovered the presence of a most powerful specific irritant poison. I used Mitscherlich's method of detection, and although I cannot yet actually determine the poison with which the gum on the envelope had been impregnated, I proved its terrible effect by experiments. A rabbit inoculated with a single drop of the solution died, in fourteen seconds, of complete paralysis of the muscles, while a drop placed on a piece of meat and given to a cat proved fatal within one minute."

"Then there was poison on the envelope?" I gasped, astounded.

"Yes, but only upon that particular envelope. While left alone in the room awaiting mademoiselle, I secured four other of the same envelopes from the stationary rack on her escritoire. These I took home at once, made solutions, and tested them upon rabbits without effect. This proved that one envelope alone was poisoned."

"Then she was actually poisoned?" I said, surprised at his ingenuity and careful investigation.

"Undoubtedly so. The most curious feature is the mysterious character of the poison. At first I suspected strychnia; but as that attacks the sensitive portion of the spinal nervous system, and the symptoms were so totally different, I was compelled to abandon that theory, as also another I formed — namely, that the paralysis of the motor nerves might be due to curare. After some hours of study and experiment, however, I found that the poison was one extremely difficult of detection when absorbed into the system — that its symptoms were none of those ordinarily attributed to irritant poisons by Tanner and the other toxicologists — that it was a poison not commonly known, if, indeed, known at all."

"Then you think that Yolande was the victim of a deliberate attempt upon her life?"

"Of that I am absolutely convinced. Having taken possession of the letter, I could not well mention it or make inquiries regarding it. I thought it would be best to leave such inquiries to you, who are her intimate friend. I went there to-day in order to satisfy myself regarding the mark on the lip, and also to secure some of the other envelopes. Both of these objects I fortunately accomplished, and have succeeded in establishing the fact that she was poisoned in a most ingenious and secret manner by some person who is evidently no novice in the use of that most deadly and mysterious substance."

"But whom do you suspect?"

He blew a cloud of smoke from his lips, and, with his eyes fixed upon the panelled ceiling, answered:

"Ah! that's the enigma."

"Well," I said, after a pause, "you seem so hostile towards the Countess, I'm wondering if you suspect her?"

"I can't very well, even though there are several curious circumstances which seem to point in that direction. The great fact in favour of her innocence is that she sent for you. Therefore I should like to obtain more direct evidence before actually condemning her. Some of the circumstances are distinctly suspicious, even damning, yet others go far to prove the exact contrary."

"But I can't see what object she could have in getting rid of her daughter," I observed, much puzzled by this extraordinary theory.

"Unless she feared some awkward revelations which Yolande might make in a moment of desperation. To me there is still a good deal of mystery surrounding both mother and daughter."

"I quite agree, Dick. But do you think it possible that a mother could deliberately attempt to kill her daughter by such dastardly means? I don't."

"Such a thing is not unknown in the annals of crime," he answered, knocking the ash slowly from his cigar. "You see, it is practically plain that Yolande is in possession of some secret, and has grown nervous and melancholy. Of the nature of that secret we have no idea. If it were disclosed it might seriously affect the Countess; hence it would be to the latter's advantage if her daughter's lips were sealed."

"But, my dear fellow, I know the Countess well. She's one of the most charming of women, and utterly devoted to Yolande. Your suggestion seems incredible."

"How incredible it appears to you is of no import, my dear Ingram," he answered calmly. "You asked me to investigate the strange affair for you, and I've done so to the best of my ability. I found that the young lady had been poisoned, in a most secret and ingenious manner, by someone well acquainted with the use of the unknown drug. That the envelope was carefully prepared is quite plain, but by whom it is impossible to say—"

"Not by her mother," I declared, interrupting him. "I can't believe that."

"It is for you to discover that. You can ask her a little later about the letter, without giving her any clue to the fact that I have secured it. She must remain under the impression that the letter was duly posted by one of the servants."

"But she is leaving Paris," I said.

"You can see her this evening and make the necessary inquiries, surely?"

"No," I responded. "I shall not see her again."

"Then it is true, as I've already suggested, that you've quarrelled?"

"No," I declared, "we have agreed to part again—that's all."

He was silent for a moment, contemplating the end of his cigar. Then he observed:

"Well, if I may be permitted to say so, old fellow, I think you've chosen a very wise course. You, in your official position, ought not to be mixed up with any mystery of this sort."

"I know, Dick—I know quite well," I responded hastily. "You, however, do not love a woman as I love Yolande."

"Love be hanged!" he cried, laughing. "Love is like the influenza—painful while it lasts, but easily forgotten."

"This matter is too serious for joking," I said, a trifle annoyed by his flippancy.

"Ah, I've heard that story once or twice before! It is astonishing what a difference a month makes in the course of the malady. Take my tip, old chap, and think no more of her. Depend upon it, your charming Yolande with the pretty hair, that used to be admired so much in Brussels, is not worth the position of wife to a good fellow like you."

"That's all very well," I sighed. "I know I was a fool to have called upon her, but I was compelled."

"What compelled you?"

"A circumstance over which I had no control," I answered, for I did not intend to explain to him the accusation made against her by Kaye.

"And you at once fell in love with her again? Ah! such meetings are always extremely dangerous."

"Yes; that is only too true. I know I have been foolish, and now must suffer."

"Rubbish!" he cried. "Why, my dear fellow, Edith loves you, and is perfectly devoted to you. She is charming, pretty, smart, with all the qualities necessary for the wife of a successful diplomatist. Some day, when you get your promotion, you will be gazetted minister to one or other of the South American Republics, and with her as your wife you'll be perfectly happy."

"You seem to have already carved out my future for me, Dick."

"I've only prophesied the ordinary course of things."

"I shall, I feel certain, never marry Edith," I answered, shaking my head. "It is entirely out of the question."

"Well, we shall see. A man hardly ever marries his first love, you know. There always seems an evil fortune connected with first loves."

"How coldly philosophical you are, Dick! Is it because you've never been in love?"

"Never been in love?" he echoed. "Why, my dear old fellow, I've been in love a hundred times, but it's never been sufficiently serious to cause me to pop the question. I'm quite catholic in my tastes, you see. I'm fond of women as a sex."

What he said was perfectly true. He was a popular favourite among the English colony in Paris, and was an inveterate diner-out. Indeed, his well-set-up figure was constantly to be seen at all smart gatherings, and I had overheard many a dainty Parisienne whisper nice things about him behind her fan.

"You'll find a pair of eyes fascinating you one of these days, never fear," I said. "Then it will be my turn to smile."

"Smile away, old chap; you'll never offend me. We are too old friends for that."

Chapter Twelve
The English Tea-Shop

There was a rap at the door, and Harding entered with a telegram addressed to me. I tore open the flimsy blue paper, and saw that it was in cipher from Berlin. The sender, I knew, was Kaye.

"What's up?" my friend asked. "Some affair of State?"

"Yes," I answered mechanically, as I went across to the safe, and took out the decipher-book which gave the key to the cipher used by members of the secret service. By its aid I had quickly transcribed the message, which read:

"*Suspicions regarding Yolande de Foville proved beyond doubt. She is a French agent employed indirectly by the Quai d'Orsay. Am returning to-night. In the meantime instruct Osborne to keep strict observation upon her movements.*

"*K.*"

"Anything serious?" asked Deane, watching my face.

I held my breath, and managed to recover my self-possession.

"No," I answered, "nothing of any grave importance. I sit here to deal with a strange variety of public business, ranging from despatches from home down to vice-consul's worries."

"We are not at war yet," he laughed, "and we trust to you diplomatists to keep us out of it."

I smiled, rather sadly I think. Little did my friend dream how near we actually were to hostilities with France. But in the school of diplomacy the first lesson taught is that of absolute secrecy; hence I told him nothing. To be patient, to preserve silence, to be able to give to an untruth the exact appearance of the truth, and to act a lie so as to deceive those with the most acute intelligence on earth, are qualifications absolutely necessary—together, of course, with the stipulated private income of four hundred a year—for the success of the rising diplomatist.

"We are trying to keep England out of war," I said. "Indeed, that is the principal object of our existence. Were it not for the efforts of Lord

Barmouth, we should have been at war with the Republic long ago. Why, scarcely a week passes but the political situation changes, and we find ourselves, just as the French also find themselves, sitting on the edge of the proverbial volcano. Then, by careful adjustment and marvellous tact and finesse, matters are arranged, and once more the ships of State sail together again into smooth waters. Only ourselves, in this Embassy, are really alive to the heavy responsibilities resting on the shoulders of our trusted Chief. Many a sleepless night he passes in his own room opposite, I can assure you."

"And yet he is always merry and good-humoured, as though he hadn't a single care in the world."

"Ah, that is owing to his long training as a diplomatist. He shows no outward sign of anxiety, for that would betray weakness or vacillation of policy. An ambassador's face should never be an index to his thoughts."

He tossed his cigar-end away and rose, asking: "Where are you feeding to-night? Can you dine with me at Ledoyen's—or at the Café de Paris, if you prefer it?"

"Sorry I can't, old chap," I responded. "The Chief and I have a dinner engagement at the Austrian Embassy. I'd much rather be with you; for, as you know, I'm tired to death of official functions."

"You're bound to attend them, I suppose?"

"Yes, worse luck," I replied. "To be a diplomatist one must, like a Lord Mayor, possess an ostrich's digestion."

"Well, good-bye, old chap. Sorry, you can't come," he said, smiling. "But do buck up! I don't want to have you as a patient, you know. Take my advice, and just forget your pretty charmer. She's leaving to-morrow, and there's no reason on earth why you should meet again."

"But about that letter?" I suggested. "We surely ought to clear up the mystery?"

"Let it pass," he urged. "Don't call there again, but simply forget her. Remember, you have Edith."

His words recalled to me the fact that I had received a letter from her that morning, and that it was still in my pocket unopened.

"Yes, I know," I exclaimed rather impatiently. "I shall, of course, try to forget. But I fear that I shall never succeed—never!"

"Take my advice and forget it all," he cried cheerfully, clapping me on the back. "Good-bye."

We clasped hands in a firm grip of friendship. Then he walked out, and I was left alone.

I went to the window, and looked down into the roadway. It was a blazing afternoon, and the streets seemed deserted. All Paris was at Trouville, Dieppe, or Arcachon, or drinking the more or less palatable waters in Auvergne. Paris in July is always more empty than is London in that month, and it is certainly many degrees hotter, even though the plashing fountains of the Place de la Concorde may give one a pleasant feeling of refreshment in passing, and the trees of the boulevards shed a welcome shade not found in the dusty streets of dear old grimy London.

As I stood gazing aimlessly out of the window, it suddenly occurred to me that I had still in my pocket the letter which I had found on Yolande's little writing-table—the letter making an appointment for five o'clock that day. I glanced at my watch, and found it was already half-past four.

Then, taking out the note, I carefully read it through, and, after a few moments' debate within myself, determined to stroll round and ascertain who it was who wished so particularly to speak with her.

I do not think, now that I reflect calmly, that this determination was prompted by any feeling of jealousy, but rather by a strong desire to discover the truth regarding her connection with the Quai d'Orsay. Anyhow, I brushed my hair, settled my cravat, replaced the decipher-book in the safe, and, taking my hat, strolled out into the blazing afternoon.

Would she herself keep the appointment, I wondered? Surely not! She was too busy making preparations for a hasty departure. Nevertheless, she might have sent a message to her mysterious correspondent regretting her inability to be present. Anyhow, I was determined to watch and ascertain for myself.

The English tea-shop in the Rue Royale is known, I daresay, to a good many of my lady readers who go shopping in the Madeleine quarter, bargain-hunting in the Louvre, or strolling about the grand boulevards watching Parisian life in all its many phases. Tea such as that to which English people are accustomed is difficult to obtain in Paris hotels. It usually turns out to be slightly discoloured hot water, served in a teapot upon the spout of which hangs a more or less useless strainer. With the addition of sugar and milk, the beverage becomes both weak to the eye and nauseous to the palate, while in the bill at a first-class hotel the unfortunate visitor finds himself charged two francs for "one tea simple." The English shop in the Rue Royale, known to the Englishman in Paris as the "Bun-shop," is like Henry's, or the American bar at the Chatham, where presides the ubiquitous Johnnie with the small moustache, one of the institutions of the English colony. It is a rendezvous for the ladies, just as the Chatham bar is crowded at four o'clock by Englishmen resident in the gay capital, with a sprinkling of those misguided and decadent Paris youths who term themselves Orleanists and play at political conspiracy.

The "Bun-shop" is generally full from four to five, be it summer or winter. In the season it is patronised largely by chic Parisiennes and their male encumbrances, generally laden with small parcels; while in summer the British tourists in their blouses and short tailor-made skirts, which serve alike for the boulevards and the Alps, seem to scent it out and make it their habitual house of call.

When I strolled in, the crowd at the little tables mostly hailed from those essentially British hotels in the Rue Caumartin. Being a Britisher, I naturally hesitate to criticise the get-up of the tourist to Paris. But it is always a matter of speculation to those of us who live abroad why our compatriot, who would not be seen in a golf-cap in the Strand or Piccadilly, invariably sports one when he patronises the boulevards, and conducts himself, when in what he calls "gay Paree," in a fashion which often makes one think that he has left his manners behind in England together with his silk hat. The fair-faced English girl in cotton blouse and straw hat is always a common object in the "Bun-shop," and on this afternoon she was predominant, and the chatter in English was general.

I found one of the little tables free, and, discovering an illustrated paper, sat with it before me, making an examination of each little group visible from my seat. Not a single person, however, excited my suspicion. Apparently no one was waiting, save a girl in black, a Parisienne evidently, who, being joined presently by a gentleman, finished her tea and went forth.

The clock showed it to be already five, and as I sat sipping my cup and feigning to read the *Graphic*, I became more and more convinced that Yolande, finding herself unable to keep the appointment, had sent an excuse.

About me sounded the gossip which one always hears among the feminine tourists in Paris: the criticisms of the Louvre museum, the eulogies of the "lovely things" in the Rue de la Paix, and the delight at wonderful bargains obtained at the Bon Marché. It is always the same. The tide of tourists is never-ceasing; and the impression which Paris makes upon the Englishman or Englishwoman is always exactly similar. Those who spend a fortnight in the City of Pleasure always believe life there to be a round of gaiety punctuated by fêtes de nuit with Moulin Rouge attractions. These idolaters should live a year in Paris, when they would soon discover that the French capital quickly becomes far more monotonous than their own much-abused London.

The hands of the clock moved very slowly, and by degrees I got through the whole of the cup-marked illustrated literature of the establishment. Many of the merry gossips had risen and departed, and at half-past five only two little groups remained.

At length a smart victoria stopped before the door, and a dark, rather handsome, middle-aged, elegantly dressed woman descended, and, entering, took a seat. Her style was not English, that was certain; and by the fact that she took lemon with her tea I judged her to be Russian, although she addressed the waiter with an accent purely Parisian. Her footman stood at the door with the carriage-rug over his arm. From the inquisitive expression of her face I judged it to be the first time she had visited the tea-shop.

Could she be waiting for Yolande? I made a close examination of her face, and saw that although she was just a trifle made-up, as are most Parisiennes, she was nevertheless good-looking. She sipped her tea leisurely, nibbled a biscuit, and was readjusting her veil by twisting it beneath her chin, when suddenly the silhouette of a figure appeared in the open doorway.

I glanced up quickly over the top of my piper, and in an instant recognised the new-comer, who looked very smart in his well-cut frock-coat, silk hat, and light grey suède gloves. He hesitated for an instant on the threshold and glanced swiftly around. No sooner had his eyes fallen upon the woman sitting there than he turned instantly, went out, and was next moment lost to sight.

The man who had stood in the doorway during that brief moment, and who had apparently retreated owing to the presence of the woman whose carriage was awaiting her, was none other than the individual whose arrival in Paris was so inexplicable—the man known as Rodolphe Wolf.

Chapter Thirteen
The Spy's Report

So swiftly did the figure disappear from the doorway of the pâtisserie that I doubt whether the elegant woman there seated had been aware of his presence. She was sitting with her face half turned from the door, and, unless by means of the mirror, she could not possibly have witnessed his sudden hesitation and disappearance. That he intended entering there, and had been prevented by her presence, was manifest. He had no desire to be seen by her, that was quite evident.

Again it seemed as though Yolande's mysterious correspondent was actually this man, whose presence in Paris had caused her so much anxiety.

A sudden impulse led me to go forth and keep watch upon his movements, and as I passed out I took note of the fine equipage, and saw that upon the harness was a duke's coronet, beneath which was a cipher so intricate that I could not unravel it. The woman within was evidently some notability, but a foreigner; otherwise I should have recognised her, knowing as I did, by sight, all smart Paris. Her attitude, seated at that little table sipping her tea and lemon, was so calm that I felt assured she was not there for the purpose of meeting Yolande, but only for rest and a cup of that refreshing decoction so dear to the feminine palate. Nevertheless, I was puzzled to know who she was, and why her presence had had such a terrifying effect upon the man who had come and fled like a shadow.

I hurried along in the direction he had taken, down to the Place de la Concorde. Whether he had really detected my presence or not I was undecided. I believed and hoped not. I had had a paper before my face at the moment of his appearance, and it had seemed to me that when his eyes fell upon the lady sipping her tea, he did not pause to make further investigation. I was looking for him eagerly among the hurrying foot-passengers, when, just as I turned the corner by the grey wall of the Ministry of Marine, I saw his thin, tall figure cross the road and mount upon the impériale of one of the omnibuses going towards the Bastille. At the same moment a second omnibus passed, travelling in the same direction, down the Rue de Rivoli, and without hesitation I jumped upon it, and, also mounting the impériale, was thus able to follow him without much risk of detection. I kept my eyes upon his glossy silk hat some distance ahead as we travelled along the fine, broad thoroughfare, past the Continental, the Tuileries Gardens, the Louvre, and the quaint old Tour St. Jacques, until both vehicles pulled up at the corner of the wide Place de l'Hôtel de Ville, where he descended.

I quickly ran down the steps, and, sauntering along with affected carelessness, followed him across the Place and along to the Quai des Celestins, where he suddenly halted, glanced quickly around as though desiring to escape observation, and then entered an uninviting-looking door of one of those rickety dwellings which are among the most ancient and most unwholesome in Paris. The door he entered seemed to be the private entrance to a dingy little shop that sold fishing-tackle, wicker eel-traps, and such-like necessities for the angler. The manner in which he entered was distinctly suspicious, but I congratulated myself that, while he had not detected me, I had run him to earth.

He was a smart, rather foppish man of military appearance, though somewhat foreign-looking; thin-faced, black-haired, with a small, black, pointed beard, and a pair of cold grey eyes, sharp and penetrating; an erect, rather imposing, figure, which if once seen impressed itself upon one. Outwardly he bore the stamp of good breeding and superiority, and he now called himself Rodolphe Wolf. It was strange—very strange.

I noted the house he had entered, then, turning, walked slowly along the Rue St. Paul, and so regained the upper end of the Rue de Rivoli; and as I strolled along my thoughts were indeed complex ones. Sight of that man recalled a chapter of my life which I had hoped was sealed for ever. Of all men in the world he was the very last I should have dreamed of meeting. But as he had not detected me, for the present I possessed the advantage.

That thin, superior-looking man who had strolled so airily along the Quai, smart in his silk hat and pearl-grey gloves, and carrying his cane with such a jaunty air, was a man whose name had once been known throughout Europe—a man, indeed, of world-wide notoriety. In those days, however, he did not call himself Rodolphe Wolf. He had changed his name, it was true, but he could never succeed in changing his personality. Besides, the name he used had given me, who alone knew his secret, a clue to his identity. When Sibyl had mentioned the name and described him as a chance acquaintance at the Baronne's, I felt convinced as to the truth. Yolande, too, seemed aware of his change of name, for so sudden had been my announcement that he was in Paris that she had been completely taken by surprise, and had made no attempt to declare herself ignorant of my meaning.

At the corner of the Caserne, in the Rue de Rivoli, I sprang into a fiacre, and told the man to drive to the Café de la Paix, where, seated upon one of the little wicker chairs in the warm sunset, I drank my mazagran and allowed my thoughts to run back to the time when this man had played so important a part in my life. All those strange circumstances came back to me as vividly as though they had happened but yesterday. He had once been my friend, but now he was my bitterest enemy.

Count Rodolphe d'Egloffstein-Wolfsburg, or as he now preferred to be called, Rodolphe Wolf, was in Paris. He had returned as though from the grave, and was apparently living in seclusion in an exceedingly unfashionable apartment over the fishing-tackle shop beside the Seine. It was over two years since report had declared him to be dead, and I had congratulated myself upon an escape from what had seemed an inevitable disaster; yet that report was false. He was alive, and I had no doubt that he meant mischief.

Yet why did Yolande fear him? This fact puzzled me. They had been acquainted in the old days, it was true, but what cause she had to hate him I could not discern. Something had passed between them of which I had remained in ignorance. Strange, too, that the Austrian Ambassador should introduce him at the Baroness's reception! With what motive? I wondered. Surely he must know from the Diplomatic List that I was now in Paris, and that at any sign of hostility on his part I should expose him and explain the whole truth. He was playing a dangerous game, whatever it was; and I, too, felt myself to be in deadly peril.

I sat there trying to review the situation with calmness, but could see no solution of the problem. The truth was that, believing him to be dead, I had given no heed to that sealed chapter of my history, and now the ghastly truth had fallen upon me as a thunderbolt. Sibyl had met and liked him. She had in her ignorance declared d'Egloffstein-Wolfsburg to be a charming fellow. There was a touch of grim humour in the situation.

Fate seems sometimes to conspire against us. At such times it is no use kicking against the pricks. The proper course is to accept misfortune with the largest amount of good-humour possible in the circumstances, and just to treat one's sorrows lightly until they pass. This is, I am aware, counsel excellent in kind, but extremely difficult to follow. At that moment I felt crushed beneath the weight of sudden misfortune. All my future seemed dark and hopeless, without a single ray of happiness.

The mystery surrounding Yolande's actions, the suspicion resting upon the Countess of having made a dastardly attempt upon her daughter's life, the manner in which knowledge of our secret despatch had been obtained and our diplomatic efforts thereby checkmated, and the reason of the sudden appearance in Paris of my most bitter enemy, formed a problem which, maddening in its complexity, appeared to admit of no solution.

Two men of my acquaintance came up and shook my hand in passing, but what words I uttered I have no idea. My thoughts were, at that hour, when the Place de l'Opéra was bathed in the crimson afterglow, far away from the busy whirl of central Paris, away in that peaceful forest glade where took place that incident by which I so narrowly escaped with my life. The whole scene came before me now. I remembered every detail of that night long ago.

Bah! My cigar tasted bitter, and I flung it across the pavement into the gutter. Would that I could have put from me all recollection as easily as I cast that remnant away! Alas! I knew that such a course was impossible. The ghost of the past had arisen to overshadow the future.

Next day at noon I sat with the Ambassador in his private room discussing the political outlook. He had exchanged telegraphic despatches with Downing Street during the morning, and I knew from the deciphers which I had made that never in the course of my career as a diplomatist had the European situation been so critical.

Try how we would in Madrid, in Berlin, and in Vienna, we could obtain absolutely no confirmation of our suspicions that Ceuta had been sold by Spain to France. At the first rumours of the impending sale of this strategic point the machinery of our secret service in the various capitals had been set to work, and under the ubiquitous Kaye no stone had been left unturned in order to get at the real truth of this grave menace to England's power in the Mediterranean.

His Excellency, leaning back in his favourite cane chair, was grave and thoughtful, for again he had declared:

"All this is owing to those confounded spies! Here, in Paris, nothing can be conducted fairly and above-board. I really don't know, Ingram, what will be the outcome."

"Do you consider the situation so very critical, then?" I asked.

"Critical? I certainly do. It is more than critical. With this scurrilous Press against us, popular feeling so extremely antagonistic towards England, and the difficulties in the Transvaal, only a single spark is required to produce an explosion. You know what that would mean?"

"The long-predicted European war?"

He nodded, and his grey face grew greyer. I had never seen him more gloomy than at that moment. While we were talking, Harding rapped at the door and asked:

"Will Your Excellency see Mr Grew?"

The Ambassador turned quickly, exchanged a glance with me, and answered at once in the affirmative. For two persons His Excellency was at all times unengaged—for Kaye and for his trusted assistant, Samuel Grew.

A few moments later a rather under-sized, bald-headed, gentlemanly little man entered and seated himself, at the Chief's invitation. He was well-dressed, round-faced, with longish grey whiskers, and in his manner was the air of a thorough cosmopolitan, with just a trifle of the bon viveur.

"Well, Grew," inquired His Excellency, "anything fresh?"

"I have come to report to Your Excellency upon my visit to Ceuta."

"What!" the Ambassador exclaimed in astonishment. "Have you actually been there and returned?"

"Certainly," the other answered, smiling. "I can move swiftly when necessary. I was in Barcelona when I received my telegraphic instructions, and set out at once."

"Well, tell us the result of your observations," urged Lord Barmouth, instantly interested.

"I went down to Algeciras, and crossed to the much-discussed penal settlement by boat. Before I could do so, I was compelled to get a permit from the commander of the Algeciras garrison, and only then was allowed to board the steamship, whose every nut, screw, and chain was screaming for a little oil, whose hands stretched themselves on deck in the sun and left the work to the captain and his engineer, while they sang songs and smoked cigarettes. There were very few passengers, mostly women, who sang until the steamer cut across the Straits in the teeth of the wind; then they ceased to sing and commenced to pray. In little more than two hours we were just off Ceuta—a long, straggling Spanish town, the convict station high up on the eastern hill, with stone-work fortifications, that would hardly endure three hours' attention from modern guns, down to the water's edge, and beyond, to the west, well-cultivated fields full of young wheat or barley. Arrived on shore, I was summoned to a shed, where a severe official in uniform examined my papers, recorded my age and other details in a book, returned the passport, and told me that if I wished to leave Ceuta at any time I must go to the commandant and get his written permission to do so. Later on, the native who showed me the way to the Governor's house made an explanation that was less satisfactory than he intended. 'You see, señor,' he said, 'we have a great many convicts here, and they are very like you. I mean to say,' he went on, feeling that he had not expressed himself happily, 'that they are often dressed to look like gentlemen.' I then changed the conversation."

"And how about the fortifications?" His Excellency inquired.

"I have full plans and photographs of them," answered the member of the secret service. "The photographs are on films, as yet undeveloped, and I at once posted them to an address in Bâle, so as to get rid of them from my possession. The plans, on tissue paper, I have here in my walking-stick," he added, smiling grimly and holding up to our view his rather battered ebony cane with a silver knob.

"Aren't you afraid of anyone prying into that?" I asked.

"Not at all. The knob is removable, as you see," and he unscrewed it, revealing a small cavity with a compass set in the top. "But no one ever suspects the ferrule. There is a hidden spring in it;" and, inverting the stick, he opened the ferrule, disclosing a small cavity in which reposed some tiny pieces of tissue closely resembling rolled cigarette papers.

It is against the British principles of openness and fairness to employ secret agents; but in these days, when spies abound everywhere and the whole of Europe is a vast network of political intrigue, we cannot afford to sit inactive and remain in contented ignorance.

"You will make a full report later, with photographs and plans, I presume?" His Excellency suggested.

"Yes. But knowing the importance of the matter I came straight to make a verbal report to Your Excellency. I arrived in Paris only an hour ago. At present Ceuta does not impress the eye of the person who knows something of England's fortified stations. Gibraltar stands on guard across the water, presenting nothing but a towering, bare rock, honeycombed with hidden batteries, to which all Ceuta lies exposed. While Gibraltar is of solid rock, the vegetation round and in Ceuta hints at a more mixed material, and an immense amount of money would be required to make fortifications that would fulfil all modern requirements. The expenditure might work wonders, for the town has the sea on all sides, and could be completely isolated by flooding the strip of land that fronts the Bay. The present garrison consists of five thousand soldiers, including a regiment of Moors, who in point of physique are the best men in the place. Ceuta itself is rather a pretty town, so thoroughly Spanish that the few Moors and Arabs met in the streets are objects of interest. The houses are small, and often built round the cool patios dear to southern Spain. The balconies stretch so far across the streets that groups of girls sit all day, except in the hours of noon, chatting with their neighbours across the way."

"And what does your visit lead you to conclude?" inquired His Excellency, all attention to this statement of the well-trained secret agent.

"I am of opinion that the present condition of Ceuta need inspire no uneasiness. Our latest and heaviest guns completely command the town; and if, in an hour of universal commotion, the unexpected happened, and Spain gave up her possession, very long and expensive work would be required to render the position tenable."

"And have you made arrangements for further information?" asked Lord Barmouth.

"Yes. We shall be at once informed of any fortification of Ceuta conducted at a cost out of proportion to Spanish resources—say at the expense and on behalf of a Power that would hope to acquire it suddenly."

"Good," observed the Chief in a tone of approval. "I congratulate you, Mr Grew, upon your smartness in this affair. But you have not told me whether you discovered any French agents there?"

"None. I went in the guise of a Frenchman, with a French passport, and searched for any compatriots, but found none whom I could suspect."

"Well," responded the Ambassador, rising, as a sign that the audience was at an end, "it behoves us to be constantly on the alert in face of the network of French intrigue that threatens England in the land of the Moors, and consequently at one end of the Mediterranean."

Then the keen, bald-headed, little man, highly pleased by the Chief's word of commendation, bowed and withdrew, taking with_ him the precious walking-stick in which were concealed the plans of the Spanish fortifications.

His Excellency sighed when the man had gone, and after a pause exclaimed seriously:

"I can't help regarding the affair, Ingram, as something more than a political ballon d'essai. The silence of our friends both in the Boulevard de Courcelles and the Rue de Lille is very ominous."

Chapter Fourteen
Smart Paris

On the following afternoon, as Lord Barmouth had some business with the Minister of Foreign Affairs over at the Quai d'Orsay, I accompanied Lady Barmouth and Sibyl to a rather queer function. It was a unique opportunity offered to visit in detail one of the most attractive palaces in La Ville Lumière; to while away a few hours very agreeably with a well-chosen variety entertainment presented by some of the most popular artists on the Paris stage; and to aid a philanthropic enterprise, L'Oeuvre Sociale, conceived, I suppose, in a compassionate love of humanity and carried on in a touching spirit of self-abnegation. The palace was that of Prince Roland Bonaparte, in the Avenue d'Jena. Through the galleries, salons, and magnificent library the crush was enormous. The afternoon was hot and the atmosphere stifling; nevertheless, in the cause of charity we of the diplomatic circle must always be en évidence, even though we would rather be away from the crowd in the country or by the sea.

It was evident when we arrived that the visit to the hotel was one of the great attractions of the fête, for many lady visitors, especially the American contingent, examined and admired the handsome staircase, with its green marble columns, its vast collection of pictures, sculpture, bronzes, tapestries, and curiosities, the salons filled with souvenirs of the First Empire and of the Imperial family, and the incomparable library—that of Louis XIV—in exquisitely carved wood.

We mounted to the vestibule on the first floor, where a concert-room had been fitted up, and there with difficulty found seats among the crowded audience.

Aristide Bruant himself was concluding one of his popular songs of the street:

> La moral' de c'tte oraison-là,
> C'est qu' les p'tit's fill's qu'a pas d' papa,

Doiv'nt jamais aller à l'école,
À Batignolles,

and bowed himself off amid thunders of applause. As a Paris singer has not to submit his lines to a paternal County Council, they are frequently a trifle more free than those to which English audiences are in the habit of listening. Nevertheless, it must be remembered that this charity function was a very smart affair, all the best-known people remaining in Paris being present. After Bruant, an outburst of applause greeted the renowned Spanish dancer, La Belle Otero, who danced and sang, followed by pastourelles of the eighteenth century, romances by Florian and Marie Antoinette, and songs by Paulus. Lastly, there bounded upon the stage Eugénie Buffet, the "chanteuse des rues," together with her troupe. She sang that weird song of Paris life so popular at the cafés, called "À la Villette," commencing:

Il avait pas encor' vingt ans,
I' connaissait pas ses parents,
On l'app'lait Toto Laripette,
À la Villette.
Il était un peu sans façon,
Mais c'était un joli garçon:
C'était l'pus beau, c'était l'pus chouette,
À la Villette.

The audience had heard much of the song, but few of those present had ever ventured into the insignificant café where she sang it nightly. Consequently there was distinct novelty in it. She sang it through, to the accompaniment of her street musicians, until she came to the final verse:

La derniér' fois que je l'ai vu,
Il avait l'torse à moitié nu,
Et le cou pris dans la lunette,
À la Roquette.

Then, with a sudden outburst of enthusiasm, the whole audience threw hundreds of sous and francs to the singer.

Sibyl, seated beside me, her ladyship having found a seat with the Baronne de Chalencon some distance away, turned to me, saying:

"The air is simply suffocating here. Shall we go?"

"Certainly," I answered, glad myself to escape from the semi-asphyxiation. We rose and passed out together. On the stairs we met Prince

Roland, delighted with the success of the entertainment, ascending, with, as usual, hat on the back of his head and hands in pockets.

"Ah, mon cher Ingram!" he cried, greeting us. "And you are here with mademoiselle?"

Sibyl congratulated him upon his great success, whereupon he answered, with a broad smile:

"It seems, mademoiselle, that my hotel is not large enough for charity."

And he passed on, leaving us to laugh at his rather witty mot. In Paris everyone knows the Prince, for he is one of the central figures in Society. Below we encountered the Baronne de Nouilles, who with Madame Bornier was sharing the feminine literary honours of Paris at the moment. The Baronne's poems were well known, especially "Il n'y a plus d'îles bienheureuses." She greeted us merrily, for Sibyl was her especial favourite. She was still quite young, dark, slim, and distinguished-looking. In addition to much originality and charm in her manner of writing, she possessed an insight into, and a power to judge, human nature in its many varied aspects which had been pronounced by the critics to be remarkable. She was very graceful, with auburn hair and a face such as Burne-Jones loved to paint. Indeed, she had sat for the faces of several of that artist's more recent pictures.

"What!" she cried, "you, too, find the crush too great? And I also. I am returning home. Come with me, both of you, and have a quiet cup of tea. I will explain to her ladyship;" and walking quickly across to where Sibyl's mother was standing, she uttered a few words to the Ambassador's wife. Then we all three entered her landau and drove to her house.

The Baronne was, as all Paris knows, in every way an artist, wealthy, chic, and philanthropic to a degree. Her house was, I found, a dream of exquisite taste.

When we entered, Sibyl turned to me, saying:

"These white carpets and delicate hangings make one tremble at the thought of dirty feet or smutty fingers!"

And they certainly did. The effects everywhere were highly artistic—more striking, I think, than I had ever seen in any private house. Her refined taste and rare turn of—mind were shown in every corner of that delightful house, so delicate and restful in every detail. The salon in which tea was served was all white—soft white velvet hangings, white carpet, white wood furniture, and a little gallery also in white. Along the dado-line, in white wood, were painted butterflies in pale opal shades, frail symbols of the flitting gaieties of life.

We had been chatting some little time, and the conversation between the Ambassador's daughter and the poetess had turned upon frocks, as it so often does between women devoted to La mode. They were discussing the toilette of Madame de Yturbe, one of the prettiest women in Paris, and the tendency of late towards the Empire and Directoire periods in dress, when I asked a question to which I had often failed to get a satisfactory answer.

"Who is really the smartest—the Parisienne, or the American woman, in Paris?"

"Ah, m'sieur!" cried the merry little Baronne, holding up her hands, "the Americans run us so very close in the matter of dress nowadays that I really do not know. Indeed, many Americans are in my opinion more chic than the vraie Parisienne."

"Well," observed Sibyl rather philosophically, "there is, I think, more independence and individuality in the American woman's manner of putting on her clothes. The French woman—forgive me, Baronne—accepts her frock just as it comes from the dressmaker, and looks more or less as though she has just stepped out of a bandbox. But the American knows better what suits her in the first place, and in putting on her clothes adapts them, by a judicious touch here and there, to her own particular style and taste."

"I thoroughly agree," observed the Baronne. "We have been actually beaten on our own ground by the Americans. It is curious, but nevertheless true, that we French women are being left behind in the mode, as we have been left behind in the laws. Here, in France, we are twenty years or so behind the age in regard to the laws affecting women."

"I don't understand," observed Sibyl.

"Well, in brief, our modern intellectual young man in Paris is all for woman's rights. In England you have long been aware that to educate and gradually emancipate the women-folk is one of the most important points in modern progress; but though the Feministe movement in France has been actively pushed by a small minority during the last few years, we in Paris have only just heard of your so-called New Woman."

"And do you believe, Baronne, that the movement will progress?" I inquired.

"Ah! it is difficult to say, m'sieur," she answered, with a slight shrug of her well-formed shoulders. "When the reformers' ideal has once been placed in the category of practical politics it will probably be accorded a welcome and given a deferential attention which has scarcely been vouchsafed to it on your side of the Pas de Calais. At present, as you know, a married woman in France has no right to her own earnings. They belong to the husband. A man can actually imprison his wife for two years if discovered with a lover; while a woman who has been wronged is not allowed the recherche de la paternité. In short, you English respect your womenkind, and are a free and enlightened people in comparison with us. Here, 'Liberté, Egalité, Fraternité,' are words which apply solely to the masculine sex."

We both laughed, but the Baronne was quite serious, and from her subsequent observations it was patent that I had accidentally touched upon one of her pet subjects. To confess the truth, I became rather bored by her violent arguments in favour of the emancipation of women, for when a voluble Frenchwoman argues, it is difficult to get in a word edgewise.

Presently she exclaimed:

"A couple of days ago I had a visit from an old friend who inquired whether I knew you—the Comtesse de Foville. She has left Paris."

"Yes," I said, "I think she has. Her visit has been only a brief one. They have gone for their cure at Marienbad, I believe."

"Very brief. She wrote telling me that she and Yolande would remain in Paris at least a month, and yet they've not been here a week!"

"Is this the same Yolande whom you knew in Brussels?" asked Sibyl, turning to me with a glance of surprise.

"Yes," I answered in a hard voice. Why, I wondered, had this woman brought up a subject so distasteful to me?

"You were her cavalier in Brussels, so I've heard," observed the Ambassador's daughter. "I was still at college in those days, I suppose. But is it really true that your flirtations were something dreadful?"

"Who told you so?" I inquired, in a tone which affected to scout such an idea.

"Mother said so the other day. She told me that everyone in Brussels knew you had fallen violently in love with her, and prophesied marriage, until one day you suddenly applied for a change of post, and left her. They whispered that it was owing to a quarrel."

"Well," I said with a sad smile, "you are really awfully frank."

"Just as you are with me. You're always chaffing me about my partners at dances, and making all sorts of rude remarks. Now, when I have a chance to retaliate, it isn't to be supposed that I shall let it slip."

"Certainly not," I laughed. "Now describe all my shortcomings, and make a long list of them. It will be entertaining to the Baronne, who dearly loves to hear a little private history."

"Now, m'sieur, that is really too bad," the other protested. "You Englishmen are always so very cynical."

"We find it very necessary for our existence, I assure you, madame."

"Just as Yolande was once necessary for your existence—eh?" she added mischievously, as they both laughed in chorus at my discomfiture.

"Well, and if I admit it?"

"If you admit it you will perhaps set our minds at rest as to the reason of her sudden departure from Paris yesterday," exclaimed the Baronne, with a strange expression upon her face, as though she knew more than she would admit.

"I have no idea of the reason. They have gone for their cure at Marienbad, I believe." Madame smiled, pushing a little tendril of her auburn hair from off her brow.

"You believe!" she echoed. "Are you not certain?"

"No, I'm not certain. They left hurriedly. That is all I know."

"And all you care?" asked Sibyl, regarding me very gravely.

"And all I care," I added.

"What a courteous cavalier!" exclaimed madame, laughing. Then she added: "I've known Yolande and her mother for quite a number of years. Yolande is a most charming girl."

"I've heard that she is now engaged," I observed, resolved upon a ruse. "Giraud, of the Belgian Embassy, told me the other day that she was to marry some German—I think he is—named Wolf. Do you know him?"

"Wolf!" ejaculated the Baronne, her fine eyes fixed upon me with a strange look, as though in a moment she had become paralysed by some sudden fear. The next instant, however, with a woman's marvellous self-possession, she made shift to answer:

"No, the name is quite unfamiliar to me."

"Why," cried Sibyl suddenly, "that was the name of the dark-bearded man who was so charming to me at the de Chalencon's the other night. Is he the same?"

"Yes," I said. "His character, however, is none of the best. I would only warn you to have nothing whatever to do with him—that's all."

"He was awfully kind to me the other evening," she protested.

"Well," I replied earnestly, "but you and I are friends of old standing, and I consider that I have a right to give you warning when it seems to be necessary."

"And is one actually needed regarding Rodolphe Wolf?" asked the Baronne, evidently much puzzled, for she undoubtedly knew him, even though she had declared her ignorance of his existence.

"Yes," I said, "he is a person to be avoided. More, I cannot tell you."

Chapter Fifteen
Across the Channel

A week went by, but the war-cloud still hung heavily upon the political horizon.

At my direction Grew, assisted by other members of the secret service, had searched high and low in Paris for Rodolphe Wolf; but in vain. After entering that dingy old house on the Quai, he had suddenly and unaccountably disappeared. The fishing-tackle shop was not, as I had believed, his headquarters, but he had evidently only made a visit there, and had afterwards left Paris suddenly, at almost the same time as the Countess de Foville and Yolande. The ladies had also completely eluded us. They were not in Marienbad, for inquiries had been made in that town without result.

I was in daily expectation of Kaye's return to Paris; but he did not arrive, and I had heard nothing of his whereabouts. The astute secret agent had a habit of being lost to us for weeks, and of then returning with some important piece of information; not infrequently with a copy of some diplomatic document by means of which our Chief was able to foil the machinations of England's enemies. Nevertheless, in view of the curious events which had occurred, I was anxious to learn what facts he might have ascertained in Berlin regarding Yolande.

Lady Barmouth was receiving in the grand salon of the Embassy one afternoon, the fine apartment being full to overflowing with the usual chattering cosmopolitan men and women who circle about from one embassy to another, when I suddenly encountered my friend Captain Giraud, the Belgian military attaché. He had been absent on leave for several days, and had only just returned to Paris.

"I've been to Brussels," he exclaimed, after we had exchanged greetings. "A cousin of mine has been married, and I went to the feasting."

"And now you have the usual attack of liver, I suppose?"

"Yes," he laughed. "I'm feeling a little bit seedy after all the merry-making. But, by the way, you knew my cousin, Julie Montbazon? She was often a guest of the Countess de Foville at the château."

"Of course I remember her. She was tall, fair-haired, and spoke English extremely well," I said.

"The same. Well, she has married the son of Tanchot, the banker, of Antwerp—an excellent match."

"And the Countess and Yolande, what news of them?"

"They are in Paris, are they not?"

"No, they left suddenly some days ago."

"Well, they are not to be blamed," he said, smiling. "No one stays in Paris during this heat if they can possibly avoid it. Yolande told me she was going to Marienbad."

"She told me so, too. But they have altered their plans, it seems."

"Oh! So you have met again?" he cried, opening his eyes widely. "I thought your friendship had ended long ago?"

"So it had."

"Then it has been resumed?"

"No, it has not," I replied.

"Are you certain?" he inquired, with sudden earnestness. He had been one of my most intimate friends in Brussels in the old days, and knew well the secret of our broken engagement.

"Quite certain."

"And they have left for some destination unknown to you?"

"Yes."

"But why did you seek her again, my dear Ingram? It was scarcely wise, was it?"

"Wisdom has to be thrown to the winds in certain circumstances," I answered. "I was in this instance compelled to see her."

"Compelled?" he echoed, puzzled. "Then you did not call upon her of your own free will?"

"No. I called, but against my own inclination."

"And are you absolutely certain, mon cher Ingram, that all is broken off between you—that you have no lingering thought of her?"

"Quite. Why?"

He paused, as though in doubt as to what reply he should make to my question.

"Because," he said slowly, at last—"well, because if my information is correct, her character has changed since you parted."

What could he know? His words implied that he was aware of the truth regarding her.

"I don't quite understand you," I said eagerly. "Be more explicit."

"Unfortunately I cannot," he answered.

"Why?"

"Because I never condemn a woman, either upon hearsay or upon suspicion."

A couple of merry fellows, attachés of the Russian Embassy, strolled up, and we were therefore compelled to drop the subject. Their chief, they told us, was about to leave Paris for his country house in Brittany—a fact interesting to Lord Barmouth, as showing that the political atmosphere was clearing. One ominous sign of the storm had been the persistent presence of all the ambassadors in Paris at a time when usually they are in the country or by the sea. The representative of the Czar was the first to move, and now without doubt all the other representatives of the Powers would be only too glad to follow his example, for the month was August, and the heat in Paris was almost overpowering enough to be described as tropical.

In the diplomatic circle abroad the most accomplished, the merriest, the most courteous, and the best linguists are always the Russians. Although we at the British Embassy were sometimes in opposition to their policy, nevertheless Count Olsoufieff, the Russian Ambassador, was one of Lord Barmouth's most intimate friends, and from the respected chiefs downwards there existed the greatest cordiality and good feeling between the staff of the two embassies, notwithstanding all that certain journalists might write to the contrary. Volkouski and Korniloff, the two attachés, were easy-going cosmopolitans, upon whose shoulders the cares of life seemed to sit lightly, and very often we dined and spent pleasant evenings together.

We were gossiping together, discussing a titbit of amusing Paris scandal which Volkouski had picked up at a dinner on the previous night, and was now relating, when suddenly Harding approached me.

"His Excellency would like to see you at once in his private room, sir."

I excused myself, having heard the dénouement of the story and laughed over it, and then mounted the grand staircase to the room in which my own Chief was standing with his hands behind his back, gazing thoughtfully out of the window. As I entered and closed the door, he turned to me saying:

"The political wind has changed to-day, Ingram, and although the mystery regarding Ceuta remains the same, the outlook is decidedly brighter. I had a chat with de Wolkenstein and Olsoufieff over at the Quai d'Orsay an hour ago, and the result makes it plain that the tension is fast disappearing."

"Olsoufieff leaves for Brittany to-morrow," I said.

"He told me so," answered the Ambassador. "Yet with regard to Ceuta I have learned a very important fact, which I must send by despatch to the Marquess. Anderson, however, left for Rome to-day, and we have no messenger. You, therefore, must carry it to London by the night service this evening. If you object, Vivian can be sent."

"I'll go with pleasure," I responded, glad of an opportunity of spending a day, and perhaps even a couple of days, in town. We who are condemned to exile abroad love our dear old London.

"Then if you will get out the cipher-book I'll write the despatch."

I unlocked the safe, handed him the book, and then stood by, watching as he reduced the draft despatch which he had already written to the puzzling array of letters and numerals. The operation of transcribing into cipher always occupies considerable time, for perfect accuracy is necessary, otherwise disastrous complications might ensue.

At last, however, His Excellency concluded, appended his signature, and took from a drawer in his big writing-table a large envelope bearing a formidable red cross. Despatches placed in those envelopes are for the eye of the principal Secretary of State for Foreign Affairs alone, and are always carried by the Royal messengers in the chamois-leather belt worn next their skin. They are essentially private communications, which British ambassadors are enabled to make with the great statesman who, untiring by night and by day, controls England's destinies. The messengers carry the ordinary despatches to and fro across Europe in their despatch-boxes, but what is known in the Foreign Office as a "crossed despatch" must be carried on the person of the messenger, and must be delivered into the actual hand of the person to whom it is addressed.

When the communication was placed in its envelope, duly secured by the five seals of the Ambassador's private seal—a fine-cut amethyst attached to his plain watch-guard of black silk ribbon—he handed it to me to lock in the safe until my departure. This I did, and after receiving some further verbal instructions went to my rooms to prepare for the journey. I dined early, called at the Embassy for the despatch, which I placed in my waist-belt, and left the Gare du Nord just as the summer twilight had deepened into dusk.

I was alone in the compartment on that tedious journey by Amiens to Calais. The night service between Paris and London never holds out a very inviting prospect, for there is little comfort for travellers as compared with the saloon carriages of the Chemin de Fer du Nord and the fine buffet cars of the Wagon Lit Company which run in the day service between the two greatest capitals of the world. The boats by the night service, too, are not all that can be desired, especially if a strong breeze is blowing. But on arrival at Calais on the night in question all was calm; and although the boat was one of the oldest on the service, nevertheless, not the most delicate among the lady passengers had occasion to seek the seclusion of a cabin or claim the services of the portly, white-capped stewardess.

In the bright moonbeams of that summer's night I sat on deck smoking and thinking. What, I wondered, did Giraud know concerning Yolande? It was evident that as my friend he had my interests at heart, and wished to warn me against further association with her, even though he had done it clumsily and without the tact one would have expected of a man so well schooled in diplomacy. I remembered how at one time he was frequently a guest at the Château of Houffalize; indeed, we had been invited there at the same time on several occasions for shooting and wild-boar hunting in the Ardennes forest.

Yes, it seemed apparent that he knew the truth, that Yolande was actually a secret agent. But she had disappeared. Perhaps, after all, it was as well. I had no desire that Kaye and his smart detectives should hunt her through Europe, unless it could be actually proved that through her the secret of our policy towards Spain with regard to Ceuta had been betrayed to those Powers which were ever at work to undermine British prestige.

But how could she possibly have obtained the secret? That was the crux of the whole situation. The despatch from the Marquess of Malvern to Lord Barmouth had been a crossed one, and it had never left the person of the foreign service messenger until placed in my Chief's hands with the seals intact. The mystery was absolutely inscrutable.

The moonbeams, reflected by the dancing waters, and the many lights of Dover harbour as we approached it, combined to produce an almost fairy-like picture. Indeed, in all my experience of the Channel I had never known a more perfectly calm and brilliant night, for the sea was almost like a lake, and on board the passengers were promenading as they chatted and laughed, pleasantly surprised to find the passage such an enjoyable one.

But as I lolled in my deck-chair, my eyes fixed upon the silver track of the moonbeams, a figure suddenly passed along the deck between my vision and the sea. There were a good many passengers, for a P&O steamer had come in at Marseilles, and about a couple of hundred travellers from the Far East were hurrying homeward. Every moment they were passing and repassing me; therefore I cannot tell what it was that attracted my attention to that particular silhouette dark against the silvery sea.

I only saw it during a single second, for next instant it had passed and become lost in the crowd of promenaders on deck. It was that of a woman of middle height, wearing a long travelling-cloak heavily lined with fur and a small sealskin toque. The fur collar of her coat was turned up around her neck, and thus hid the greater part of her face; indeed, I saw little of her countenance, for it was only a grey blotch in the shadow; yet her dark eyes had glanced at me inquiringly, as though she wished to mark well my appearance. Her height and gait struck me as somewhat unusual. I had seen some person before closely resembling her, but could not remember the occasion. She had passed me by like a shadow, yet somehow a strange conviction had in an instant seized me. That woman had followed me from Paris. She had stood on the platform of the Gare du Nord watching me while I had walked up and down awaiting the departure of the train.

I rose and searched the deck from end to end, but could not rediscover her. I went below, wandering along the gangway, past the engines, where sometimes passengers seek shelter from the chill winds, but she was not there. As far as I dared, I peered into the ladies' cabin, but saw no one resembling her. In every part of the vessel I searched, but she had disappeared as though by magic. Indeed, a quarter of an hour later I was questioning myself as to whether I had really seen that figure or whether it had been merely a chimera of my excited imagination.

But there was no doubt that a tall, well-dressed woman had passed me and had peered into my face; and equally certain was it that, apparently fearing detection, she had disappeared and hidden herself somehow. Upon a vessel at night there are many dark corners where one can escape observation; besides, the most likely spot for a hiding-place was one or other of the private deck-cabins.

Try as I would, I could not rid myself of the recollection of that face. Now that I reflected, I remembered that when I saw her on the railway-platform I noticed she was dark-eyed, with a thin, elongated, rather striking, careworn face; a figure almost tragic in expression, yet evidently that of a woman of the world Her nationality was difficult to distinguish, but by her tailor-made travelling-dress and her rather severe style, I had put her down as English. Her glance in the semi-darkness had, however, been a curious one, and the reason was rendered the more puzzling by her sudden disappearance.

As we reached the pier at Dover I stationed myself at the gangway, and closely scrutinised every person who went ashore, waiting there until the last passenger had left. But no one resembling her appeared. She seemed to have vanished from the boat like a shadow.

I went ashore, and ran from end to end of both trains, the Chatham and Dover and South Eastern, but could not find her. Then, entering a compartment in the latter train, I travelled to Charing Cross, much puzzled by the incident. I could not doubt but that this thin-faced woman had followed me for some mysterious purpose.

Chapter Sixteen
Dawn

When in the early morning I drove into Downing Street and entered the office of the chief of the night staff, I was informed that the Marquess of Malvern was in town; therefore I drove on to Belgrave Square.

The Prime Minister's house was a large, old-fashioned, substantial-looking mansion, devoid of any outward show or embellishment, and with very little attempt at ornamentation in the interior. Everything was solid and good, but long out of date. The gimcrack painted deal abominations, miscalled art-furniture, had not been invented in the day when the town house of the great family had been renovated in honour of the marriage of the fourth Marquess, the present Prime Minister's grandfather, and very little had been altered by the two generations who had succeeded him. The time-mellowed stability of the place was one of its greatest charms. The footman led me upstairs through the great reception-room which every foreign diplomatist in London knows so well, where the furniture was at present hidden beneath holland shrouds, and down a long corridor, till we found the valet, who, in obedience to the strict orders of his master, went and awakened him. The Marquess, attentive to the affairs of State by night as well as by day, was always awakened on the arrival of a crossed despatch from any of Britain's representatives at the Foreign Courts.

"His lordship will see you in his dressing-room in a few moments, sir," the valet said when he returned, as he ushered me into a small room close at hand.

I had sat there before on previous occasions when I had been the bearer of secret reports from my Chief. I had only to wait a few moments, and the great statesman—a tall, thin, grave-faced gentleman, wrapped in his dressing-gown, opened the door and stood before me.

"Good-morning, Mr Ingram!" he exclaimed affably; for to all the staff of the Foreign Office, from ambassador down to the lower-grade clerk, the Marquess was equally courteous, and often gave a word of encouraging approval from his own lips. Many times had he been heard to say, "Each of us work for our country's good. There must be neither jealousy nor pride among us." The esprit de corps in the Foreign Office is well known.

I bowed, apologised for disturbing him at that early hour—it was half-past five—and handed him the despatch.

"You've been travelling while I've been sleeping," laughed the director of England's foreign policy, taking the envelope and examining the seals to assure himself they were intact. Then he scrawled his signature upon the receipt which I handed him, tore open the envelope, and glanced at the cipher.

"Have you any idea of the contents of this?" he inquired.

"No, it is secret. Lord Barmouth wrote it himself."

"Then kindly come this way;" and he led me down a long corridor to a large room at the end—his library. From the safe he took his decipher-book, and after a few minutes had transcribed the despatch into plain English.

I saw from his face that what he read was somewhat displeasing, and also that he was considerably surprised by the news it contained. He re-read the lines he had written, twisting his watch-guard nervously within his thin white fingers. Then he said:

"It seems, Ingram, that you have some extremely difficult diplomacy in Paris just now—extremely difficult and often annoying?"

"Yes," I said, "there are several problems of late that have required great tact and finesse. But we at the Embassy have the utmost confidence in our Chief."

"Lord Barmouth is a man of whom England may justly be proud. Would that there were many more like him in our service!" said the Prime Minister. "Kindly ask him to keep me posted constantly regarding the progress of the matter he has just reported. It is serious, and may necessitate some drastic change of policy. It is for that reason that I wish to be kept informed."

"Do you require me to return to my post to-day?"

"Certainly not," he replied quickly. "Now you are in England you may remain a couple of days or so, if you wish. I am well aware how all of you long for a day or two at home."

I thanked his lordship; and then, after a short and pleasant chat upon the political situation in Paris and the mystery regarding Ceuta, I went out, mounted into my cab, and drove down to the St. James' Club, where I made myself tidy, and breakfasted.

When I had finished my second cup of tea and glanced through the morning paper, eight o'clock was striking. I rose, went to the window, and looked out upon Piccadilly, bright and brilliant in the morning sun. With hands in my pockets I stood debating whether I should act upon a suggestion that had been constantly in my mind ever since leaving Paris. Should I take Edith by surprise, and go down to visit her?

The fact that the Marquess had given me leave so readily showed that the outlook had become clearer, notwithstanding the fact that my Chief had transmitted, for the eye of the Foreign Minister only, the secret despatch of which I had been the bearer.

At that early hour there was no one in the club, yet as I wandered through those well-remembered rooms my mind became filled with pleasant recollections of merry hours spent there in the days before my duty compelled me to become an exile abroad. I thought of Yolande, and tried to decide whether or no I really loved her. A vision of her face arose before my eyes, but with a strenuous effort I succeeded in shutting it out. All was of the past. Besides, had not Kaye proved her to be a secret agent, or, to put it plainly, a spy? Daily, hourly, I had struggled with my conscience. In the performance of what was plainly my duty I had visited her, and had nearly fallen into the trap she had so cunningly baited, for she no doubt intended, after all, to become my wife; and in this she was acting, I felt confident, in concert with that man who was my bitterest enemy—the man who now called himself Rodolphe Wolf. No, I had treated Edith unfairly, and therefore resolved to run down to Norfolk and visit her. With that object, an hour later I left London for Great Ryburgh, the small village where she delighted to live reposeful days in company with her maiden aunt, Miss Henrietta Foskett. In due course I arrived by the express at Fakenham, drove in a fly to the quiet little village, and descended before the large, low, roomy old house with mullioned windows and tall chimneys, which lay back from the village street behind a garden filled with those old-world, sweet-smelling flowers so much beloved by our grandmothers.

I walked up the garden-path, knocked, and was admitted by the neat maid, Ann, who for fifteen years had been in Miss Foskett's service.

It has always seemed to me that except by their immediate heirs, maiden aunts are often nearly forgotten among a bustling younger generation always striving and toiling. They are left to dust their own china and sharply to superintend the morals and manners of their general servant, save when the holiday-times of the year come round, when their country houses are more apt to recur to their relatives' minds; their periodical letters, in the delicate pointed Italian hand, essential in the days of their youth as the hall-mark of gentility, are then more eagerly replied to, for Aunt Jane's or Aunt Maria's proffered hospitality will generally furnish an economical change of air.

Edith's case was not an unusual one. Her father, a wealthy landowner in Northumberland, had died in her youth, while five years ago, just before she left college at St. Leonard's, her mother, who was constantly ailing, also succumbed. She was left entirely alone; but she had succeeded to a handsome income, derived from property in the city of Newcastle. Her Aunt Henrietta, her mother's only surviving sister, had constituted herself her guardian. Miss Foskett had been able through stress and change to cling to the old house—the old place, once so full, from which so many had gone out to return no more.

I knew that interior well. There was a haunting sense of pathos in those old rooms, and the ancient furniture was arranged in unyielding precision.

When Ann ushered me into the musty-smelling drawing-room, I glanced round and shuddered. Aunt Henrietta's rules were the household rules of her mother before her, and she severely reprobated the domestic slackness and craving for mere comfort and luxury of the present generation. Her lace curtains, carefully dressed, were hung up, and fires banished from all her fireplaces, on the first of May. Untimely frost and snow had no power to move the prim old wool-work screen, glazed and framed, that hid the steel bars of the grate; the simpering ladies, in their faded blue and scarlet dresses, looked unsympathetically at the light carpet, the white curtains, the anti-macassared armchairs, the round table with books, miniatures, and a flowering plant, whatever the state of the thermometer.

Through the windows a pleasant vista was presented across a well-kept lawn with broad pasture-lands beyond, and the spire of Testerton church rising in the distance behind the belt of trees. While I sat there awaiting Edith, who was no doubt amazed at the announcement of my presence, and was now rearranging her hair, as women will, I glanced up at the feeble watercolours and chalk drawings traced by the hand of "dear Aunt Fanny, who had a wonderful talent for drawing." It occurred to me that Fanny's great-nieces, with perhaps less artistic excuse, now studied at the Slade, copied at the National Gallery, and lived in flats with some feminine friend on tea and pickles. Such girls give lunches and teas to stray bachelors, and own a latchkey. But such doings could hardly be thought of among Fanny's muddled trees and impossible sunsets, with Fanny's pictured eyes smiling sweetly, if a trifle inanely, from behind her bunches of fair, hanging curls, at grandmother's mild face and folded hands on the opposite wall.

Notwithstanding the inartistic character of the place, there was everywhere a tranquillity and an old-world charm. Through the open window came the scent of the flowers, the hum of insects in the noonday sun, and the call of the birds. How different was the life there from my own turbulent existence in the glare and glitter of the gayest circle in Paris! I sighed, and longed for quiet and rest at home in dear old rural England.

Suddenly the door opened, and Aunt Henrietta, a prim, shrunken, thin-faced old lady in stiff black silk, and wearing a cap of cream lace, came forward to greet me.

"Why, you have taken us entirely by surprise, Mr Ingram!" she said in her high-pitched voice. "When Ann told me that it was you, I would scarcely believe her. We thought you were in Paris."

"I had to come to London on business, so I thought I would run down to see how you all are," I answered. "I hope my visit is not inconvenient?"

"Oh no," answered the old lady. "I've told Edith, and she will be down in a moment. She's been worrying for the past week because she has received no letter from you."

"Well, I've come personally, Miss Foskett," I laughed. "I hope my presence will partly make up for my failure as a correspondent."

Her grey, wizened face puckered into a smile. I knew that she had not altogether approved of Edith becoming engaged to me. But her niece was of age, mistress of her fortune, and, I shrewdly suspected, contributed handsomely towards the expenses of that small, prim household.

Although Aunt Hetty was of a somewhat trenchant type, and shook her head over the wilful vagaries of a world that had outgrown her philosophy of life, yet she still preserved a motherly instinct of patient love for all mankind. She was, in common with most maiden aunts, a great church-goer and firm supporter of the parish clergy of Great Ryburgh; but in parochial matters I believe she was more dreaded than loved for the uncompromising force of her doctrine and demeanour. She was severe on the faults and failings of her inferiors, and apt to discriminate in her almsgiving. Frequent curtseys and a little adroit flattery from "the poor" were a surer road to her purse than morose merit, however great.

The old lady straightened out an antimacassar that chanced to be a trifle awry, then, spreading out her skirts slowly, seated herself, and began to relate to me gossip concerning people whom I knew in the neighbourhood—the squire, the doctor, the parson, and other local worthies, all of whom, taken together, made up her quiet little world.

At last the door opened again, and next instant, as I sprang up, I became conscious of a fair vision in a simple white gown standing before me. The touch of her soft, tiny hand, the love-glance of those beautiful eyes, the glad smile of welcome, the music of that voice, came upon me as a sudden revelation. Her perfect type of English loveliness became disclosed to me for the first time. She was absolutely incomparable, although never before that moment had I realised the truth. But in that instant I became aware that she held me irrevocably beneath her spell.

I took her hand, and our eyes met. My gaze wavered beneath hers, and what words I uttered in response to her greeting I cannot tell. All that I knew was that I was unworthy of her love.

Chapter Seventeen
Edith Austin

For a time our conversation was somewhat stilted. Then Aunt Hetty rose suddenly, with a loud rustling of her stiff silks, made the excuse that she had to speak with the servants, and discreetly left the room.

The instant the door had closed, Edith moved towards me, and we became locked in one another's arms. She was full of inexpressible sweetness and perfect grace. The passion that had at once taken possession of her soul had the force, the rapidity, the resistless violence of the torrent; but she was herself as "moving delicate," as fair, as soft, as flexible as the willow that bends over it, whose light leaves tremble even with the motion of the current which hurries beneath them.

Love lit within my breast a clear fire that burned to my heart's very core. Edith could scarce speak, so overjoyed was she at my visit; but at last, as I pressed her to me, and rained kisses upon her brow, she said, looking up at me with a glance of reproach:

"You have not written to me for ten whole days, Gerald! Why was that? Last night I sent you a telegram asking if you were ill."

"Forgive me, dearest," I urged. "This last week I've been extremely busy. There have been serious political complications, and, in addition, I've had a perfect crowd of engagements which duty compelled me to attend."

"You go and enjoy yourself at all sorts of gay receptions and great dinners, and forget me," she declared, pouting prettily.

"I never forget you, Edith," I answered. "Don't say that. You are ever in my thoughts, even though sometimes I may be too much occupied to write."

"Do you assert then that for the past ten days you have absolutely not had five minutes in which to send me news of yourself?" she cried in a tone of doubt.

"Well, perhaps I had better admit that I've been neglectful," I said, altering my tactics. "But, you see, I knew that I should come here to-day, so I thought to take you by surprise. Are you pleased to see me?"

"Pleased!" she echoed, raising her lips to mine. "Why, of course I am! You seem always so far away, and I always fear—" and she paused without concluding her sentence.

"Well, what do you fear?"

"I fear that amid all that whirl of pleasure in Paris, and amid all those smart women you must meet daily, you will forget me."

"I shall never do that," I answered reassuringly.

She was silent for a moment. Her countenance had assumed a very grave expression.

"Ah," she said, with a slight sigh, "you do not know how I sometimes suffer, Gerald. I am always fearing that some other woman may rob me of you."

"No, no, dearest," I answered, laughing. "Never contemplate that, for such a theft is not possible. Remember that my duty in a foreign capital is to represent my country at the various social functions, and to endeavour to promote good feeling wherever I can. A diplomatist who is not popular with the women never rises to the post of ambassador. To be gallant is essential, however one may despise and detest the crowd of voluble females upon whom one must dance attendance."

"I often sit here and picture you in your smart diplomatic uniform flirting with some pretty foreign woman in a dimly lit arbour or conservatory," she observed, still very grave. "My life is so very quiet and uneventful in comparison with yours;" and she sighed.

"The charge against me of flirtation is entirely unfounded," I declared, holding her hand and looking earnestly into her clear eyes, now filled with tears. "It is true that sometimes, for purposes connected with our diplomacy, I chat merrily with some grande dame in an endeavour to pick up information regarding the latest change in the political wind; but with me the art of pleasing women is a profession, as it is with every man in the Diplomatic Service."

"I know," she said in a strained tone. "And in those hours of pleasure you forget me. Is not that so?"

"I do not forget a certain summer evening up in Scotland when we walked out after dinner and strolled together down by the rippling burn," I said in a low voice, pressing her closer to me. "I do not forget what words I uttered then, nor do I forget your response—that you loved me, darling."

"But there are others, more attractive than myself, whom you must meet constantly at those brilliant receptions of which I read in the newspapers," she cried, bursting into tears.

"They are foreign women," I declared, "and I hate them all."

"Ah," she cried in a tremulous voice, "if I could only believe what you tell me is the truth!"

"It is the truth, dearest," I said, kissing her tears away. "We are parted; but the quiet, even life you live here is far happier and more healthful than one passed in the stifling atmosphere of politics and perfume in which I am compelled to exist. The ladies' newspapers tell you of the various entertainments in Paris, and describe the gay toilettes and all that kind of thing; but those journals say nothing of the unfortunate diplomatists who are compelled to ruin their digestions and wreck their constitutions by late hours in the service of their country."

She was silent, and I felt her hand trembling in mine. I looked upon her fair face, and lovingly stroked the dark tendrils of hair from her brow. What she had said had aroused within me some qualms of conscience; but, loving her, I strove to reassure her of my perfect and unwavering fidelity. Women, however, are difficult to deceive. They possess a marvellous instinct where love is concerned, and are able to read their lover's heart at a glance. No diplomatist, however expert in the art of prevarication, can ever hope to mislead a woman who is in love.

"I often doubt, Gerald, whether you really love me as truly as you have declared," she said in a low tone, at last. "Perhaps it is because you are absent, and I think of you so much and wonder so often what you are doing."

"My absence is compulsory," I answered, adding earnestly: "I love you, Edith, however much you may doubt my protestations."

"Ah!" she answered, smiling through her tears. "If I could only believe that what you say is true! But it is said that you people at the embassies never speak the truth."

"To you, dearest, I speak the truth when I say that I love no other woman save yourself. You are mine—you are all the world to me."

"And yet you have neglected to write to me for ten whole days! The man who really loves is not so forgetful of the object of his affections." She was piqued at my neglect. Such was the simplicity, the truth, and the loveliness of her character that at first I had not been aware of its complexity, its depth, and its variety. The intensity of passion, the singleness of purpose, and the sweetly confiding nature presented a combination which came near to defying analysis. I now saw in her attitude at this moment the struggle of love against evil destinies and a thorny world; the pain, the anguish, the terror, the despair, and the pang unutterable of parted affection. My heart went out to her.

"But I thought you had forgiven," I said seriously. "I have come myself to spend a few hours with you. I have come here to repeat my love;" and, bending, I kissed the slim, delicate little hand I held.

But she withdrew it quickly; for there was a sudden movement outside in the hall, and Aunt Hetty entered fussily with the news that luncheon was waiting, and that she had ordered an extra cover to be laid for me.

The dining-room was just as antiquated as the musty drawing-room, and just as inartistic, save that the oak beams in the low ceiling were mellowed by age and the dark panelling presented a more cosy appearance than the awful green and red wall-paper of the state apartment. I knew Miss Foskett's cuisine of old, and seated myself at table with some misgiving. True to my expectation, the meal proved a terribly formal one, with Aunt Hetty seated at the head of the table directing Ann by movements of her eyebrows, talking but little except to intersperse some remarks sarcastic or condemnatory; while to us were served several extremely indigestible specimens of English culinary art.

Aunt Henrietta, a strict observer of all the conventionalities, was never tired of referring to the exemplary youth of her day; but above all she had, in the course of her lonely life, developed the keenest and most obtrusive nose for a lie. She was one of those who would, uninvited, join in a casual conversation and ask the luckless conversationalist to verify his statements with chapter and verse. She would stop in the streets and challenge with soul-searching doubts the remark that it was a "Fine day." Aristophanes invented an adjective to describe this ancient and modern product; it is a long word, but it describes her: (a Classical Greek phrase), which, being interpreted, is, "early-prowling-base-informing-sad-litigious-plaguey." She was fond of picking one up in a quotation if one changed a mere "yet" for a "but"; and would nag all round until she had silenced the conversation. Knowing her peculiarities, I hazarded but few remarks at table, and carefully avoided making any distinct statement, lest she should pounce upon it.

At last, with a feeling of oppression relieved, we rose, not, however, before Aunt Hetty had invited me to remain the night, and I had accepted. I should be compelled, I knew, to leave Charing Cross by the night mail on the morrow, much as I desired to remain a few days in that rural retreat beside the woman I loved.

For an hour or so we idled together beneath the trees in the quaint old garden, where Edith had caused the gardener to swing the hammock I had sent her from Paris. When the sun began to lose its power she put on her large flop hat of Leghorn straw trimmed with poppies, and we strolled together through the quiet village, between its rows of homely cottages, many of them covered with creepers and flowering plants, until we came to the winding Wensum river, which we followed by the footpath lined with poplars, past the old mill, and away into the country. Hand-in-hand we wandered, neither uttering a word for some little time, both of us too full of our own thoughts.

Suddenly, in Guist Wood, where the stream with its cooling music wound among the polished stems of the beeches, with the sunshine glinting down upon them through the veil of leaves, we halted, standing ankle deep in soft moss and nodding wild-flowers. Her beauty and her silence had struck a new, intolerable conviction of guilt into my heart.

She turned her flawless face to mine as though with firm resolve, and then in a hoarse, strained voice told me plainly that her love for me was all a mistake.

"A mistake that you love me, Edith!" I repeated, holding both her hands tightly in mine, and looking straight into her clear, dark, fathomless eyes.

"Yes," she insisted. Her colour went, and her eyes fell away from mine.

"Then why have you so changed?" I asked quickly. "I have always, since that evening beside the burn, regarded you as my affianced wife."

She closed her lips tightly, and I saw that tears welled in her eyes.

"My happy dream is over," she said bitterly, "and the awakening has come."

"No," I cried, "you cannot say that, Edith. You do not mean it, I'm sure! Remember the early days of our love, and recollect that my affection for you is as strong now as then—indeed, stronger to-day than it has ever been."

She was silent. In that moment my new-found happiness of those days in Scotland all came back to me. I remembered that summer-time of long lingering beneath the shadowy glades of the glen; of moonlight wanderings along the lanes, of love-trysts under the rising sun, by rose-garlanded and dew-spangled hedgerows. Ah! many had been the vows we had plighted in the deep heart of Scottish hills during those golden summer days, and many were the lovers' kisses taken and given under the influences of those long balmy evenings, when merely to idle was to be instinct with the soul of passion and of poetry.

"I remember those days," she answered. "They were the dawning days of our love. No afterglow of passion can ever give back the subtle charm of those sweet hours of unspoken joy. But it is all past, Gerald, and there is now a breach between us."

"What do you mean?" I asked anxiously. "I do not understand."

"I have already told you," she answered in a hard voice. "You love another woman more than you love me. Ah, Gerald! you cannot know how I have suffered these past months, ever since the truth gradually became apparent. All through these summer days I have wandered about the country alone, revisiting our old haunts where we had lingered and talked when you were here twelve months ago. Years seem to have passed over my head since that day in June when you last stood here and held my hand in yours. But now you have slipped slowly from me. I have drunk deeply of the cup of knowledge, and life's cruellest teachings have been branded upon my heart."

"But why?" I cried. "I cannot see that you have any cause whatever for sadness. True, we are compelled to be apart for the present, but it will not be so always. Your life is, I know, a rather monotonous one, but soon all will be changed—when you are my wife."

"Ah," she sighed, "I shall never be that—never!"

"Why not?"

"Because I see—I see now," she faltered, "that I am not fitted to become a diplomatist's wife. I have no tact, no smartness, no experience of the kind that is so absolutely necessary for the wife and helpmate of a man who is rising to distinction. I should only be a burden. You will find some other woman more brilliant, more chic, and thoroughly versed in all the ways of Society. You must marry her;" and with a woman's weakness she burst into tears.

"No, no!" I cried, kissing her upon the brow and drawing her closely to me in an effort to comfort her. "Who has been putting such ideas into your mind, darling? Who has told you that love can be curbed, trained, and controlled? Love does not stop to question right or wrong; it is spontaneous, irresponsible, and born of itself in one's heart. And I love you," I whispered into her ear.

She was silenced, as a true woman must always be by her lover's voice, no matter how specious may be his protestations; for there is no argument that can withstand the magic of the lover's touch or the light in the eyes of the man a woman loves, and the glamour of low, caressing words that steal their way to her innermost heart.

"Are you sure, quite sure, that you really love me sufficiently to sacrifice yourself for my sake?" she faltered through her tears.

"Sacrifice myself!" I echoed. "It is no sacrifice, darling. We love each other, and in future the course of our lives must be along the same path, no matter what may be the obstacles."

"I wish I could think so," she said; while a faint smile, sweet and tender as the sunshine of May, gleamed for a moment about her eyes and lips.

The heart of a woman who loves is the most complex and subtle thing on earth; and often when most she protests, she most longs to be faithless to the spirit of her own protestation.

I looked at her now fully and firmly. There was, I think, terror in my eyes—the terror of losing her, which her last words had suddenly conjured up.

"But cannot I convince you?" I cried. "Will you not accept what I tell you as the truth, darling? Will you not believe that I love you still?"

I stooped, and taking her fair face in my hands, tenderly kissed her brow, just as I had kissed her in the days when our love had dawned.

"I have tried," she answered bitterly, "but cannot. Alas! it is a woman's part to suffer;" and her breast heaved slowly and fell again.

How pathetic were her great dark eyes, how attractive was the delicate face with its refined outline, how tenderly seductive those tremulous lips which no man had kissed save myself! That she suffered an agony of heart because of the suspicion that I no longer loved her truly was more than plain. It became her creed—the creed of the martyr and the enthusiast, which comes to some women by nature with the air they breathe, and is an accentuation of one of the finest instincts of human nature.

"But you shall not suffer thus, my darling!" I cried. "You shall not, for I love you truly, honestly, and well. You shall be my wife. You have already promised, and you shall not draw back, for I love you—I love you!"

Chapter Eighteen
By Day and by Night

She put up both her small white hands as though to stay the torrent of passionate words which I poured forth; but I grasped her wrists and held her to me until I had told her all the longings of my soul.

What she had said had caused me a stab of unutterable pain, for my conscience was pricked by the knowledge that I had for a brief moment forsaken her in favour of Yolande. But she could not know the real truth. It was only by her woman's natural intuition that she held me in suspicion, believing that by my neglect to write I had proved myself attracted by some member of that crowd of feminine butterflies who flit through the embassies, showing their bright colours and dazzling effects.

At last she lifted her face, and in a low, faltering voice said:

"I do not wish that we should part, Gerald. I have no one but you."

"And God knows—God knows, darling, I have no one but you!" I cried brokenly; and as I uttered these words she cast her arms about my neck, clinging to me, sobbing, with her face lying close against my breast.

"My darling—my own darling!" was all I could murmur as I kissed away the tears that rained down her checks. I could say nothing more definite than that.

"You will not be false, will you?" she implored at last. "You will not break your promise, will you?"

"I will never do that, dearest," I assured her. "I love you, upon my word of honour as a man. I have loved you ever since that day when we first met at the house-party up in Scotland—the night of my arrival when you sat opposite me at dinner. Do you remember?"

"Yes," she answered, smiling, "I remember. My love for you, Gerald, has never wavered for one single instant."

"Then why should you be unhappy?" I asked.

"I really cannot tell," she answered. She turned her face, and I saw that there was a shadow across it, as though the sunshine of her life had gone behind a bank of cloud. "All I can compare this strange foreboding to is the shadow of an unknown danger which seems of late to have arisen, and to stand in a wall of impenetrable blackness between us."

"No, no!" I hastened to urge, "the sweet idyll of our blameless love must be preserved. That fancy of yours is only a vague, unfounded one."

She shook her head dubiously.

"It is always with me. During my long, solitary wanderings here I think of you, and then it arises to overshadow me and crush out all my happiness," she said in a tone of sorrow.

"Your life is dismal and lonely here," I said. "You've become nervous and melancholy. Why not have a change? Persuade your aunt to bring you to Paris, or, if not, to some place near, where we may meet often."

"No," she replied in a harsh tone. "My presence in Paris is not wanted. You are better without me. You must leave England again to-morrow—and you must forget."

"Forget!" I gasped. "Why?"

"It is best to do so," she faltered with emotion. "I am unfitted to become your wife."

"But you shall—you must!" I cried. "You have already given me your promise. You will not desert me now!"

She made no response. I pressed her again for an answer, but she maintained silence. Her attitude was one of firm resolve, and gave me the distinct impression that she had gained some knowledge of the reason of our brief estrangement.

"Tell me the reason of your sudden disbelief in my declarations," I urged, looking earnestly into her eyes. "Surely I have given you no cause to regard our love as a mere irresponsible flirtation?"

"I have no reason to disbelieve you, Gerald," she answered seriously; "yet I recognise the impossibility of our marriage."

"Why is it impossible? We are both controllers of our own actions. You will not remain here with your aunt all your days?"

"We may marry, but we should not be happy, I feel certain."

"Why?"

"Because if I were your wife I could not bear to think you were out each night dancing attendance upon a crowd of foreign women at the various functions which you are in duty bound to attend."

I smiled at her argument. Ignorant of the world and its ways, and knowing nothing of Society beyond that gossiping little circle of tea-drinkers and tennis-players which had its centre in the town of Fakenham, and had as leader the portly wife of the estimable incumbent, she saw herself neglected among the brilliant crowd in Paris as described by the so-called "Society" papers.

I hastened to reassure her, and as we strolled on through the wood and, following the meandering of the river, emerged upon the broad grass-lands before Sennowe Hall, I used every argument of which I was capable in order to dispel her absurd apprehensions. My protestations of love I repeated a hundred times, striving to impress upon her that I was actually in earnest; but she repelled me always, until of a sudden I halted beneath the willows, and, placing my arm around her slim waist, narrowly girdled by its crimson ribbon, I drew her again to me, saying:

"Tell me, Edith, plainly, whether or no you love me. These cold words of yours have struck me to the heart, and I feel somehow that in my absence you have found some other man who has your gratitude, your respect, and your love."

She raised her hand, as though to stay the flow of my words.

"No, no!" I went on passionately. "You must hear me, for you seem to be gradually slipping away from me. You must hear me! Cast away this cold sweetness that is enough to madden any man. Give me a right to your love; give me a right to it! You cannot be indifferent to such a love as mine unless you love someone else."

"Stop!" she cried, moved by a sudden generous impulse. "I love no one else but you."

"And you admit that you still love me? You will be the same to me as before?" I cried eagerly.

"If you will swear that there is no thought of another woman in your heart," she answered seriously.

A pang of conscience smote me; but inwardly I reassured myself that all the fascination of Yolande had been dispelled and that my love was free.

"I swear," I said; then slowly I bent until our lips touched.

Hers met mine in a fierce, passionate caress, and by that I knew our compact was sealed.

"I admit," she said, "that my instinct, if it were instinct, was wrong. You have, after all, proved yourself loyal to me."

"And I shall remain so, darling," I assured her, kissing her again upon the brow. "For the present you must be content to remain with your aunt; but nevertheless, try to persuade her to come to Paris. Then we can spend many happy days together."

"She hates the Continent and foreigners," answered my love with a brightening smile. "I fear I can never persuade her to move from here. She went to Switzerland twenty years ago, and has never ceased condemning foreign travel."

"If she will not come, then why not engage a chaperon? You surely know some pleasant woman who would be pleased to have a holiday jaunt."

"Well," she answered dubiously, "I'll try, but I fear Aunt Hetty will never hear of it."

"The life in the profound stillness of that house and the rigid seclusion from all worldly enjoyment are producing an ill effect upon your health, darling," I said presently. "You must have a change. It is imperative."

But she only sighed, smiled rather sadly, and answered in a low voice:

"The quietness of life here is nothing to me, as long as I am confident that your love for me is just the same as it was when you first told me the secret of your heart."

"It is," I assured her—"it is, darling. I love you—and you alone."

There was an instant's hesitation, and then her arms stole gently to my neck, and her lips were pressed to the cheek I bent to them, but only for a second; then my lips were upon hers, clinging to them softly, passionately; and in those moments of ecstasy I drew my soul's life from that sweet mouth.

Heedless of time, we stood there in each other's embrace, repeating our vows of love and devotion, until the sun went down behind the low hills beyond Raynham, and the broad pastures were flooded by the purple glow of the dying day. Happy and content in each other's affection, we were careless of the past, and recked not of the future. Edith loved me, and I wished for naught else in all the world.

Now as I sit committing this strange story of my life—this confidential chapter in the modern history of Europe—to paper, I recall every detail of those hours we spent down by the riverside, and contrast it with the curious events which followed—events which were so strange as to be inexplicable until the ghastly truth became revealed. But I loved, and my affection was reciprocated. That surely was sufficient, for I knew that I had gained the purest, most beautiful, and sweetest woman I had ever met.

At last the fading sunlight impressed upon us the fact that the dinner-hour was approaching; and, knowing Miss Foskett's punctuality at meals, we were compelled to strike along the footpath over Dunham Hill, and take the shortest cut across the fields through the little hamlet of Gateley, and thence by a grass-grown by-road back to Great Ryburgh, where we arrived just as the gong sounded.

When we re-entered the dining-room, Aunt Hetty glanced at us keenly, as though she wished to make some sarcastic comment upon our long absence; but our pleasant demeanour apparently silenced her, and she contented herself by taking her seat at table and inquiring of me if I had had a pleasant walk, and whether I found the country agreeable after the dusty boulevards of Paris.

"Of course," I answered, "I always find England charming, and I'm very frequently homesick, living as I do among foreigners always. But why don't you come abroad for a month or so, and bring Edith?"

"Abroad!" screamed the old lady, holding up her hands. "Never! I went to Lucerne once, and found it horrible."

"But that was some years ago, was it not? If you went now, you would find that travelling has greatly improved, with a through sleeping-car from Calais to Basle; hotels excellent, and food quite as good as you can obtain in England. During the past few years hotel-keepers on the Continent have awakened to the fact that if they wish to be prosperous they must cater for English visitors."

"Oh, do let us go abroad, aunt!" urged Edith. "I should so much enjoy it!"

"Paris in summer is worse than London, I've heard, my dear," answered Miss Foskett, in her high-pitched tone.

"But there are many pretty places within easy reach of the capital," I remarked. "Edith speaks French; therefore you need have no hesitation on that score."

"No," said the old lady decisively, "we shall not move from Ryburgh this summer, but perhaps next winter—"

"Ah!" cried Edith joyously. "Yes, capital! Let us go abroad next winter, to the Riviera, or somewhere where it's warm. It would be delightful to escape all the rain and cold, and eat one's Christmas dinner in the sunshine. You know the South, Gerald? What place do you recommend?"

"Well," I said, "any place along the Riviera except, perhaps, Monte Carlo."

"Monte Carlo!" echoed Aunt Hetty. "That wicked place! I hope I shall never see it. Mr Harbur told us in his sermon the other Sunday about the frightful gambling there, and how people hanged themselves on the trees in the garden. Please don't talk of such places, Edith."

"But, aunt, there are many beautiful resorts in the neighbourhood," her niece protested. "All along the coast there are towns where the English go to avoid the winter, such as Cannes, Nice, Mentone, and San Remo."

"Well," responded Miss Foskett with some asperity, "we need not discuss in August what we shall do in December. Ryburgh is quite pleasant enough for me. When I was your age I employed my time with embroidery and wool-work, and never troubled my head about foreign travel. But nowadays," she added with a sigh, "I really don't know what young people are coming to."

"We've advanced with the times, and they've emancipated women in England," responded Edith mischievously, glancing merrily across at me.

Miss Foskett drew herself up primly, and declared that she hoped her niece would never become one of "those dreadful creatures who ape the manners of men;" to which my love replied that liberty of action was the source of all happiness.

Fearing that this beginning might end in a heated argument, I managed to turn the conversation into a different channel.

"If all we read in the newspapers is true, it would seem," observed Aunt Hetty presently, "that you diplomatists have a most difficult task in Paris."

"All is not true," I laughed. "Much of what you read exists only in the minds of those imaginative gentlemen called Paris correspondents."

"I suppose," remarked Edith, smiling, "that it is impossible for either a diplomatist or a journalist to tell the truth always."

"Truth, no doubt, is all very well in its place, and now and then in diplomacy, but only a sparing use should be made of it as a rule," I answered. "But there should be no waste. Only those should be allowed to handle it who can use it with discretion, and who will ladle it out with caution."

"Mr Ingram, I am surprised!" interrupted Miss Foskett, scandalised.

"It is our creed," I went on, "that truth should be always spoken in a dead or foreign language, no home-truths being for a moment tolerated. Now think what a happy land this England of ours would be if only we were not so wedded to the bare, cold truth! Suppose for its own good purposes our Government has thought right to make a hasty dash for the back seats in the international scrimmage, and to adhere to them with all the tenacity of a limpet, why, for all that, should the Opposition journals blurt out the fact for our humiliation, when by a few deft scratches of the pen the leader-writer might easily make us believe that no back seat had ever in any circumstances been occupied by Britain, and that the nose of the lion had never been pulled out of any hole into which it had once been inserted? The itch for truth is, judged from a diplomatists point of view, responsible for the ruin of our policy towards our enemies."

"Shocking, Mr Ingram! I'm surprised to find that you hold such views," said Miss Foskett in a soured tone; while Edith laughed merrily, declaring that she fully agreed with my argument, much to her aunt's discomfiture.

The old lady loved the harsh truth as propounded by the precisionist.

And so the dinner proceeded, each of us vying with the other to dispel Aunt Hetty's deep-seated prejudices and narrow-minded views of the world and its ways.

Coffee was served in the drawing-room, where Edith went to the piano and sang in her sweet contralto several of my favourite songs, after which, at an early hour, as was usual with the household at Ryburgh, we all retired.

To sleep so quickly after dinner was to me impossible; therefore, on gaining my room, I lit a cigar, and, taking a novel from my bag, sat reading. The book proved interesting; and time had passed unnoticed, until of a sudden my attention was attracted by the sound of low voices. I listened, glancing at the clock, and noticed that it was nearly two in the morning.

A suspicion of burglars at once flashed across my mind. I blew out my candles, so as not to attract attention, noiselessly opened the wooden shutters before my window, and cautiously gazed out. The lawn, garden, and wide sweep of country beyond lay bathed in the bright moonlight, and at first I distinguished no one. Peering down, however, until I could see the path running in the shadow just below my window, I distinguished two figures with hands clasped, as though in parting. I looked again, scarce believing my own eyes. But I was not mistaken. One figure was that of a woman, her dark cloak open at the throat, revealing her white dress beneath; while the other was the tall dark figure of a man in a long black overcoat, the collar of which was turned up as though to conceal his features. Even though they stood together in the dark shadow, the astounding truth was plain to me. The woman who had kept that midnight assignation was Edith Austin, my well-beloved.

My heart stood still.

Chapter Nineteen
Whispered Words

The revelation held me rigid. I stood there, peering down, watching their movements, and straining my ears to catch the whispered words. As I feared to open the window lest the noise should attract them, I could do no more than remain a spectator of Edith's perfidy. To me it seemed as though she had been walking with him, and he had accompanied her back to the house. As he held her hand, he was bending, whispering some earnest words into her ear. She did not attempt to withdraw; indeed, it was apparent that she was not unwilling. The conclusion to be made was that they were lovers.

Reader, can you imagine my feelings at this astounding discovery? Only six hours before we had stood beside the river, and she had vowed that for no man save myself had she any place in her heart; yet with my own eyes I was watching her while she believed me sleeping in calm ignorance of her movements. That she had been walking with him was apparent, because of the shawl she wore wrapped about her head; while the fact that the stranger carried a stout stick showed that he had walked, or was about to walk, a considerable distance. Because his hat was drawn over his brow and his coat collar turned up, I could not see his features. To me, as he stood there, he appeared to be slightly round-shouldered, but, nevertheless, a strongly built fellow, seemingly rather above the average height.

How long she had been absent from the house I could not tell. Her light step across the lawn had not attracted my attention. Only his low, gruff voice on their return had caused me to listen. There was a French window near where they were standing, and it was evident that by means of this she had secretly left the house.

Across the moon there drifted a strip of fleecy cloud, hiding the lawn and garden for a few moments; then suddenly all became brilliant again, and, looking down, I saw that she had moved, and was unconsciously in the full white light. I caught sight of her countenance, so that her identity became undeniable. He was urging her to speak, but she remained silent. Again and again he whispered into her ear, but she shook her head. At last she spoke. I heard what she said, for I had contrived to raise the sash an inch or two.

"Very well, I promise," she said. "He leaves to-morrow."

"And you will not fail?" asked the gruff voice of her clandestine companion.

"No. Adieu!"

And as I watched I saw his dark figure striding away in the full moonlight across the lawn. He did not glance back, but went straight over to the belt of elms on the left, and a few minutes later was lost to view, while the woman I loved had apparently re-entered the house by the dining-room window, and was creeping silently to her room.

The one thought that gripped my heart and froze my senses was that Edith was false to me. She had a lover whom she met at dead of night and with whom she had a perfect understanding. She had made him a promise, the fulfilment of which was to take place when I had left. Had such things been told to me I would not have believed them, but I had seen with my own eyes and heard with my own ears. The truth was too terribly plain. Edith, the one woman in the world whom I had believed to be pure, honest, and upright, was false to me. I saw it all as I reclosed the shutters, relit the candles in their old silver sconces, and paced that ancient bed-chamber. The reason of her attempt to evade me and to withdraw her promise of marriage was only too apparent. She, the woman whom I loved and in whom I had put all my faith, had a lover.

As I reflected upon our conversation of that afternoon I saw in her uneasiness and her responses a self-condemnation. She dreaded lest I should discover the secret within her breast—the secret that, after all, she did not love me. The dark silhouette of that man standing forth in the brilliant light of the moon was photographed indelibly upon my memory. His outline struck me as that of a man of shabby attire, and I felt certain the hat drawn down upon his face was battered and worn. Indeed, I had a distinct conviction that he was some low-born lout from the neighbourhood—a conviction aroused, I think, by her announcement that I was to leave on the morrow. She would have freedom of action then, I reflected bitterly. And her promise? What, I wondered, had she promised? The fellow had evidently been persuading her until she had at last given him her pledge. His gait was that of a man who knew the place well, the swinging step of one used to walking easily in rough places. His stick, too, was a rough ash, such as a town-bred lover would never carry, while his voice had, I felt certain, just a tinge of the Norfolk accent in it. That they should meet at dead of night in that clandestine manner was surely sufficiently suspicious, but those words I had overheard sounded ever in my ears as I paced from end to end of that old room with its sombre, almost funereal, hangings.

A great bitterness fell upon my heart. The woman whom I really loved had played me false; and yet, when I reflected, I could not help admitting that perhaps, after all, I deserved this punishment. I had wavered from her and gone back to my old love, it was true. But I loved Edith well and truly, whatever might have been the fascination of the smart, gesticulating, foreign beauty. She was mine in heart and mine alone.

All my belief in woman's affection or devotion had, in that instant, been dispelled. The truth had fallen upon me as a crushing blow, which staggered me, wrecking all my hopes and plans for the future.

I tossed my things heedlessly into my bag, in readiness for early departure in the morning. I had been a fool, I knew. I was ever a fool where women were concerned. In the old days in Brussels my affection for Yolande had been strong and impetuous, burning with all the ardour of a first love; yet the awakening had come, and I had tardily discovered that she had played me false. And in Edith's case, although I entertained towards her such a real and deep affection as a man only extends to a woman once in his lifetime, unfaithfulness had once again been my reward.

I flung away my cigar. My agony of heart was too acute to be accurately described in words. You, my reader, who may have experienced the sudden breaking of your most cherished idol, can only rightly understand the chagrin, the intense bitterness, the spiritual desolation of that night watch.

My candles were as nearly as possible burnt out. At length I took my hat, and, creeping noiselessly downstairs, passed through the dining-room, and let myself out by the window which Edith had entered. The first grey of dawn was spreading, and a sudden desire for fresh air had seized me. I felt stifled in that old room with its gloomy furniture and hangings. With the cool wind of early morning fanning my heated temples, I struck straight across the lawn in the direction taken by the mysterious lover. For some distance I traversed the boundary of the grounds, until I discovered a break in the oak fence, and, passing through it, found myself out upon the broad, undulating meadows which stretched away to the Beacon Hill and the tiny hamlet of Toftrees, noted for its ancient hall and quaint church steeple. Heedless of where my footsteps led me, I went straight on, my mind full of the discovery I had made, my heart overflowing. Away to my left, from behind the low dark hills, the sky became flushed with the crimson light of dawn; but all was still save the distant crowing of a cock and the howl of a dog in the far distance. Behind me the bell of Ryburgh church solemnly chimed the hour, followed by other bells at greater distances. Then all was quiet again save for the soft rustling of the trees. The morning air was delicious, with a sweet fragrance everywhere.

Suddenly, leaping a fence, I found myself upon the old coach-road that ran over the hills to Lynn, and continued along it without thought of distance or destination. I passed a carter with his team, and he wished me good-morning. His words aroused me, and I saw that I was nearing an unfamiliar village.

"What place is this?" I inquired.

"It's Harpley, sir."

I thanked him and went my way. I had never heard of the place before; but as I entered it the first rays of sunlight shot across the hills, and it certainly looked picturesque and typically English in the light of the dawn. I must have walked fully eight miles, and, being tired and thirsty, I noticed at the entrance of the village a small inn, upon which was the sign The Houghton Arms. The door stood open, and a burly man, evidently the landlord, was busy chopping wood in an outhouse at the side.

"Nice mornin', sir," he observed, looking up at me, probably astonished to see anyone who was not a labourer astir at such an early hour.

I returned his greeting, and inquired whether it was too early for a cup of tea and a rest.

"Not at all, sir," he answered, laying down his axe and conducting me within.

The place, in common with all village hostelries, smelt strongly of the combined fumes of shag and stale beer. Village innkeepers have a habit of polishing their well-seasoned furniture with sour beer; hence the odour, which, to the patrons of such places, seems appetising. The perfume is to them as the hors d'oeuvre.

The man, having shown me into a little parlour behind the tap-room, called loudly to "Jenny," who turned out to be his wife. After this I had not long to wait before a pot of tea and a couple of poached eggs were at my disposal.

They were a homely pair, these two, full of local chatter. Harpley, the man informed me, was nine and a half miles from Great Ryburgh, and I saw by his manner that he was much exercised in his mind to know whence I had come and the reason for my being about at such an hour. The rural busybody was extremely inquisitive, but I did not permit his bucolic diplomacy to triumph. While I drank the tea and ate the eggs the landlord stood leaning against the door-lintel with his arms folded, garrulously displaying his Norfolk brogue. He evidently regarded me as one of those summer visitors from London who stay at the farmhouses, where hypocrisy terms them "paying guests," and I allowed him to adhere to his opinion. I learned from him that at six o'clock there was a train from Massingham station, half a mile away, which would convey me direct to Fakenham. This I resolved to take, for I could then return to Miss Foskett's by a quarter to seven. A map of the county was hanging on the wall, and I had risen to look at the spot to which the landlord was pointing, when a footstep sounded in the narrow passage, and, turning, I caught sight of the dark figure of a man making his way out. The hat, the black overcoat, the figure, all were familiar. His head was turned away from me, so that I could not see his features, but in an instant I recognised him.

He was Edith's mysterious lover!

Chapter Twenty
From Downing Street to Paris

I sprang quickly to the door, and looked down the passage out into the village street; but he had already made his exit. By the time I had reached the porch of the inn he was already striding quickly along the dusty highway. He turned to glance back, and I perceived that he was thin-faced, with high cheekbones and a small black beard. He was carrying his thick stick jauntily, and walking smartly, with an easy gait which at that moment struck me as being distinctly military.

"Who is that man?" I inquired eagerly of the landlord, who stood beside me, evidently surprised at my sudden rush towards the door.

"A stranger, sir. I don't know who he is."

"When did he arrive?"

"He came by the last train to Massingham last night, sir, and had a bed here. My missis, however, didn't like the looks of 'im."

"Why?"

"Well, I don't exactly know. There was something about him a bit peculiar. Besides, he went out before one o'clock, and didn't return till an hour ago. Then he went up, washed, had a cup o' tea in his room, paid, and now he's gone."

"Rather peculiar behaviour, isn't it?" I suggested, hoping to find some clue to his identity from what this man might tell me. "Did he have no luggage?"

"None. He seemed a bit down on his luck. His clothes were very shabby, and he evidently hadn't had a clean collar for a week."

Then the opinion I had formed of him—namely, that he was shabby genteel—was correct.

"You're certain you've never seen him before?"

"Quite certain," he replied.

At that moment his wife entered, and, addressing her, he said:

"We're talking of that stranger who's just gone, missus. His movements were a bit suspicious, weren't they?"

"Yes. Why he should want to go out half the night wandering about the neighbourhood I can't make out, unless he were a burglar or something o' that sort," the woman answered, adding: "I shouldn't be at all surprised to hear that one of the houses about here has been broken into. Anyhow, we'd know him again among a thousand."

"What kind of man was he?"

"Tall and dark, with a beard, and a pair of eyes that seemed to look you through. He spoke all right, but I've my doubts as to whether he wasn't a foreigner."

"A foreigner!" I echoed quickly, interested. "What made you suspect that?"

"I really can't tell. I had a suspicion of it the first moment I saw him. He pronounced his 'r's' rather curiously. His clothes seemed to be of foreign cut, and his boots, although worn out, were unusually long and narrow. I brushed 'em this morning, and saw on the tabs a foreign name. I think it was 'Firenze,' or something like that."

I reflected for an instant. The word "Firenze" was Italian for Florence, the town where the boots had evidently been made. Therefore the mysterious stranger might be Italian.

"You didn't actually detect anything foreign in his style of speaking?"

"He didn't speak much. He seemed very glum and thoughtful. I sent him up some toast with his tea, but he hasn't touched it."

"He didn't say where he was going?"

"Not a word. When he arrived he only explained that he had come by the last train from Lynn, and that he wanted a bed—that's all. I should think by the look of him that he's gone on tramp."

My first impulse was to follow him; but on reflection I saw that by doing so I should in all probability lose my train, and to dog the fellow's footsteps would, after all, be of no benefit now that I knew the truth of Edith's perfidy. So I stood there chatting, discussing the stranger, and wondering who he could be.

"He's up to no good, that I feel certain," declared the landlord's wife. "There's something about him that aroused my suspicion at once last night. I can't, however, explain what it was. But a man don't prowl about all night to admire the moon."

And thus I waited until it was time to catch the train; then, wishing the innkeeper and his wife good-morning, left them and strolled in the morning sunlight to the station, arriving at Fakenham shortly before seven. I took the short cut through Starmoor Wood to Ryburgh, and, finding Miss Foskett's maid polishing the door-handle, entered and went upstairs.

Upon the toilet-table was a telegram, which the maid said had just arrived, and on opening it I found a message from the Foreign Office, which had been forwarded from the Club, asking me to call at the earliest possible moment, and to be prepared to return to my post by the afternoon service from Charing Cross. I knew what that implied. The Marquess desired me to bear a secret despatch to my Chief.

I washed, tidied myself after my dusty walk, strapped my bag, and with a feeling of regret that I was compelled to meet my false love again face to face before departure, I descended the stairs.

She was awaiting me, looking cool and fresh in her white gown, with a bunch of fresh roses she had plucked from the garden in her breast. She smiled gladly, and stretched forth her hand as though I were all the world to her. What admirable actresses some women are! Her affected sweetness that yesterday had so charmed me now sickened me. The scales had fallen from my eyes, and I was angry with myself that I had ever allowed myself to lose control of my feelings and love her. She was false—false! That one thought alone ran in my mind as she laughed merrily.

"Why, Gerald, wherever have you been? A telegram came for you by special messenger from Fakenham at half-past six, and when Ann knocked at your door she found you were out. And you went out by the dining-room window, too."

"Yes," I said, not without a touch of sarcasm, "I felt that I wanted fresh air, so I went for a stroll."

"You are an early bird," she answered. "Did you go far?"

"No, not very far. Only down the Lynn road a little way."

"I always thought that you people in Paris never got up till your déjeuner at eleven?"

"I'm an exception," I said shortly. "I prefer the morning air in the country to lying in bed."

"And the telegram? Is it anything particular?"

"Yes," I answered. "I must leave at once. I am summoned to Downing Street, and must leave London this afternoon."

"What! return to Paris at once?"

"Yes," I replied. "It is an order from the Chief. There's a train to London at 9:50, I think. I must not fail to catch that."

I had not kissed her, and I saw that she was somewhat puzzled by my coolness. Did the fact that I had let myself out by the dining-room window give her any clue to the reason why I had chosen that mode of egress?

"I thought you would remain here with us at least to-day," she pouted. "That's the worst of diplomacy. You never seem to know what you may do next."

We were standing alone in the dining-room, where breakfast was already laid and the copper kettle was hissing above the spirit-lamp. As Aunt Hetty had not entered, it was upon the tip of my tongue to charge Edith with that clandestine meeting; yet if I did so, I reflected, a scene would certainly be created. Aunt Hetty would first be scandalised and afterwards wax indignant, while my departure would doubtless be fraught with considerable unpleasantness. Therefore I resolved to keep my anger within my heart, and on my return to Paris to write a letter of explanation to this smiling, bright-faced woman who had thus played me false.

"You cannot tell how wretched I am at the thought of your departure, Gerald," she said, her dark eyes suddenly grave and serious. "Each time we part I always fear that we shall not meet again."

I smiled, rather bitterly, I think, and uttered some weak platitude without appearing to be much interested. Then with a quick movement she took my hand, but next instant was compelled to drop it, for Miss Foskett entered suddenly, and, after an explanation of my unexpected call by telegram, we seated ourselves and breakfasted.

As the woman I had so dearly loved sat opposite me I saw that she was strangely nervous and agitated, and that she was eager to question me; but with feigned indifference I chatted and laughed with the punctilious old spinster until the boy brought round the pony-trap and it was time for me to depart for Fakenham, where I could join the express for London.

Edith drove me to the station, but, the boy being with us, she could say nothing confidential until we were walking together upon the platform. Then, looking at me in strange eagerness, she suddenly asked:

"Gerald, tell me why you are so cold towards me this morning? You were so different yesterday. Have I displeased you?"

"Yes," I said in a hard voice, "you have."

"How?" she gasped, laying her gloved hand upon my arm and stopping short.

I was silent. Should I tell her, or should I say nothing about my knowledge of her perfidy?

"Why do you not speak?" she urged. "Surely if I have caused you pain I ought to know the reason!"

"You know the reason," I answered in a mechanical voice, regarding her coldly.

"No, I do not."

"In this matter it is entirely unnecessary to lie to me, Edith," I said; "I am aware of the truth."

"The truth? What truth?"

"That you do not love me," I said hoarsely.

At that instant the train rushed into the station, and my voice was almost drowned by the noise of the escaping steam. As I thought she deserved to suffer, I was not sorry for the interruption.

"Gerald!" she cried, gripping me by the hand, "what are you saying? What have I done?"

"It is enough," I answered, my voice broken by emotion, which I could no longer suppress, for my heart was at that moment bursting with grief. "Good-bye;" and turning, I raised my hat and stepped into the empty compartment, in which a porter had placed my bag.

In an instant she was leaning in at the doorway, imploring me to tell her the truth. But I evaded her questions.

The guard came and closed the door.

"Gerald!" she cried, bursting into tears, "tell me why you treat me thus when I love you so dearly! It is cruel! You cannot guess how deeply I have suffered these two hours! Will you not kiss me once before you go?" and she raised her white face to the window with an imploring expression.

"No," I said, "I cannot, Edith."

"You refuse to kiss me this once—for the last time?" she wailed.

"Yes," I answered in a strained voice. "If you desire to know the reason of this refusal you will discover it when you reflect upon your actions of last night."

"What!" she gasped, pale to the lips. "*You saw him!*"

"Yes," I answered gravely, "I saw him."

Then the train moved off, leaving her standing there pale and rigid; and without further glance at the blanched but beautiful face which only twelve hours ago I had believed to be the open countenance of the purest and sweetest woman on earth, I flung myself back into the corner, plunged in my own bitter reflections. I had told her the ghastly truth, and we had parted. Edith Austin, whom I had hoped to make my wife, was lost to me for ever.

At midday I wearily ascended the great marble staircase at the Foreign Office, those stairs which every diplomatist in London climbs, and in the corridor met Boyd, one of the Marquess's private secretaries, who informed me that a meeting of the Cabinet was being held, and that his lordship had left instructions that I was to wait until he returned, when he would give me a despatch to carry at once to Paris.

So, accompanied by Boyd and my friend Thorne, of the Treaty Department, I strolled along Parliament Street and lunched at the Ship, that old coffee-house frequented by Foreign Office and other officials. In the days before I received my appointment abroad I used to lunch there regularly, and as I entered I found many of my old colleagues at the tables.

After an hour I returned to Downing Street, and went up to the Foreign Secretary's private room. He was seated at his great table at the farther end of the sombre, green-painted apartment, the windows of which looked down upon the silent courtyard, where the cooing pigeons strut undisturbed. Upon his grey, refined face was an intensely anxious look, and by the nervous manner in which he toyed with his quill as he acknowledged my salutation I knew that the subject discussed by the Cabinet had been a momentous one. The meeting had been specially and unexpectedly convened, and I had heard below that during its sitting several despatches had been exchanged over the private wire to Windsor, facts which in themselves were sufficient to show that some complication had arisen, and that the lines of British policy had been discussed and submitted to the Sovereign for approbation.

"You are returning to Paris this afternoon, Mr Ingram?" said the Marquess. "I am just writing a private despatch to Lord Barmouth, which must be placed in his hands at the earliest possible moment. The instructions contained in it are secret—you understand?"

"I shall deliver it, I hope, before eleven o'clock this evening," I said.

"Good," he answered approvingly; and while I walked to the window and looked out upon the courtyard, the great statesman continued tracing the cipher upon the large sheet of blue despatch-paper with his creaking quill. I glanced at a newspaper to while away the time, until presently one of the secretaries entered, prepared the taper and wax, and I watched the Marquess affix the five seals upon the envelope, impressing his own arms with the large old fob seal which he wore upon his watch-guard. He affixed the last seal, held the envelope for a few moments in order that the wax should set, then handed it to me, saying:

"Remember, Ingram, none of our friends across the Channel must be allowed to get sight of this. It is entirely confidential. Please ask Lord Barmouth to telephone me to-night an acknowledgment of its safe receipt."

"Certainly," I answered, placing it in my pocket. I then bowed, and wished the Minister good-day.

"Good-day," he said, smiling pleasantly, "and a pleasant journey to you, Ingram."

Then I withdrew, and drove in a cab to the club. Arrived there, I placed the despatch in my belt next my skin, and, taking my bag, went down to Charing Cross and caught the tidal train.

The journey was uneventful, the passage smooth, and about eleven o'clock that night I mounted the stairs of the Embassy in Paris, and went to his lordship's private room. He was alone, enjoying a final cigar before turning in, and was surprised at my sudden return. I quickly explained the reason, and taking off my belt in his presence handed him the despatch.

Having assured himself that the seals were all intact, he broke them, and, taking it at once to the bureau, I got for him the key of the private cipher used only for the confidential despatches, written by the hand of the Prime Minister to the representatives abroad. Then, standing underneath the tall lamp, the Ambassador slowly deciphered it.

What he read caused him serious reflection, judging from the manner in which his countenance changed. Then, taking a match from his pocket, he crossed to the grate, lit the paper at the corner, and held it until it was all consumed.

The nature of that confidential communication none knew save the Cabinet in London and the Ambassador himself. That it was extremely important was certain, and I felt confident that some decision had been arrived at which would materially affect the European situation.

After telephoning an acknowledgment of the despatch to Downing Street, we returned together to the smoke-room, where I drank a whisky and soda, and then, lighting a cigar, left the Embassy and drove to my own rooms, wearied out after the journey.

At noon next day, when I went round to the Rue du Faubourg St. Honoré, Harding, the footman, met me in the hall, saying:

"His Excellency has just telephoned to you. He wishes to see you immediately."

I went straight to his private room, and found him seated with Kaye, the lynx-eyed chief of the secret service.

The Ambassador's face was pale as death, and his voice trembled as he hoarsely acknowledged my salutation.

"Ingram," he said in a low tone, motioning me to close the door, "we have been betrayed!"

"Betrayed? How?" I gasped.

"A copy of the despatch you brought me last night reached the Quai d'Orsay at two o'clock this morning. Our secret agent there has handed a copy of it to Mr Kaye. The wording of the instructions, as sent to me by the Marquess, is exact. Here it is;" and he held towards me a sheet of that pale yellow paper used in the French Foreign Office, upon which a transcription of the despatch had been hurriedly traced in pencil.

I glanced at it, then stood speechless. The secret despatch had never left my possession. The theft was utterly incredible.

Chapter Twenty One
The Sister Arts

"But it is absolutely impossible that the despatch has been copied!" I cried, addressing His Excellency, when at last I found tongue. "I saw it written myself, and it never left my belt until I took it out here in your presence!"

"Well," interposed Kaye grimly, turning to Lord Barmouth, "that it has really been copied is quite plain, for you have the copy in your hand. It was telegraphed to the Quai d'Orsay from Calais at half-past one o'clock this morning, and that copy reached my hands at four, half an hour after I had returned from Berlin. Our secret agent in the French Foreign Office happily lost no time in making us acquainted with our loss."

"Fortunately for us," remarked the Ambassador, pacing the floor from end to end. "Had we remained in ignorance that the secret of our policy was out, we might have found ourselves in a very awkward predicament. But how could the despatch possibly have been copied, when no other eyes have seen it except those of the Marquess and myself? The thing is incredible!"

"Ah! that's the question," observed Kaye. "The French system of espionage has very nearly approached perfection. Even though it be against our grain, as Englishmen, to employ spies ourselves, yet it is daily becoming more necessary. Every nation in the world has its elaborate secret service; therefore, England must not sleep and allow other nations to undermine her prestige."

"I cannot imagine how it is possible that our enemies could have obtained sight of the despatch, even for an instant," I said. "The only other person in the Chief's room at Downing Street while he was writing was Boyd, who helped him seal it. I then took it, drove in a cab to the club, and there placed it in my belt beneath my clothes. It never left my person until, in the smoking-room here, I took it out and handed it to His Excellency."

"The telegram was despatched from the maritime station at Calais by some person who signed his name as 'Gaston.' He is evidently known to our friends at the Quai d'Orsay."

There was a brief and painful pause. Such a catastrophe staggered belief. Surely the spies of France did not use the Roentgen rays in order to read the letters carried on one's person! It would almost appear as though they did.

"Fate seems entirely against us, Ingram," observed Lord Barmouth, breaking the silence at last. "In every effort we are thwarted by these scoundrelly spies. Our most secret instructions leak out in a way that is absolutely unaccountable. Indeed, the position has now become so critical that I dread to contemplate the result. In the matter of Ceuta we had an illustration of the marvellous astuteness of our enemies, while to-day here is an example much more alarming. And further, we must send home a despatch acknowledging ourselves checkmated. Our position is an ignominious one—most ignominious," he added vehemently.

"If I were at fault I would willingly bear any blame attaching to my actions," I said in a tone of protest; "but as far as I am aware I am utterly blameless in this matter."

"I do not seek to fix any culpability upon you, Ingram," His Lordship hastened to assure me. "While serving under me you have always done your duty with a thoroughness and tact worthy of the British diplomatist. All I can say is that it is excessively unfortunate for us all, and for the nation at large. Those instructions there, as you will see, are of the highest importance at this juncture; but we are now quite unable to act because our secret intentions have become common property. They will probably be in the *Figaro* to-morrow."

"The whole affair is at present a complete enigma," observed Kaye, who, turning to me, added: "If you cannot give us any clue whatever, I can't see what can be done."

"I can give you absolutely no clue," I answered, utterly bewildered by this amazing turn of events. "All I know is what I have just related."

The chief of the secret service turned his eyes full upon me, and asked slowly:

"You have, for instance, held no further communication with Mademoiselle de Foville?" Mention of that name caused me to start. All came back to me—how that the Ambassador had suspected her, and Kaye himself had declared that she was a spy.

"She left Paris before I went to London. I have no idea of her whereabouts."

"You do not suspect that she was in London at the same time as yourself?" he asked. "I mean, you saw nothing of her?"

"Absolutely nothing."

"And on the several occasions when you called upon her in the Rue de Courcelles you gave her no idea of the policy which His Excellency was pursuing? I know you visited her several times, for, suspecting her, I had placed a watch upon her movements."

"I told her absolutely nothing," I answered, annoyed that this man should think fit to spy upon me.

"Strange," he said thoughtfully. "Now that is really very strange, because her subsequent actions would appear to give colour to the theory that she learnt from you some secret which she was strenuously endeavouring to obtain."

"I don't quite follow you."

"Well, I have ascertained that the French Ambassador in Berlin has been receiving full reports of the progress of our actions regarding Ceuta."

"From her?" I asked quickly.

"Not exactly from her, but through her."

"Then that woman is actually a spy!" cried His Excellency.

"Without the slightest doubt," responded Kaye. "My inquiries in Berlin and Brussels have substantiated our suspicions. She is one of the smartest secret agents in Europe."

"I know that she is a friend of Wolf's, but what proof have you that she has any connection with the Ministry of Foreign Affairs?"

"I have obtained proof—absolute proof," he answered.

"In what manner?"

"By inquiries I made in Berlin. She is well known in the Wilhelmstrasse. She was compelled to fly from Germany because it leaked out that she was a French spy."

"Cannot you give me any further explanation?" I urged. "I am much interested, as she was once my intimate friend."

"Yes," interposed the Ambassador, "unfortunately so. It was once rumoured, Ingram, that you actually intended to marry her."

"Or rather," observed Kaye, "she intended, for her own purposes, to marry Mr Ingram, I think."

I pursed my lips, but made no response. My reflections at that moment were bitter enough without these observations from my friends.

"But do you suspect that she has had a hand in our latest betrayal?" I inquired a few minutes later. "You have just alleged that she is in the French service. If so, it hardly seems credible that she would give her information to the French Ambassador in Berlin."

"On that point I am not yet absolutely certain," Kaye responded. "I am, however, quite convinced that the exposure of our plans regarding Ceuta filtered to the French through their Embassy in Berlin."

"Then, contrary to supposition, de Hindenburg, the German Ambassador here, may be assisting France against us?" I said in surprise.

"It seems much like it. Our inquiries all tend towards that theory. The German Ambassador has of late had almost daily interviews with the Minister of Foreign Affairs. These are generally believed to be in connection with the Samoan difficulty or the Transvaal; but without doubt the chief subject of discussion has been the formation of a plan whereby to checkmate our policy towards Spain in the matter of Ceuta."

"Well, up to the present they have done so," the Ambassador admitted, turning sharply upon his heel from the window, out of which he had been gazing moodily. "We appear to be arriving at a most critical stage, for what with the constant Anglophobe feeling here, the vile attacks of the Paris Press, the disgusting caricatures of Her Majesty and her subjects, and the army of spies surrounding us on every side, honest, straightforward diplomacy— the diplomacy which should preserve the peace of Europe—is well-nigh impossible. In all my career in the service I never knew a blacker outlook than at this moment—never, never!"

"The complications that have arisen are due entirely to spies," I remarked.

"They are due, it appears, mainly to your friend, Yolande de Foville," he said in a harsh voice. "We have to thank that interesting young lady for rendering all our diplomacy in that direction abortive."

"You had suspicion of her the other day?" I exclaimed. "What caused you to suspect her?"

"Drummond knew her in Brussels, and mentioned her."

"As a secret agent?"

"Yes, as a secret agent. He warned me to be wary of her."

"Well," I said, "I, who knew her most intimately years ago, never suspected it for one single instant."

"Ah, Ingram," the Ambassador answered, a smile crossing his serious, hard-set face, "you were in love with her. A man in love never believes that his idol is of mere clay."

A sigh escaped me. His words were indeed true. A thought of Edith flashed across my mind. The face of that woman who was false to me rose before my vision, but I swept it aside. All was over between us. Diplomacy and flirtation are sister arts, but diplomacy and love never run hand-in-hand. I had quaffed the cup of life, with all its infinite joys and agonies, in one intoxicating draught.

Kaye rose at last and departed, promising to leave no stone unturned in his efforts to discover how the contents of the secret despatch had been obtained by the Ministry of Foreign Affairs; and then, at the Ambassador's dictation, I wrote a despatch to London explaining to the Marquess the reason why his instructions could not be acted upon. Thus were we compelled to acknowledge our defeat.

Below, in the hall, I met Sibyl dressed smartly, ready to go out.

"What!" she exclaimed, laughing, "you are back again! Why, I thought you would be at least a week in London. Did you bring that lace for me?"

"Yes," I answered, "I have it round at my rooms. I'll send it you this afternoon."

"Why are you back so soon?" she inquired, holding out her hand, so that I might button her glove. "Was London too hot?"

"The heat was insufferable. Besides, we have much to attend to just now."

"Poor father!" she exclaimed, looking up at me. "He seems terribly worried. Tell me, Mr Ingram, what has happened? I feel sure that some catastrophe has taken place."

"Oh, nothing," I reassured her. "Your father is a little anxious regarding some negotiations, that is all."

"But you will go to the Elysée to-night, won't you?"

"To-night! What is it to-night?"

"Why, the grand ball," she answered.

"Which means a new frock for you—eh?" I laughed.

"Of course," she replied. "You will come, won't you?"

"I fear I'm ever so much too tired for dancing," I responded, feeling in no humour for the crowded gaiety of the President's ball.

"But you must," she declared—"to please me. I want you to dance with me."

"Well," I said with reluctance, "I suppose I dare not be so ungallant as to refuse you."

"That's good," she laughed. "Now, as a reward, I'll drive you down to the boulevard. The victoria is outside. Where will you go?"

I reflected a moment, then told her I was on my way to my chambers.

"Very well," she replied, "I'll drop you there. I have to go down to the Rue de la Paix."

"To the couturière, of course?"

"Yes," she said, with that merry twinkle in her dark eyes, "you've guessed it the first time. It's a charming gown; but I know father will pull a wry face when he finds the bill on his table."

"But you can stand any amount of wry faces as long as you get pretty dresses, can't you?" I laughed, handing her into the carriage and taking a seat beside her.

Then she opened her sunshade and lolled back with an air of indolence and luxury as we drove along together.

Chapter Twenty Two
Perfume and Politics

Upon my table a letter was lying. The handwriting I recognised instantly as Edith's, and not without a feeling of anger and impatience I tore it open in expectation. Long and rambling, it upbraided me for leaving her without a single reassuring word, and declared that my refusal to kiss her at parting had filled her heart with a bitter and uncontrollable grief. As I read, memories of those midnight hours, of my walk to that distant village, and of my meeting with that shabby lover crowded upon me, and the impassioned words she had written made no impression upon me. I had steeled my heart against her. She had played me false, and I could never forgive.

"I know I have been foolish, Gerald," she wrote, *"but you misjudge me because of an indiscretion. You believe that the man with whom you saw me last night was my lover; yet you left me without allowing me to make any explanation. Is this right? Is it just? You know how well I love you, and that without you my life is but a hopeless blank. Can you, knowing that I love you thus, believe me capable of such duplicity as you suspect? I feel that you cannot. I feel that when you come to consider calmly all the circumstances you will find in your own honest heart one grain of pity and sympathy for the one woman who loves you so dearly. Write to me, for I cannot live without a word from you, because I love no other man but you?"*

I crushed the letter in my hand, then slowly tore it into fragments. I had no confidence in her protestations—none. My dream of love was over.

We often hear it remarked that those who are themselves perfectly true and artless are in this world the more easily and frequently deceived. I have always held this to be a commonplace fallacy, for we shall ever find that truth is as undeceived as it is undeceiving, and that those who are true to themselves and others may now and then be mistaken, or, in particular instances, duped by the intervention of some other affection or quality of the mind; but that they are generally free from illusion, and are seldom imposed upon in the long run by the show of things and by the superficies of any character.

There was a curious contradiction in Edith's character, arising from the contrast between her natural disposition and the situation in which she was placed, which corroborated my doubts. Her simplicity of language, her admission of an "indiscretion," the inflexible resolution with which she asserted her right, her soft resignation to unkindness and wrong, and her warmth of temper breaking through the meekness of a spirit subdued by a deep sense of religion,—all these qualities, opposed yet harmonising, helped to increase my distrust of her. To me that letter seemed full of a dexterous sophistry exerted in order to ward off my accusations. Her remorse was without repentance; it arose from the pang of a wounded conscience, the recoil of the violated feelings of nature, the torture of self-condemnation.

The fragments of the letter I tossed into the waste-paper basket, and, putting on my hat, went down to the Grand Café to idle away an hour among friends accustomed to make the place a rendezvous in the afternoon.

On entering, I found Deane sitting at a table alone, his carriage awaiting him at the door. He was having a hasty drink during his round of visits, and hailed me lustily.

"Sit down a moment, Ingram," he cried. "I want to see you."

"What about?" I inquired, lighting the cigarette he handed me.

"About that curious incident in the Rue de Courcelles—Mademoiselle de Foville's strange attack."

"Well, what of it?" I asked eagerly.

"Strangely enough a man, who proved to be an Englishman giving himself the name of Payne, was brought to the Hôtel Dieu three nights ago in what appeared to be a cataleptic state. He had, it seemed, been found by the police lying on the pavement in the Boulevard St. Germain, and was at first believed to be dead. Some letters in English being found upon him, I was called, and upon examination discovered exactly the same symptoms as those which mademoiselle your friend had displayed. I was enabled, therefore, to administer an antidote, and within twelve hours the man had sufficiently recovered to take his discharge. The case has excited the greatest possible interest at the hospital, for I had previously submitted a portion of the solution obtained from the envelope which mademoiselle had used to Professor Ferrari, of Florence, the greatest authority on toxicology in the world, and he had declared it to be an entirely unknown, but most potent, poison."

"Who was the Englishman? Did he tell you nothing?"

"No. Unfortunately the hospital authorities allowed him to leave before I deemed it wise to question him. I read the letters found upon him, however; but they conveyed nothing, except that he had been recently living somewhere in the neighbourhood of Hackney."

"Then you have no idea of the manner in which the poison was administered?" I said, disappointed.

"His right hand was rather swollen, from which I concluded that he had accidentally touched some object impregnated with the fatal compound."

"You don't know its composition yet?"

"No. Ferrari is trying to discover it, but at present has failed. The fact of a second person suffering from it is in itself very mysterious. I intended to call upon you this evening and tell you all about it."

"The affair is extraordinary," I admitted. "I wonder whether the same person who made the attempt upon Yolande's life is responsible for the attempt upon the Englishman? What can be the motive?"

"Ah! that's impossible to tell. All we know is that some unknown person in Paris has in his or her possession a deadly compound capable of producing catalepsy and subsequent death in a manner most swift and secret. In order to ascertain whether any other person is attacked in the same manner, I have sent letters to the Direction of all the hospitals in Paris explaining the case, and asking that if any similar cases are brought to them for treatment, I may be at once communicated with."

"An excellent precaution," I said. "By that means we shall be able to watch the progress of the mysterious criminal."

"You have heard nothing from Mademoiselle Yolande?"

"Nothing," I said.

"Hers was a curious case," he remarked. "But the man Payne's was equally strange. It appears that he made no statement to either police or hospital authorities before he left. He only said that he was walking along the boulevard and suddenly fell to the ground insensible."

"You think he had some motive in preserving silence?" I inquired quickly.

"Yes, I feel sure of it. I only wish I could rediscover him. They were foolish to allow him to take his discharge before giving me an opportunity of concluding my investigations. It was simply owing to professional jealousy. English medical men are not liked in Paris hospitals. But I must be off," he said, rising. "Good-bye."

Then he went out, and, entering his carriage, drove away.

Volkouski, the Russian attaché, was sitting close by, and I crossed to him, greeting him merrily. He was a good fellow—a thorough cosmopolitan, who had been trained in the smartest school of diplomacy—namely, the Embassy in London, which is presided over by that prince among diplomatists, Monsieur de Staal. Whatever may be said regarding the relations between Russia and England as nations, it cannot be denied that in the European capitals the staffs of the embassies of both Powers are always on terms of real friendship. I make no excuse for repeating this. The mutual courtesy of the representatives of the two nations is not, as in the case of those of France, Germany, and Austria, mere diplomatic manoeuvring, but in most instances a sound understanding and a deep personal regard. England, Russia, and Italy have interests in common, hence their representatives fraternise, even though certain journals may create all sorts of absurd scares regarding what they are pleased to term the "aggressive policy of Russia." This is a stock journalistic expression, as meaningless as it is absurd. We who are "in the know" at the embassies smile when we read those alarmist articles, purporting to give all sorts of wild plans, which exist only in the imagination of the leader-writer. There is, indeed, one London journal known in the Russian Embassies on the Continent as *The Daily Abuser*, because of its intensely Russophobe tone. Fortunately nobody takes it seriously.

I chatted with Volkouski, sipping a mazagran the while. He was, I found, full of projects for his leave. His chief had already left Paris, and he himself was going home to Moscow for a month. Every diplomatist on service abroad gets homesick after a time, and looks forward to his leave with the same pleasurable anticipation of the schoolboy going for his summer holidays. To escape from the shadow of a throne or the ceaseless chatter of an over-democratic Republic is always a happy moment for the wearied attaché or worried secretary of embassy. One longs for a respite from the glare and glitter of the official world of uniforms and Court-etiquette, and looks forward to rambles in the country in flannels and without a collar, to lazy afternoons upon the river, or after-luncheon naps in a hammock beneath a tree. To the tired diplomatist, sick of formalities, and with the stifling dust of the ballroom over his heart, the expression "en campagne" conveys so very much.

Shortly before midnight I stepped from a fiacre and ascended the broad steps of the Elysée. Tired as I was of the ceaseless whirl of the City of Pleasure, it nevertheless amused me to fix the physiognomy of the great official fêtes. They are inevitably banales, of course; but there is always a piquancy of detail and of contrast that is interesting.

If one wishes to see what a mixed crowd is like, there is no better illustration than the flocks of guests at the Elysée balls. Ah! what a crowd it was that night! What dresses! What a public! I know, of course, that it can never be otherwise under the present democratic régime. One man, who came on foot and whose boots were muddy, forgot to turn down the tucked-up ends of his trousers. People were walking about with their hands in their pockets, jostling each other without a word of excuse. Many were touching the furniture, and feeling the curtains and tapestry with that sans-gêne which so disgusted Gambetta with his former friends. You could see that they were determined not to appear astonished at anything, and that, after all, they were at home in the Elysée. They were of the detestable breed of café politicians, of loud-voiced orators at party meetings, of successful carpet-baggers, who render the ideas of equality and fraternity at times insufferable.

Before the buffet these fellows displayed themselves as goujats—cads—plain and simple. They grabbed for sandwiches, for biscuits, for glasses of champagne across the shoulders of ladies in front of them, or even elbowed them aside to get to the front row—and stop there. In the smoking-room the boxes of cigars were gone in the twinkling of an eye. One man struck his match on the wall. With these odd guests about it is not surprising that the Budget writes off a certain sum every year for articles that have disappeared from the buffets.

Whew! the heat there was insufferable!

In my search for Sibyl I passed through the antechamber. The footmen wore new livery. I saw none of those restaurant waiters who used, in the time of ce pauvre Monsieur Faure, to be employed at twenty francs the evening, supper included. Yes, things had slightly improved, but the crush was terrific. I made my way to the Salon des Aides-de-Camp, that historic chamber where, in the armchairs still furnishing the room, on the night of the coup d'état, sat, a prey to mortal anxiety, Morny, Persigny, Saint Arnaud, Piétri, Rouher, King Jérôme, and the Prince President.

The Japanese military attaché, walking before me, mixed himself up somehow with his sabre, and fell. This contretemps was greeted, as at a theatre, with laughter. Someone cried, "Oh, la la!" as if the stumble were a very clever bit of clowning indeed. The unhappy Japanese looked as if he wished the floor would swallow him.

I struggled up and paid my respects to the President, who was standing in the centre of the salon. Smiling, affable, displaying a simplicity that was real and unaffected, and yet devoid of mere familiarity, his bow and hand-shake were perfect. He struck the right note. I was impressed, moreover, by his sense of proportion. A little more cordiality, and he would cease to be Chief of the State. A little more solemnity, and he would be stilted. It is a little hard to convey the distinction; but imagine, on the one hand, a host who wants to make you forget his official position, and on the other a President of the Republic who is determined to be a good host. For well-bred people there is always a well-defined shade of difference between these two; and the President was the latter.

While turning away I suddenly came face to face with Monsieur Mollard, the chef-adjoint of the Protocol, who greeted me affably and commenced to tell me the latest story of General de Galliffet, Minister of War.

"It is amusing," he laughed. "You must hear it, M'sieur Ingram. The General arrived at his club, the Union, last night, and for some reason or another his former friends were more than usually cold in their treatment of him. After saying a bonjour to one and the other of them, and receiving a curt reply here and a snub there, the Minister of War realised this. But he took their coolness coolly. With his back to the fireplace he said quietly, by way of bringing home to his friends the absurdity of their attitude: 'You may come near me. Je ne sens pas mauvais—I don't smell bad. You see, there was no Cabinet to-day!' Is it not excellent?"

I smiled. It was a purely French joke. Mollard was always full of droll stories. Every diplomatist in Paris knew him as the keeper of the Elysée traditions, as guardian of its unwritten law by inheritance, his father having been, under other presidencies, the official known as introducteur des ambassadeurs. When a question of precedence puzzled the plebeian bigwigs at the Quai d'Orsay—the Foreign Office—it was Monsieur Mollard who would run to the archives to look it up. Nature had not, however, endowed him with a demeanour befitting his office, for he wore his uniform as awkwardly as a middle-aged volunteer officer, and looked more like a clerk than a chamberlain. But when he spoke he dragged on the mute syllables as French actors are taught to do in delivering Racine. He put three "l's" in "Excellence" and four "r's" in "Protocol." For the rest, he was a good fellow, much liked in the diplomatic circle, although many jokes had from time to time been played at his expense. Presently, after we had been talking for a few moments, I inquired whether he had seen Sibyl.

"Ah, no! I regret, m'sieur," he answered. "But a lady who is sitting over in the Salon Diplomatique has just inquired of me whether you are present."

"A lady? What is her name?"

"I know her by sight, but cannot recall her name," he responded. "She is a grande dame, however."

"Young or old?"

"Young. You will find her in the salon talking with Count Tornelli, the Italian Ambassador. You will easily recognise her. She is wearing a costume of black, trimmed with silver. She told me that she desired to speak with you particularly, and that I was to tell you of her presence."

"But you don't know her?" I laughed.

"Go and see," he answered. "You probably know her;" and, smiling, he turned away.

My curiosity being aroused, I struggled through the throng until I reached the spot indicated. Only the diplomatic corps and distinguished guests were allowed there, and the other guests, huddled together before the open door, were pointing out well-known personages.

I looked in, and in a moment saw before me the striking figure in black and silver. No second glance was needed to recognise who she was. For a moment I stood in hesitation; then, with a sudden resolve, entered, and, walking straight up, bowed low before her.

Chapter Twenty Three
Princess Léonie

"Princess," I said, "permit me to offer my félicitations on your return to Paris. This is indeed an unexpected pleasure."

"Ah, M'sieur Ingram!" she cried in charming English, holding forth her white-gloved hand, "at last! I have been hunting for you all the evening. All Paris is here, and the crush is terrible. Yes, you see I am back again."

The Italian Ambassador had risen, bowed, and turned to speak to another acquaintance; therefore, with her sanction, I dropped into his place.

"And are you pleased to return?" I inquired, glancing at her beautiful and refined face, which seemed to me just a trifle more careworn than when I had last met her eighteen months ago.

"Ah!" she answered, "I am always pleased to come back to France. I went to America for a few months, you know; thence to Vienna, and for nearly a year have been living at home."

"At Rudolstadt?"

She nodded.

"Well," I said, "it was really too bad of you to hide your existence from your friends in that manner. Everyone has been wondering for months what had become of you. Surely you found Rudolstadt very dull after life here?"

"I did," she sighed, causing the magnificent diamonds at her throat to sparkle with a thousand fires. "But I have departed from my hermitage again, you see. Now, sit here and tell me all that has happened during my absence. Then if you are good, I will, as a reward, give you just one waltz."

"Very well," I laughed. "Remember that I shall hold you to your bargain;" and then I commenced to gossip about the movements of people she had known when, two years before, she had been the most admired woman in Paris.

The Princess Léonie-Rose-Eugénie von Leutenberg was, according to the *Almanach de Gotha*—that red, squat little volume so dreaded by the ladies—only thirty years of age, and was certainly extremely good-looking.

Her pale, half-tragic beauty was sufficient to arrest attention anywhere. Her noble features were well-moulded and regular, her eyes of a clear grey, and her hair of flaxen fairness, while her bearing was ever that of a daughter of the greatest of the Austrian houses. Her goodness of heart, her gracefulness, her conversational esprit, and her genuine Parisian chic had rendered her popular everywhere; while, as with the Duchesse de Berri, one strong point of her beauty was her charming little foot, which two years ago had been declared to be the loveliest foot in France, or, in Paris, simply "Le pied de la Princesse." Her shoes and hosiery were perfect marvels of fineness and neatness, and when she walked, or rather glided, along the Avenue des Acacias, the other promenaders formed long rows on each side to behold and admire le pied de la Princesse.

I had heard it declared, too, with mysterious smiles, how le pied de la Princesse had been seen more than once at the masked balls at the Opera, and many an amusing little story had gone the round, and many a piquant tale had been told of how the Princess had been recognised here and there by the extreme smallness of her foot. One was that for a wager she had disguised herself as a work-girl with a bandbox on her arm, and, attended by her valet, likewise disguised, appeared before the Hôtel de Ville awaiting an omnibus. The vehicle stopped, and the conductor exclaimed in an indifferent tone, "Entrez, mademoiselle," without taking any further notice. Then, however, his wandering eye caught sight of a pair of tiny feet, and, looking into her face in surprise, he enthusiastically exclaimed: "Ah! ah! le pied de la Princesse!" and doffed his hat respectfully. The Princess lost her wager, but was in no little measure proud of the conquest which her foot had won over the plain omnibus-conductor.

Her life had been a somewhat tragic one. The only daughter of Prince Kinsky von Wchinitz und Tettau, the Seigneur of Wchinitz, in Bohemia, Léonie had, when scarcely out of her teens, been forced to marry the old Prince Othon von Leutenberg, a man forty years her senior. The marriage proved an exceedingly unhappy one, for he treated her brutally, and after five years of a wretched existence, during which she bore herself with great patience and forbearance, the Prince died of alcoholism in Berlin, and her release brought her into possession of an enormous fortune, together with the mansion of the Leutenbergs in the Frieung at Vienna, one of the finest in the Austrian capital, the castle and extensive estates in Schwazbourg-Rudolstadt, that had belonged to the family from feudal days, as well as the hôtel in the Avenue du Bois de Boulogne, and the beautiful Château de Chantoiseau, deep in the forest of Fontainebleau.

She was very charming, and there was an air of sadness in her beauty that made her the more interesting. We were friends of long standing. Indeed, I had known her in the days when I was junior attaché and fancied myself in love with every woman. I had admired her, and a firm friendship existed between us, although I think I can say honestly that I had never fallen in love with her. More than once, when those false and scandalous tales had been whispered about her—as they are whispered about every pretty woman in Paris—I had constituted myself her champion, and challenged her traducers to prove their words.

As we sat there chatting, watching the gaily uniformed corps diplomatique, and bowing ever and anon as some man or woman came up to congratulate her on her return to Paris, she told me of the dreariness of her life in the gloomy, ancestral Castle of Rudolstadt, and how, finding it unendurable at last, she had suddenly resolved to spend the remainder of the summer at Chantoiseau.

"I have been there already a fortnight, and everything is in order," she said. "I am inviting quite a number of people. You must come also."

"But I scarcely think it is possible for me to be absent from Paris just now," I answered in hesitation.

"I will take no refusal," she said decisively. "I will talk to Lord Barmouth to-night before I leave. Me never refuses me anything. Besides, in two hours you can always be at the Embassy. You will remember, the last time you were my guest, how easy you found the journey to and from Paris. Why, you often used to leave in the morning and return at night. No, you cannot refuse."

"I must consult His Excellency before accepting," I replied. "In the meantime, Princess, I thank you for your kind invitation."

"Princess?" she exclaimed, raising her eyebrows. "Why not Léonie? I was Léonie to you always in the days gone by. Is there any reason why you should be so distant now? Unless—" and she paused.

"Unless what?" I inquired, looking at her swiftly.

"Unless you have a really serious affair of the heart," she said.

"I have none," I answered promptly, suppressing a sigh with difficulty.

"Then do not use my title. I hate my friends to call me Princess. Recollect that to you I am always Léonie."

"Very well," I laughed, for she was full of quaint caprice.

I had pleasant recollections of my last visit to the château, and hoped that if the theft of the instructions contained in the despatch I had brought from London produced no serious international complication, I should obtain leave to join her house-party, which was certain to be a smart and merry one.

She told me the names of some she had invited. Among those known to me were the Baroness de Chalencon, Count de Hindenburg, the German Ambassador, and his wife, and Count de Wolkenstein, Austrian Ambassador, as well as several other men and women of the smartest set in Paris.

"You will be a real benefactress," I laughed. "Everyone here is stifled; while Dieppe is too crowded; Aix, with its eternal Villa des Fleurs, is insupportable; and both Royat and Vichy are full to overflowing."

"Ah, mon cher Gerald!" cried the Princess, lifting her small hands, "it is your English tourists who have spoilt all our summer resorts. If one has no place of one's own in which to spend the summer nowadays, one must herd with the holders of tourist tickets and hotel coupons."

I admitted that what she said was in a great measure true. Society, as the grande dame knows it, is being expelled by the tourists from the places which until a year or two ago were expensive and exclusive. Even the Riviera is fast becoming a cheap winter resort, for Nice now deserves to be called the Margate of the Continent.

Having arranged that I should do my best to accept her invitation, our conversation drifted to politics, art, and the drama. She seemed in utter ignorance of recent events, except such as she had read about in the newspapers.

"I know nothing," she laughed. "News reaches Rudolstadt tardily, and then only by the journals; and you know how unreliable they are. How I've longed time after time to spend an evening in Paris to hear all the gossip! It is charming, I assure you, to be back here again."

"But for what reason did you shut yourself up for so long?" I asked. "It surely is not like you!"

She grew grave in an instant, and appeared to hesitate. Her lips closed tightly, and there was a hard expression at the corners of her well-shaped mouth.

"I had my reasons—strong ones."

"What were they?"

"Well, I was tired of it all."

"Léonie," I said, looking at her seriously, "pray forgive me, but you do not intend to tell me the truth. You were tired of it years ago, when the Prince was alive."

"That was so," she answered, with a glance of triumph; "and I went home to my father and shut myself up at Wchinitz."

"But you must have had some stronger motive in burying yourself again as you have recently done. You did not write to a soul, and no one knew where you were. You simply dropped out; and you had some reason for doing so, otherwise you would have told the truth to your most intimate friends."

"You are annoyed that I should have left you without a word—eh?" she asked. "Well, I will apologise now."

"No apology is necessary," I answered. "It is only because we are such good friends that I venture to speak thus. I feel confident that you have sustained some great sorrow. You are, somehow, not the same as you were in Paris two years ago; now, tell me—"

"Ah! Do not talk of it!" she cried huskily, rising to her feet. "Let us drop the subject. Promise me, Gerald, not to mention it again, for I confess to you that it is too painful—much too painful. I promised you a waltz. Come, let us dance."

Thus bidden, I rose, and she, twisting her skirts deftly in her hand, leaned lightly upon my arm as I conducted her to the great ballroom. A very few moments later we glided together into the whirling, dazzling crowd.

"You will not speak of that again, Gerald?" she urged in a hoarse whisper, looking earnestly up to my face, as her head came near my shoulder. "Promise me."

"If it is your wish, Léonie," I responded, puzzled, "I will ask no further question."

Chapter Twenty Four
In the Forest of Fontainebleau

Sixty kilometres from Paris, just off that straight and noble highway that runs through the heart of the magnificent forest, and passes through the old-world town of Fontainebleau — where Napoleon signed his abdication — through the mediaeval, crumbling gates of Moret, and away far south to Lyons, rises the fine old Château of Chantoiseau. Half-way between the clean little village of By, standing in the midst of its well-kept vineyards, and the river-hamlet of Thomery, it occupies a commanding position on the summit of a cliff, where far below winds the Seine, on past Valvins and Samois, until it becomes lost like a silver thread among the dark woodlands in the direction of Paris.

The position of the splendid old place is superb. From its windows can be obtained a view of the great forest stretching away to the horizon on the left, while to the right is the valley of the Seine, and across the river spread the smiling vineyards with their white walls — the vineyards of Champagne. The house, a long, rambling place with circular towers, has been historical for many centuries. Once the property of Madame La Pompadour, in the days when the splendours of the Palace of Fontainebleau were world-renowned, a latter-day interest also attaches to it, inasmuch as it was the headquarters of the German Crown Prince during the advance of the Prussians upon Paris. Its grounds, sloping down, enclose part of the forest itself; therefore, during the blazing days of August one lives actually in the woods. The forest is an enormous one, and even to-day there still remain many parts unexplored, where the wolf and wild boar retreat in summer, and where even that most ubiquitous forester, the viper-hunter — the man whose profession it is to kill vipers and sell them at the local mairie — has never penetrated. In the whole of the great forest, however, no spot is more charming or more picturesque than that in which the château is situated. It is not a show-place, like Barbison or the Gorges de Franchard, but entirely rural and secluded — on the one side the open valley, on the other the dark forest, where in the tunnel-like alleys the trees meet overhead, and where the shady highroads to the painter colony at Marlotte and to Bois-le-Roi are perfect paradises for the cyclist.

Chantoiseau itself is not a village, not even a hamlet, only a big old-fashioned cottage in which the forest-guards live. Above it, on the high ground beyond, stands the fine old château. Many of those who read my story have driven or cycled in the forest, and many have no doubt given the great old place a passing glance before plunging deep into those leafy glades that lead to Fontainebleau. If when you have driven past you have inquired of your cocher, "Who lives there?" he has probably only shrugged his shoulders and replied: "Servants only. Madame la Princesse, alas! seldom comes," and you have gone on your way, as many others have done, wondering why such a beautiful old place should be neglected by its owner.

One hot evening at sundown, about three weeks after the President's ball, I strolled slowly beside the Princess down the hill, entering the forest by that well-kept cross-road which leads by the Carrefour de la Croix de Montmorin straight to the pretty village of Montigny on the Loing.

Contrary to expectation, no immediate result had accrued from the mysterious theft of the secret instructions to Lord Barmouth; hence I had obtained leave and accepted my hostess's invitation, although I was compelled to spend two days each week at the Embassy, going up to Paris in the morning and returning by the six o'clock express from the Gare de Lyon. That some result of the exposure of our policy must certainly make itself felt we knew quite well, but at present the political atmosphere seemed clearer, and by the fact that several of the ambassadors had left Paris considerable confidence had been established. Yet in those sultry August days the war-cloud still hung over Europe and the representative of Her Majesty was compelled, as he ever is, to exercise the greatest tact and the utmost finesse in order to preserve peace with honour. Truly, the office of British Ambassador in Paris is no sinecure, for upon him rests much of the responsibility of England's position in Europe and her prestige among nations, while to him is entrusted the difficult duty of negotiating amicably with a nation openly and avowedly hostile to British interests and British prosperity.

Those summer days, so sunny, happy, and pleasant, in the forest depths at Chantoiseau, were, nevertheless, perplexing ones for the rulers of Europe. The stifling air was the oppression before the storm. I had more than once chatted in the billiard-room with my fellow guests, the German and Austrian Ambassadors, and both had agreed that the outlook was serious, and that the storm-cloud was upon the political horizon.

But life at the château was full of enjoyment. The Princess, a born hostess, knew exactly whom to invite, and her house-parties were always congenial gatherings. There was riding, cycling, tennis, boating, billiards;

indeed, something to suit all tastes, while she contented herself with looking on and seeing that all her guests enjoyed themselves.

A riding-party had gone over to Montigny, and after tea the Princess had suggested that I should accompany her for a stroll down into the forest to meet them. She was dressed simply in a washing-dress of pale blue linen, and wore a sailor-hat, so that with her fair hair bound tightly she presented quite an English appearance, save perhaps for her figure and gait, both of which were eminently foreign. The feet that all Paris had admired two years ago were encased in stout walking-boots, and she carried a light cane, walking with all the suppleness of youth.

Soon we left the full glory of the mellow sunset flooding the Seine valley, and entered the forest road where the high trees met and interlaced above, and where the golden light, filtering through the screen of foliage, illuminated here and there the deeper shadows, struck straight upon the brilliant green of the bracken, married with the greyness on the lichen-covered trunks, and kissed the leaves with golden lips. Birds were twittering farewells to the day, and here and there a red-brown squirrel, startled by our presence, darted from bough to bough with tail erect, while on each side of the road was a carpet of moss and wild-flowers. The sweet odour of the woods greeted our nostrils, and we inhaled it in a deep draught, for that gloomy shade was delightfully cool and refreshing after the blazing heat of the stifling day. As I had been compelled to attend to some official correspondence, I had not joined the riding-party. The Princess had given some half-dozen of us tea in the hall, and, while the others had gone off to play tennis, she and I had been left alone.

Suddenly, as we walked along in the coolness, she turned to me, saying in a tone of reproach:

"Gerald, you have hidden from me the true seriousness of the situation at your Embassy. Why?"

"Well," I answered, facing her in surprise, "we do not generally discuss our fears, you know. Others might profit by the knowledge."

"But surely you might have confided in me?" she said gravely.

"Then de Wolkenstein has told you?"

"He has told me nothing," she answered. "But I am, nevertheless, aware of all that has come to pass. I know, too, that since my absence at Rudolstadt you have fallen in love."

"Well?" I inquired.

She shrugged her well-formed shoulders as if to indicate that such a thing was beyond her comprehension.

"Is it a disaster, do you think?" I asked.

"You yourself should know that," she replied in a strained tone. "It seems, however, that you do not exercise your usual discretion in your love-affairs."

"What do you mean, Léonie?" I demanded quickly, halting and looking at her. Who, I wondered, had told her the truth? To which of my loves did she refer—the spy or the traitress?

"I mean exactly what I have said," she answered quite calmly. "If you had confided in me I might perhaps have used my influence in preventing the inevitable."

"The inevitable!" I echoed. "What is that?"

"A combination of the Powers against England," she replied quickly. "As you know well enough, Gerald, I have facilities for learning much that is hidden from even your accredited representatives. Therefore, I tell you this, that at this moment there is a plan arranged to upset British diplomacy in all four capitals and to ruin British prestige. It is a bold plan, and I alone outside the conspirators am aware of it. If carried out, England must either declare war or lose her place as the first nation in the world. Recollect these words of mine, for I am not joking at this moment. To-day is the blackest that Europe has ever known."

She had halted in the path, and spoke with an earnestness that held me bewildered.

"A conspiracy against us!" I gasped. "What is it? Tell me of it?"

"No," she answered. "At present I cannot. Suffice it for you to know that I alone am aware of the truth, and that I alone, if I so desire, can thwart their plans and turn their own weapons against them."

"You can?" I cried. "You will do it! Tell me the truth—for my sake. I have been foolish, I know, Léonie; but tell me. If it is really serious, no time must be lost."

"Serious?" she echoed. "It is so serious that I doubt whether the present month will pass before war is declared."

"By England?"

"Yes. Your country will be forced into a conflict which must prove disastrous. The plan is the most clever and most dastardly ever conceived by your enemies, and this time no diplomatic efforts will succeed in staving off the tragedy, depend upon it."

"Are both Wolkenstein and de Hindenburg aware of the plot?"

"I presume so. I have watched carefully, but have, however, discovered nothing to lead me to believe that they understand how near Europe is to an armed conflict."

"Then your information is not from Wolkenstein?"

"No, from a higher source."

"From your Emperor?"

She nodded.

"Then this accounts for your sudden reappearance among us?" I said.

"You may put my presence down to that, if you wish," she replied. "But promise me, on your word of honour, that you will not breathe a single word to a soul—not even to Lord Barmouth."

"If you impose silence upon me, Léonie, it shall be as you wish. But you have just said that you can assist me. How?"

"I can do so—if I choose," she responded thoughtfully, drawing the profile of a man's face in the dust with the ferrule of her walking-stick.

"You speak strangely," I said—"almost as though you do not intend to do me this service. Surely you will not withhold from me intelligence which might enable me to rescue my country from the machination of its enemies?"

"And why, pray, should I betray my own country in order to save yours?" she asked in a cold tone.

I was nonplussed. For a moment I could not reply. At last, however, I answered in a low, earnest tone:

"Because we are friends, Léonie."

"Mere friendship does not warrant one turning traitor," she replied.

"But Austria is not the prime mover of this conspiracy," I said. "The rulers of another nation have formed the plot. Tell me which of the Powers is responsible?"

"No," she answered with a slight hauteur. "As you have thought fit to preserve certain secrets from me, I shall keep this knowledge to myself."

"What secrets have I withheld from you?" I inquired, dismayed.

"Secrets concerning your private affairs."

I knew well that she referred to my passion for Yolande. For a moment I hesitated, until words rose to my lips and I answered:

"Surely my private affairs are of little interest to you! Why should I trouble you with them?"

"Because we are friends, are we not?" she said, looking straight into my face with those fine eyes which half Europe had admired when le pied de la Princesse had been the catchword of Paris.

"Most certainly, Léonie," I agreed. "And I hope that our friendship will last always."

"It cannot if you refuse to confide in me and sometimes to seek my advice."

"But you, in your position, going hither and thither, with hosts of friends around you, can feel no real interest in my doings?" I protested.

"Friends!" she echoed in a voice of sarcasm. "Do you call these people friends? My guests at this moment are not friends. Because of my position—because I am popular, and it is considered chic to stay at Chantoiseau—because I have money, and am able to amuse them, they come to me, the men to bow over my hand, and the women to call me their 'dear Princess.' Bah! they are not friends. The diplomatic set come because it is a pleasant mode of passing a few weeks of summer, while still within hail of Paris; and the others—well, they are merely the entourage which every fashionable woman unconsciously gathers about her."

"Then among them all you have no friend?" Again she turned her fine eyes upon me, and in a low but distinct tone declared:

"Only yourself, Gerald."

"I hope, Léonie, that I shall always prove myself worthy of your friendship," I answered, impressed by her sudden seriousness.

Her face had grown pale, and she had uttered those words with all possible earnestness.

Then we walked on together in the silence of the darkening gloom of the forest. The ruddy light of the dying day struggled through the foliage, the birds had ceased their song, and the stillness of night had already fallen. We were each full of our own thoughts, and neither uttered a word.

Suddenly she halted again, and, gripping my arm, looked up into my face. I started, for upon her pale countenance I saw a look of desperation such as I had never before seen there.

"Gerald!" she cried hoarsely, "why do you treat me like this? You cannot tell how I suffer, or you would have pity upon me! Surely you cannot disguise from yourself the truth, even though your coldness forces me to tell you with my own lips. You know well my position—that of a woman drifting here and there, open to the calumnies of my enemies and the scandalous tales invented by so-called friends; a woman who has borne great trials and who is still, alas! unhappy! Of my honesty you yourself shall judge. You have heard whispers regarding my doings—escapades they have been called—and possibly you have given them credence. If you have, I cannot help it. There are persons around us always who delight in besmirching a woman's reputation, especially if she has the misfortune to be born of princely family. But I tell you that all the tales you have heard are false. I—"

Suddenly she covered her face with her hands; the words seemed to choke her, and she burst into tears.

"No, no, Léonie!" I said with deep sympathy, bending down to whisper in her ear and taking her hand in mine. "No one believes in those foul calumnies. Your honour is too well known."

"You do not believe them—you will never believe them, will you?" she asked quickly through her tears.

"Of course not. I have denied them many times when they have been repeated to me."

"Ah!" she cried, "I know you are always generous to a woman, Gerald."

Then again a long silence fell between us. Presently, with a sudden impulse, she raised her tear-stained face to mine, and with a look of fierce desperation in her eyes implored:

"Gerald, will you not give me one single word? Will you still remain cold and indifferent?" As she said this, her breast rose and fell in agitation.

I drew back, wondering at her beseeching attitude.

"No, no!" she cried. "Do not put me from you, Gerald! I cannot bear it—indeed I can't! You must have recognised the truth long ago—" and she paused. Then, lowering her voice until it was only a hoarse whisper, she added, "The truth that I love you!"

I looked at her in blank amazement, scarce knowing what to reply. I had admired her just as half Paris had admired her, but I certainly had never felt a spark of deep affection for her.

"Ah!" she went on, reading my heart in an instant, "you despise me for this confession. But I cannot help it. I love you, Gerald, as I have never before loved a man. In return for your love I can offer you nothing—nothing save one thing," she added in a strange, mechanical voice, almost as though speaking to herself. "In return for your love I can save your country from the grievous peril in which it is now placed."

She offered me her secret in return for my love! The thing was incomprehensible. I stood there dumbfounded.

"This is a moment of foolishness, Léonie. We are both at fault," I said, as soon as I again found tongue. "Think of the difference in our stations—you a princess, and I a poor diplomatist! I am your friend, and hope to remain so always—but not your lover."

"But I love you!" she cried fiercely, raising her blanched and pitiful face until her lips met mine. The passion of love was in her heart. "You may despise me, Gerald; you may cast me from you; you may hate me; but in the end you will love me just as intensely as I love you. To endeavour to escape me is useless. Since the die is cast, let us make the compact now, as I have already suggested. I have confessed to you openly. I am yours, and I implore of you to give me your love in return. You are mine, Gerald—mine only!"

Chapter Twenty Five
England's Enemies

Late that night, after the Princess and most of her guests had retired, I entered the billiard-room to get my cigarette-case, which I had left there while playing pool earlier in the evening, and on opening the door found the two Ambassadors Wolkenstein and Hindenburg seated together in the long lounge-chairs in earnest conversation. They were speaking in German, and as I entered I overheard the words "in such a manner as to crush the English power on the sea." They were uttered by the German representative, and were certainly ominous. It was apparent that both men were aware of the gigantic conspiracy of which the Princess had told me—the plot which aimed at the downfall of our nation. I could see, too, that my sudden entry had disconcerted them, for they both moved uneasily and glanced quickly at each other as though fearing I had overheard some part of what had passed between them. Then Wolkenstein with skilful tact cried in French:

"Ah, my dear Ingram! we thought we alone were the late birds to-night. Come here and chat;" and at the same time he pulled forward one of the long cane chairs, into which, thus bidden, I sank.

What, I wondered, had been the exchange of view's between these two noted diplomatists? The faces of both were sphinx-like. Our talk at first dealt with nothing more important than the journey across the forest to Barbison which our hostess had arranged for the morrow. I knew, however, that the conversation held before my entrance had been about the European situation. Those men were England's enemies. My impulse was to rise abruptly and leave them; but it is always the diplomatist's duty to remain cool, and watch, even though he may be compelled to hobnob with the bitterest opponents of his native land. Therefore I remained, and, concealing my antipathy, lit a cigar and lay back in my chair, carelessly gossiping about the usual trivialities which form the subject of house-party chatter.

"The Princess looked rather pale to-night, I thought," exclaimed Count de Hindenburg suddenly. "She seemed quite worried."

"With a château full of guests the life of a hostess is not always devoid of care," I remarked, blowing a cloud of smoke toward the ceiling.

I alone knew the reason of her paleness and anxiety, and was eager to ascertain what deductions these two shrewd men had made.

"To me," observed the representative of the Emperor Francis Joseph, "it seemed as though the Princess had been shedding tears. Didn't you notice that her eyes were just a trifle swollen?" and, turning to me, he added: "She scarcely spoke to you at dinner. Are you the culprit, Ingram?"

Both men laughed.

"Certainly not," I denied. "Madame has a touch of nerves, I suppose—that's all. Such a malady is common among women."

"She looked quite worn out by fatigue," declared Wolkenstein.

"Because she is never still a single moment in the day. Her thoughts are always for her guests—how to amuse them and to give them a pleasant time. It was the same two years ago," I said.

"Remarkable woman—quite remarkable!" exclaimed de Hindenburg. "She had sufficient trouble with the rheumatic old Prince to turn any woman's hair grey; but, on the contrary, she seems now to become younger every day. She's still one of the prettiest women in Europe."

"Everyone admits that, of course," I said.

They exchanged glances, and I fancied that these looks were unusually significant. A flood of recollections of the sunset hour in the forest surged within my mind—how I had striven with firmness to release myself, and how I had been forced to turn away and leave the Princess. In that deep gloom, when the rosy afterglow was fading and the light within the leafy glade so dim that all objects were indistinct, I had seen her wild passion in all its magnificence. Her eyes had burned with the fierce, all-consuming fire of love, her cheeks were white and cold, and her words as reckless as they were passionate. She had charged me with entertaining affection for some other woman—a woman unworthy of my love, she had said with distinct meaning, as though she knew the duplicity of Yolande; and she had sworn an oath with clenched hands to compel me to reciprocate her passion.

The scene between us was one of unreason and of folly. She had been overwhelmed by the impulse of the moment, and I had bowed and left her, my heart full of conflicting emotions, my head reeling. She had suddenly twisted her soft arms about my neck and clung to me, whispering her love and declaring that I was cruel, cold, with a heart like adamant. But I had flung her off, and we had not met until two hours later, when I sat at her right hand at dinner, during which she had scarcely addressed a single word to me.

My companions had, of course, noticed this, and appeared to have cleverly guessed my refusal to accept the offer of the Princess. They little knew the terms upon which she had attempted to make a compact with me—that she was ready to betray them in return for my love.

I smoked on in silence and in wonder. The situation certainly presented a problem which I was utterly unable to solve. That the affections of such a woman as the Princess von Leutenberg were not to be trifled with I knew well, for women of her temperament are capable of anything when once they love with a fierce, uncontrollable, reckless passion such as she had seen fit to display that evening in the deep silence of the forest. Her proposition had, indeed, been a startling one. She had offered me the secret of the plot in return for my love!

With my two companions I chatted on until nearly two o'clock; then we separated, and I passed through the long oak corridors to my room. Upon the dressing-table I found a note lying. It was sealed with black wax, with the Leutenberg arms. I tore it open. It gave out an odour of fresh violets, and I saw instantly that the handwriting was Léonie's.

"*I have been foolish in my confession to you, Gerald,*" she wrote in French. "*But my heart was so full that I could conceal the truth no longer. I saw from your manner at dinner to-night that you despise me, and intend to hold me at a distance as an unwelcome woman who has flung herself into your arms. But I cannot help it. The misfortune—nay, the curse upon me—is that I love you. Would to Heaven that I did not! Because of you I have forgotten eatery thing—my duty to myself as a woman, my duty to my family as one of a noble house, my duty to my country, my duty to my Creator. When I left Paris long ago, I crossed the Atlantic, resolved to forget you; but all was in vain. I returned to Rudolstadt and shut myself up in retirement, striving to wean myself from the mad passion which had arisen within me. All, however, was futile, and at last I broke the bonds and returned to Paris. A month has gone by, and now I have told you the truth; I have confessed. To-morrow morning at eleven I shall walk alone through the forest, along the road that leads to By. My offer to you—an offer made, I admit, in desperation—still stands. If you accept it you will be enabled to save your country from her enemies, and we shall both find peace and happiness; if not, then the plot will be carried out, and at least one woman's life will be wrecked—the solitary and unhappy woman who writes these lines and whose name is Léonie.*"

She had written that letter calmly and coolly, for the handwriting showed no haste. Evidently she had penned it in the seclusion of her chamber, and Suzanne, her maid, had placed it upon my dressing-table.

I stood with the letter in my hand. My eyes caught my own reflection in the long silver-framed mirror, and I was struck by the haggard, anxious expression upon my own countenance. My personal appearance startled me.

Well I knew the character of this pale and beautiful woman whom all Paris had admired. The impression she gave everyone was that of perpetual and irreconcilable contrast. I had long ago recognised her high mental accomplishments, her unequalled grace, her woman's wit and woman's wiles, her almost irresistible allurements, her moments of classic grandeur, her storms of temper, her vivacity of imagination, her petulant caprice, her tenderness and her truth, her childish susceptibility to flattery, her magnificent spirit, and her princely pride. She had dazzled my faculties, perplexed my judgment, bewildered and bewitched my fancy. I was conscious of a kind of fascination against which my moral sense rebelled.

With all her perverseness, egotism, and caprice, she, nevertheless, I knew, mingled a capacity for warm affection and kindly feeling, or, rather, what one might call a constitutional good-nature, and was lavishly generous to her favourites and dependants. She was a Princess in every sense of the word, her right royal wilfulness and impatience often fathering the strangest caprice. There were actually moments when she seemed desirous of picking a quarrel with such immensities as time and space, and, with the air of a lioness at bay, regarded those who dared to remember what she chose to forget.

She had given me but little time to decide. To-morrow at eleven she would slip away from her guests and await me in that long, tunnel-like passage leading through the forest to the ancient town of Moret, at the confluence of the willow-lined Loing with the broad Seine. Its walls and gates, dating from the time of Charlemagne, still remain, and right in the heart of the little town stands the square old donjon keep, now ivy-grown and with its moat full of a profusion of sweet-smelling tea-roses.

I could save England if, in return for her secret, I gave her my love. Has any man ever found himself in similar perplexity?

Calmly I reasoned with myself, turning again to her letter, and feeling convinced that this sudden passion of hers was but a momentary caprice. No woman, if she were cool and reasonable, would have acted as she had done, for she must have recognised that the difference in our stations rendered marriage impossible.

My duty to my country was to learn the truth about this gigantic conspiracy; yet, at the same time, my duty towards myself and towards the Princess was to leave Chantoiseau at once and forget all that had occurred.

Signs had not been wanting in Paris during the past few days to corroborate what she had told me regarding the conspiracy of certain Powers against the prestige of their hated rival England. There was a lull in diplomatic affairs that was ominous; a distinctly oppressive atmosphere which foreboded a storm.

Far into the night I sat thinking, trying to devise some plan by which I could obtain knowledge of her secret without committing myself. But I could find none—absolutely none.

At early morning, before the others were astir, I took a stroll down the hill to where the clear Seine wound beneath the chalk cliff. The larks were soaring high, filling the air with their song. The boatmen going downstream shouted wittily to each other between their hands, and the bronzed villagers on their way to work in the vineyards chanted merrily the latest popular airs. Life is easy and prosperous among the peasantry around the Fontainebleau forest. In those clean white villages of the Department of Seine et Marne there is little, if any, poverty. I wandered through the pretty, flower-embowered village of Thomery, and, crossing the river by the long iron bridge, entered the smiling little hamlet of Champagne—a quaint and comely group of small cottages, where lived the vineyard-workers. This hamlet is famous for miles round because of a particularly venomous breed of vipers which infest the sun-kissed lands in its neighbourhood. Although only six o'clock, the prosperous little place was already busy, and as I wandered through the village, past the grey old church, and along the wide, well-kept road beside the river, I smiled to think that the name of that old-world place was known everywhere from Piccadilly to Peru, and was synonymous with wealth, luxury, and riotous living.

Heedless as to where I went, so deeply engaged was I in conflicting feelings and in trying to determine whether I should keep that appointment on the footpath to Moret, at last I found myself in Samoreau, where, crossing by the ferry, I returned to the forest, and at eight o'clock was back again, idling with several of the guests on the lawn in front of the château.

After drinking my coffee, I sat in the window of one of the petit salons that overlooked the valley and took up a pen, meaning to write to my hostess, for I had resolved to send her a note of regret, and return at once to Paris. I could remain there no longer.

Scarcely had I taken the note-paper from the escritoire, when the Baroness de Chalencon entered, fussy as usual and full of the excursion to Barbison.

"Léonie tells me you are not accompanying us," she cried in French. "I've been searching for you everywhere. Why, my dear Gerald, you must come."

"I regret, Baronne, that I can't," I answered. "I have to go to Paris by the midday train."

"How horribly unsociable you are!" she exclaimed. "Surely you can postpone your journey to Paris! Wolkenstein and the others have declared that we can't do without you."

"Express to them my regrets," I said. "But to-day it is utterly impossible. I must be at the Embassy this afternoon. I have important business there."

"Well, I suppose if you failed to put in an appearance, a crisis in Europe would not result, would it?" she observed with a touch of grim irony. "At the Rue de Lille or the Rue de Varenne," she added, meaning the German and Austrian Embassies, "they take things far more easily than you do. That's the worst of you English—you are always so very enthusiastic and so painfully businesslike."

"I am compelled to do my duty," I answered briefly.

"Most certainly," answered the Baroness. "But you might surely be sociable as well! This is not like you, M'sieur Ingram."

"I must apologise, Baronne," I said. "But, believe me, it is impossible for me to go to Barbison to-day. I have urgent correspondence here to attend to, and afterwards I must run up to Paris."

When she saw that I was firm, she reluctantly left me, saying as she disappeared through the door:

"I really don't know what is coming to you. You are not at all the light and soul of the summer picnics, as you once used to be."

"I'm growing old," I shouted with a laugh.

She halted, turned back, and, putting her head inside the room again, retorted in a low, distinct voice:

"Or have fallen in love—which is it?"

I treated her suggestion with ridicule, and in the end she retired, laughing merrily, for at heart she was a pleasant woman, with whom I was always on excellent terms of friendship.

Then I sat down again to write, hoping to remain undisturbed. But although I held the pen poised in my hand I could think of no excuse. Three carriages drew up before the château, the coachmen wearing those handsome scarlet vests, conical hats, and many gold buttons, which together represent the mode in Fontainebleau and at Monte Carlo; and the guests, a merry, laughing, chattering crowd, mounted into the vehicles. Big picnic baskets, with the gilt tops of champagne bottles peeping out, were placed in a light cart to follow the excursionists, and two of the guests—men from Vienna—mounted the horses held by the grooms. Then, when all was ready, the whips cracked, there was a loud shouting of farewells to the hostess, who stood directing her servants, and the whole party moved off and away to the leafy forest lying below.

I looked down from the window, and saw the Princess standing on the drive—a sweet, girlish figure in her white dress, her slim waist girdled with blue, and her fair hair bound tightly beneath her sailor-hat. She scarcely looked more than nineteen as she stood there in the morning sunlight, smiling and waving her little hand to her departing guests.

She glanced up suddenly, and I drew back from the window to escape observation. So gentle so tender, so fair was she. And yet I feared her—just as I feared myself.

Chapter Twenty Six
A Woman's Heart

Reader, I do not know what influence it was that overcame me in that breathless hour of perplexity and indecision: whether it was the fascination of her beauty; whether it was owing to the fact that I unconsciously entertained some affection for her; or whether it was because my sense of duty to my country urged me to endeavour to learn the secret of the conspiracy formed against her by the Powers of Europe. To-day, as I sit here writing down this strange chapter of secret diplomacy, I cannot decide which of these three influences caused me to throw my instinctive caution to the winds and keep the appointment in the leafy forest glade that led through the beeches to Veneux Nadon and on to quiet old Moret.

Instinctively I felt myself in danger—that if I allowed myself to become fascinated by this capricious, impulsive woman, it would mean ruin to us both. Yet her beauty was renowned through Europe, and the illustrated papers seemed to vie with each other in publishing her new portraits. Her confession to me had been sufficient to turn the head of any man. Nevertheless, with a fixed determination not to allow myself to fall beneath the fascination of those wonderful eyes, I strolled down the forest-path and awaited her coming.

Soon she approached, walking over the mossy ground noiselessly, save for the quick swish of her skirts; and then with a glad cry of welcome, she grasped my hand.

"Ah!" she exclaimed, a slight flush mounting to her delicate, well-moulded cheeks, "you received my note last night, Gerald? Can you forgive me? I am a woman, and should not have written so."

"Forgive!" I repeated. "Of course I forgive you anything, Léonie."

"You think none the worse of me for it?" she urged, speaking rapidly in French. "Indeed, I allowed my pen to run away, and now I regret it."

I breathed more freely. Her attitude was that of a woman who, conscious of error, now wished it to be forgotten.

"To regret is quite unnecessary," I assured her in a low voice of sympathy. "We are all of us human, and sometimes we err."

Silence fell between us for a few moments. It struck me that she was striving strenuously to preserve her self-restraint.

"You will destroy that letter, promise me," she urged, looking piercingly into my face. "It was foolish — very foolish — of me to write it."

"I have done so," I answered, although, truth to tell, it still remained in my pocket.

"And you will not despise me because in an hour of foolishness I confessed my love for you?"

"I shall never despise you, Léonie," I answered. "We have always been good friends, but never lovers. The latter we never shall be."

She looked at me quickly, with a strange expression.

"Never?" she asked, in a tone so low that I could scarcely catch the word.

"Never," I responded.

Her laces stirred as her breast rose and fell, and I saw that she herself was endeavouring to evade my query, although at the same time her heart was full of the same impetuous passion which had so much amazed me on the previous night. I had spoken plainly, and my single word, uttered firmly, had crushed her.

It occurred to me that I had made a mistake. I had not acted diplomatically. I knew, alas! that I was, and always had been, a terrible blunderer in regard to women's affections. Some men are unlucky in their love-affairs. I was one of them.

We walked slowly together side by side for some distance, neither uttering a word. At last I halted again, and, taking her hand, bent earnestly to her, saying:

"Now, Léonie, let us put aside any sentimentality and talk reasonably."

"Ah!" she said, her eyes flashing quickly, "you do not love me. Put aside sentiment indeed! How can I put it aside?"

"But a moment ago you suggested that we should forget what passed between us yesterday."

"I did so in order to test you — to see whether you had a spark of affection for me in your heart. But the bare, cold truth is now exposed. You have not!"

Her face was ashen, and her magnificent eyes had a strange look in them.

"Could you respect me and count me your friend, Léonie, if I feigned an affection which did not really exist within me?" I asked. "Reason with yourself for a moment. Had I been unscrupulous towards you I might yesterday have told you that I reciprocated your affection, and—"

"And you do not?" she cried. "Tell me the truth plainly, once and for all."

"You offered me in exchange for my love a secret which would enable me to defeat the enemies of my country, and probably cause my advancement in the diplomatic service. You offered me the greatest temptation possible."

"No;" she said, putting up her hand, "do not use the word temptation."

"I will call it inducement, then. Well, this inducement was strong enough to persuade me to break the bond of friendship between us, and to cause me to occupy a false position. But I have hesitated, because—"

"Because you do not love me," she said quickly, interrupting me.

"No, Léonie," I protested. "Between us it is hard to define the exact line where friendship ends and love begins. Our own discretion should be able to define it. Tell me, which do you prefer—a firm friend—or a false lover?"

"You are too coldly philosophical," she answered. "I only put it to you from a common-sense standpoint."

"And which position is to be preferred?" she asked. "Your own, as that of a diplomatist with a paltry fifty thousand francs or so a year, and compelled to worry yourself over every trifling action of those who represent the Courts of your enemies; or that of my husband, with an income that would place you far above the necessity of allowing your brain to be worried by everyday trifles?"

She paused, and her lips trembled. Then with a sudden desperate passion she went on:

"People say that I am good-looking, and my mirror tells me so; yet you, the man I love, can see in me no beauty that is attractive. To you I am simply a smart woman who is at the same time a princess—that is all."

"I am no flatterer, Léonie," I cried quickly. "But as regards personal beauty you are superb, incomparable. Remember what Vian said when he painted your portrait for the Salon—that you were the only woman he had ever painted whose features together made a perfect type of beauty."

"Ah! you remember that!" she said, smiling with momentary satisfaction. "I thought you had forgotten it. I fear that my beauty is not what it was five years ago."

"You are the same to-day as when we first met and were introduced. It was at Longchamps. Do you remember?"

"Remember? I recollect every incident of that day," she answered. "You have been ever in my mind since."

"As a friend, I hope."

"No, as a lover."

"Impossible," I declared. "Do reason for an instant, Léonie. At this moment I am proud to count myself among your most intimate personal friends, but love between us would only result in disaster. If we married, the difference in our stations would be as irksome to you as to me; and if I did not love you, the link would only cause us both unhappiness, and, in a year or two, estrangement."

"Only if you did not love me. If you loved me it would be different."

"You would still be a princess and I a struggling diplomatist."

"It would make no difference. Our love would be the same," she answered passionately. "Ah, Gerald, you cannot tell how very lonely my life is without a single person to care for me! I think I am the most melancholy woman in all the world. True, I have wealth, position, and good looks, the three things that the world believes necessary for the well-being of women; but I lack one—the most necessary of them all—the affection of the man I love."

"I can't help it, Léonie!" I cried. "Indeed, it is not my fault that my friendship does not overstep the bounds. Some day it may, but I tell you frankly and honestly that at present it does not. I am your friend, earnest and devoted to you—a friend such as few women have, perhaps. Were I not actually your friend I should now, at this moment, become selfish, feign love, and thus become your bitterest enemy."

"You are cold as ice," she answered hoarsely, in a low tone of disappointment.

Her countenance fell, as though she were utterly crushed by my straightforward declaration.

"No, you misunderstand," I replied, taking her hand tenderly in mine, and speaking very earnestly. "To-day the romance that exists within the breast of every woman is stirred within you, and causes you to utter the same words as you did at sixteen, when your first love was, in your eyes, a veritable god. You will recall those days—days when youth was golden, and when the world seemed a world of unceasing sunshine and of roses without thorns. But you, like myself, have obtained knowledge of what life really is, and have become callous to so much that used to impress and influence us in those long-past days. We have surely both of us taught ourselves to pause and to reason."

She hung her head in silence, as if she w'ere a scolded child, her looks fixed upon the ground.

"My refusal to mislead you into a belief that I love you is as painful to me as it is to you, Léonie," I went on, still holding her hand in mine. "I would do anything rather than cause you a moment's trouble and unhappiness, but I am determined that I will not play you false. These are plain, hard words, I know; but some day you will thank me for them—you will thank me for refusing to entice you into a marriage which could only bring unhappiness to both of us."

"I shall never thank you for breaking my heart," she said in a sad voice, looking up at me. "You cannot know how I suffer, or you would never treat me thus!"

"The truth is always hardest to speak," I answered, adding, in an attempt to console her: "Let us end it all, and return to our old style of friendship."

"I cannot!" she said, shaking her head—"I cannot!" and she burst into tears.

I stood beside her in the forest-path, helpless and perplexed. Was it possible, I wondered, that the plot of the Powers against England existed only in her imagination, and that she had invented it in order to use it as a lever to gain my affections? She was a clever, resourceful woman—that I knew; but never during the course of our friendship had I found her guilty of double-dealing or of attempting to deceive me in any way whatever. More than once, when she reigned in Paris as queen of Society, she had whispered to me secrets that had been of the greatest use to us at the Embassy; and once, owing to her, we had been forearmed against a dastardly attempt on the part of an enemy to assist the Boers to defy us. A niece of the Emperor of Austria, she was received at the various Courts of Europe, and visited several of the reigning sovereigns; therefore, she was always full of such tittle-tattle as is ever busy among those who live beneath the shadow of a throne, and was far better informed as to political affairs than many of the ambassadors; yet withal she was eminently cautious and discreet, and, if she wished, could be as silent as the grave. Nevertheless, although signs were many that the war-cloud had again arisen and was once more hanging heavily over Europe,

I could not bring myself to believe that the plot now hatched was quite as serious as she made it out to be. The world of diplomacy in Paris is full of mares' nests, and alarms are almost of daily occurrence. When events do not conspire to create them, then those ingenious gentlemen, the Paris correspondents of the great journals, sit down and invent them. The centre of diplomatic Europe is Paris, which is also the centre of the canards, those ingeniously concocted stories which so often throw half Europe into alarm, and for which the sensational journalists alone are responsible.

"Come, Léonie," I said tenderly at last, "this is no time for tears. I regret exceedingly that this interview is so painful, but it is my duty towards you as a man and as your friend to be firm in preventing you from taking a step which after a short time you would bitterly repent."

"If you become my husband I shall never repent!" she cried. "You are the only man I have ever loved. I did not love the Prince as I love you! I know," she added, panting—"I know how unseemly it is that I, a woman, should utter these words; but my heart is full, and my pent-up feelings are now revenging themselves for their long imprisonment."

I felt myself wavering. This woman who had thrown herself into my arms, was wealthy beyond the wildest dreams of avarice, world-renowned for her beauty and high intellect—a woman altogether worthy and noble. Each moment her powers of fascination grew stronger, and I felt that, after all, I was treating her affection with slight regard, for I was now convinced that her love was no mere caprice or sudden passion.

Yet, after all, my belief in woman's honesty and purity had been shaken by the discovery that Yolande was a spy and that Edith, after all her protestations, had a secret lover. These two facts caused me, I think, to regard the Princess with some suspicion, although at the same time I could not disguise from myself the truth that her emotion was real and her passion genuine.

"Your confession is but the confession of an honest woman, Léonie," I said with tenderness. "But what has passed between us must be forgotten. You tempt me to assume a position that I could not maintain. Think for a moment. Is it right? Is it just either to yourself or to me?"

"Will you not accept the offer I made you yesterday?" she asked in the tone of one desperate, her eyes fixed upon mine in fierce earnestness.

"Will you not learn the secret and save your country from ignominy?"

I held my breath, and my eyes fixed themselves on hers. Her tear-stained face was blanched to the lips.

"No, Léonie," I answered. "Anxious as I am to save England from the net which her unscrupulous enemies have spread for her, I refuse to do so at the cost of your happiness."

"And that decision is irrevocable?" she asked, with a quick look of menace.

"It is irrevocable," I replied.

"Yes, I know," she said in a hoarse whisper—"because another woman holds you in her toils! Well, we shall see!" and she laughed bitterly, the swift fire of jealousy flashing for an instant in the brilliant eyes that half Europe had delighted to praise. "I love you," she continued, "and some day you will love me. Meanwhile, my secret is my own."

Chapter Twenty Seven
The Unexpected

A fortnight passed uneventfully. After that morning walk with the Princess I left Chantoiseau and returned to Paris. My presence at the château after what had passed between us was as dangerous to her as to me. I wrote her a letter of farewell and went back to the capital that same afternoon.

In response, she had sent me a wildly worded note by a manservant, in which she declared that the reason I cast aside her love was because of the attractions of some other woman. This letter, together with the letter she had sent to my room, I kept locked in a drawer in the little den which served me as study and smoking-room. Now that they were safe under lock and key, I resolved to forget their curious and romantic history.

But the one matter uppermost in my mind was the alleged plot by the Powers against England. As I had given the Princess my word of honour not to mention it to a soul, I was unable to consult Lord Barmouth, and was compelled to wait and watch for signs that the conspiracy was in progress.

Those days were full of fevered anxiety. His Excellency was absent in the country, and the duties of the Embassy devolved upon myself. The facts that the German Ambassador had travelled suddenly to Berlin to consult the Minister of Foreign Affairs, and that urgent despatches were being exchanged daily between the Austrian Embassy and Vienna, seemed to me to establish the truth of Léonie's statement. I met my friends Volkouski and Korniloff, the Russian attachés, in the Grand Café one evening, and we spent an hour together over our consommation down at the Alcazar, in the Champs Elysées; but they apparently knew nothing, or, if they did, naturally hesitated to expose their secret. Hither and thither I sought for evidence, and with my suspicions aroused found confirmation of the Princess's story in every diplomatic action. The German Emperor made a speech in Berlin in which, with many references to his grandfather and the Fatherland, he assured Europe that never in recent history had peace been so firmly established among nations; and both from Rome and St. Petersburg came news of unusual inactivity. That calm foreboded a storm.

As those hot, anxious days went slowly past I strove to form some theory as to the manner in which the conspiracy had been arranged and as to the persons chiefly responsible, but could find none.

Had not Léonie plainly told me that this dastardly plot among jealous nations aimed directly at the undermining of the British power, the ruin of England's prestige, and the destruction of her supremacy on the sea? I, as a diplomatist, knew too well the vulnerability of our Empire. We have patriotism, it is true, for the sons of England will ever shed the last drop of their blood in the defence of their beloved country; but something more than patriotism is now necessary for successful defence. In these days, when Europe is daily arming and small republics, backed by certain of the Powers, amuse themselves by twisting the Lion's tail, an efficient British army is necessary, as well as a navy that must be stronger than that of the rest of the world. We at the embassies know how, by descending to methods which we as Englishmen scorn to use, our enemies are often able to outwit and checkmate us; and we know also that in England foreign spies are allowed to come and go at will, and that the interesting gentlemen whom we welcome are gradually elaborating their plans for the invasion of our shores.

Many there are who laugh at the idea of an invasion of England, but every diplomatist in Europe knows well that the problem is discussed in every military centre on the Continent, and that in certain quarters strategists have drawn up plans by which the catastrophe can undoubtedly be accomplished. Therefore, in spite of the sneers of those who rest upon a false belief in their insular security, we should be in a condition not only to defend, but to defy—a condition which, to our sorrow, does not at present exist.

The Princess had offered me such information as would enable me to crush the conspiracy against us, and I had refused her terms. Sometimes, as I sat alone in my room thinking, I felt that I had made a mistake, and that I ought, in the interests of my country, to have accepted. Then, at others, I felt glad that I had had the courage to refuse her conditions, and to leave her as

I had done. As she had learned the truth from the Emperor Francis Joseph of Austria, the secret must be known in the Court circle at Vienna.

Yet unfortunately it was impossible for me to go there, and equally impossible, after giving my word of honour to Léonie, to explain my fears to Kaye and allow the secret service to make inquiries. I knew from many signs that catastrophe was imminent, but was utterly powerless to avert it.

Reader, place yourself for a single moment in my position—your own honour at stake on the one hand, and that of your country on the other. It seemed base to speak, base to keep silence.

I shall not easily forget what I suffered during this period of anxious inactivity. The weeks went by, Lord Barmouth came back sun-tanned and jovial, and all the other representatives of the European Courts returned one by one after their summer leave. Parisians, driven away by wet weather, deserted the plages, the châteaux, and the various inland watering-places; and from Dieppe and Trouville, Arcachon and Luchon, Vichy and Aix, Royat and Contrexéville the crowds of mothers and daughters, with a sprinkling of fathers, came gaily back to their favourite boulevards, their favourite magasins, and their favourite cafés. Paris was herself again—for the winds were cold, the leaves in the boulevards were falling in showers, and the wet pavements were rendered disagreeable on account of them.

One afternoon towards the end of November I entered my little flat with my latchkey, and walked straight into my sitting-room, when, to my surprise, a beautiful girl rose from the chair in which she had been sitting, and, without speaking a word, held out her hand.

"You—Edith!" I gasped, utterly taken aback.

"Yes," she said in a strained voice. "Will you not welcome me? Your man said he expected you every moment, and asked me to await you. I ought not to have come here, to your chambers, I know, but being in Paris I could not resist."

"I never dreamed that you were here. Is your aunt with you?"

"Yes," she replied. "I have at last managed to persuade her to winter on the Italian Riviera."

"Where?"

"At San Remo. Our vicar at Ryburgh stayed there for a month last winter, and gave us a most glowing account of it. Judging from the photographs, it must be a most delightful place—quite an earthly paradise for those wishing to avoid the English frost and fogs. Do you know it?"

"Yes," I answered, seating myself in a chair opposite her. "I've been there once. It is, as you anticipate, perfectly charming. You will no doubt enjoy yourself immensely."

Her lips compressed, and her eyes were fixed upon mine.

"I shall, I fear, not have much enjoyment," she sighed sadly.

"Why?"

"You know why well enough," she answered in a tone of bitter reproach.

"Because we are parted," I said. "Well, Edith, I, too, regret it. But need we discuss that incident further? We are still friends, and I am glad that you have not passed through Paris without sparing an hour to call upon me."

"But it is to discuss it that I came here," she protested quickly. Her rich fur cape had slipped from her shoulders and lay behind her in my big armchair. In her black tailor-made gown and her elegant hat, which bore the unmistakable stamp of having been purchased since her arrival in Paris, she looked smart and attractive. Her pure, open face was exquisite to behold, even though a trifle thinner and paler than on that summer's day when we had wandered by the river and she had pledged her love to me. But as she sat before me toying with her bracelet, from which a dozen little charms were hanging, the remembrance of her base deception flashed through my brain. I held her in suspicion—and suspicion of this kind is the seed of hatred.

"I cannot see what there is to discuss," I answered coldly, at the same time ringing and ordering tea for her. "Nor can I see," I added, "what good there is in reopening a chapter in our lives which ought to be for ever closed."

"No, Gerald," she cried, "don't say that! Those words break my heart. It is not closed. You do not understand."

"To speak of it only causes pain to both of us," I said. "Cannot you visit me as a friend and resolve not to discuss the unfortunate affair?"

"No," she declared quickly, "I cannot. I have come to you to-day, Gerald, to explain and to ask your forgiveness. My aunt is confined to her room with a headache, and I have managed to slip away from the hotel and come to you here."

"Well?" I asked rather coldly.

I confess that her visit annoyed me, for I saw in her attitude a desire to make such explanations as would satisfy me; but, taught by experience, I was resolved to accept no word from her as the truth. She had deceived me once; and although she was the only woman I had really loved honestly and well, her wiles and fascinations had no longer any power over me.

"Gerald," she exclaimed, as she rose suddenly, crossed the space between us, and, after placing her arms about my neck, sank upon her knees at my side, "I ask your forgiveness."

She spoke in a manner the most intense; and I saw how nervous and anxious she was. Yes, she had altered considerably since that day at Ryburgh when we had strolled together in the sunset and I had told her of my love, her features were sharper, paler, and more refined. Grief had left its imprint upon that sweet, pure countenance, which had always reminded me so vividly of Van Dyck's "Madonna" in the Pitti at Florence. Do you know it? You will find it—a small picture too often unnoticed, only a foot square, hung low down in the Saloon of the Painters. It shows a marvellously beautiful face, perfect in its contour, graced by a sweet and childlike mouth with the true Cupid's bow, and with eyes dark and searching. This perfect type of beauty so markedly resembled Edith that its photograph might almost be accepted as a portrait of her.

There, on her knees, she twice besought my forgiveness. But I remained silent. To forgive was impossible, I knew; nevertheless, I had no desire to cause her pain. Her face told me that she had already suffered sufficiently in the months that had elapsed since I had bidden her farewell at the little railway-station in rural England.

"Speak!" she cried. "Tell me, Gerald, that you love no one else beside myself—that—that you will forgive me!"

Turning to her, I grasped her hand, and, looking straight into those eyes which I had once believed to be so full of truth, honesty, and affection, I answered earnestly:

"I love no woman on earth except yourself, Edith. But to forgive is quite impossible."

"No!" she cried wildly—"no! you cannot be cold and callous if you really love me. See! here at your feet I beseech of you to allow me to prove my innocence and show my love for you!"

"I once believed implicitly in you, Edith," I said very gravely, still holding her hand; "but the discovery that you met your lover clandestinely beneath the very window of my room has so shaken my confidence that it is utterly impossible for you ever to re-establish it."

"But he is not my lover!" she protested, her blanched face upturned to mine. "I swear he is not; nor has he ever been."

"I have no proof of your declaration," I answered, shaking my head dubiously.

"Except my oath," she gasped in desperation. "Cannot you accept that? I swear by all I hold most sacred," she cried, lifting her head and raising her face to Heaven—"I swear that I entertain no spark of affection for that man, and that he has never been my lover!"

"Then who is he?" I demanded. "What is his name?"

Chapter Twenty Eight
On the Crooked Way

She held her breath. Her hand trembled within my grasp. Then, after a moment, she faltered:

"He is not my lover. Is not my declaration sufficient?"

"No, it is not," I responded harshly. "If he is nothing to you, as you allege, then why did you meet him secretly at night, and make an appointment to meet again after I had left Ryburgh?"

"Because I was forced to—because—"

"Because you have allowed that shabby adventurer to love you!" I interrupted. "Because you have played me false!"

"I deny it!" she protested, a gleam of defiance flashing for an instant in her eyes. "I have never played you false, Gerald. The charge against me is utterly false and unfounded."

"Then perhaps you will explain this wandering visitor's business with you."

"I would tell you all—all that has passed between us, but I dare not. My every action is watched, and if I breathed a single word to you he would know; and then—"

"And what would happen then, pray?" I asked with some surprise, for I now saw that she entertained a deadly fear of her midnight visitor; it was evident that he held some mysterious power over her.

"The result would be disastrous," she replied in a mechanical tone of voice.

"In what way?"

"Not only would it upset all the plans I have formed, but would in all probability be the cause of my own ruin—perhaps even of my suicide," she added.

"I don't understand you, Edith," I said, turning again to her, in the hope that she would confide in me. "How would it cause your ruin? If you hesitate to tell me the truth, then it is certain that you fear some exposure."

"You are quite right," she answered, meeting my gaze unflinchingly; "I do fear exposure."

"Then you admit your guilt? You admit that what I have alleged is the actual truth?"

"I do not, for a single instant. The charge is false, and without the slightest foundation," she asserted. "You saw me speaking with him, you may have overheard our conversation, and you no doubt believe that he is my lover. But I tell you he is not."

"His movements were mysterious," I said dubiously. "I followed him."

"You followed him!" she gasped, all colour leaving her face in an instant. "You actually followed him! Where did he go?"

She spoke as though she feared that I had discovered the truth as to his identity and calling.

"To a village some little distance away," I replied ambiguously; "and I there discovered one or two things which increased my interest in him."

"What did you discover? Tell me," she urged, grasping my hand anxiously.

"What I discovered only led me still further to the belief that he held you within his power."

"I have already admitted that," she exclaimed. "I am perfectly frank in that respect."

"And you will not tell me the reason? If you refuse to be open and straightforward with me, there surely can be no love between us. Confidence is the first step towards the union of man with woman."

"I will tell you the reason," she replied in a strange voice, almost as though she were speaking to herself. "It is because a secret exists between us."

"Ah!" I cried, "I thought so. The secret of a love-affair—eh?"

"It concerns a love-affair, it is true, but not our own."

"Oh, now this is interesting!" I cried with bitter sarcasm. "You are bound to each other because of your common knowledge of the love-affair of a third person. That is curious, to say the least of it. No," I added, "I'm afraid,

Edith, I cannot accept such a remarkable explanation, notwithstanding the ingenuity displayed in its construction."

"In other words, you insinuate that I am lying to you!" she exclaimed, her cheeks flushing with indignation.

"I do not use the term 'lying,'" I said with a smile; "the word 'prevarication' is more applicable. A woman never lies."

"You are not treating me seriously," she complained quickly. "I have come here to tell you all that I can, and—"

"And you have told me practically nothing," I interposed.

"I have told you all that I dare at present," she answered. "Some day, ere long, I hope to be in a position to make full confession to you, and then you will fully understand my action and appreciate the extreme difficulty and deadly peril in which I find myself at this moment."

"You admit that you have a confession to make?"

"Of course I admit it. I wronged you when I met that man on the very night you were a guest beneath our roof. It is but just that you should know the whole of the ghastly truth."

"That is what I am endeavouring to obtain from you," I said. "I want to know who that shabby fellow was, and why he took such pains to keep his presence in Great Ryburgh a secret."

"He had some good reason, I presume," she replied.

"Do you declare that you know absolutely nothing of his movements?" I inquired.

"I know but little of them."

"How long have you been acquainted?"

"Two years—perhaps a little longer."

"And has he visited you often?"

"No, at infrequent intervals."

"Always at night?"

"Always."

"He evidently is a shrewd fellow, who does not wish his presence in that chattering little village to be known," I said with a laugh. Then I added: "You went for moonlight rambles with him, I suppose?"

"He wished to talk with me, and on such occasions we took one or other of the paths across the fields."

"Very interesting," I said. "And all this time you were causing me to believe that you were mine alone! Are you surprised at my refusal to forgive?"

"I should be if I were guilty of playing you false," she answered with slight haughtiness, as though my words wounded her self-respect.

"If you were not guilty you would never endeavour to conceal your lover's name, as you are now doing!" I exclaimed.

"It is because I dare not tell you," she replied, with a look of desperation on her face. "Were I to utter a word in explanation of the true state of affairs, all would be over, and both you and I would suffer."

"How should I suffer?" I asked with some interest.

"The affair is much more curious and complicated than you imagine," she said. "Knowledge of the truth could only bring ruin upon you."

"Rubbish!" I cried roughly, starting up. "What have I to fear?"

"No, Gerald," she implored, gripping my hand tightly, "do not treat this matter with indifference. It is, I tell you, a grave one for both of us."

"In what way?"

"Ah," she sighed, "if only I might tell you! If only I dared!"

"If you love me as you did on that evening when we wandered beside the river, you would brave all these mythical dangers and tell me the truth, Edith," I said, bending towards her in a persuasive manner.

"But, as I have explained, I cannot. I will not—for your sake!"

"How can knowledge of it possibly affect me?" I cried.

She paused for a moment and then answered: "There are certain hidden influences at work, of which you, Gerald, have no suspicion. I alone am aware of the truth. Cannot you place sufficient confidence in me—in the woman who loves you—to leave the matter in my hands? Surely our interests are mutual!"

"I have, I regret, no confidence," I said bluntly.

"Ah! because you are jealous," she replied quite calmly. "Well, that is but natural in the circumstances. You discovered *him*, and you believe him to be my lover. Nevertheless, your jealousy should not lead you into any rash action which might wreck your life."

"You speak as though you are anxious with regard to my personal safety. What have I to fear?"

"You have to fear the machinations of unscrupulous enemies," she said anxiously. "You are living in ignorance of the peril that daily threatens you, and I—who love you so well—am unable to give you a single hint which might warn you of the pitfall so cunningly concealed."

There was an earnestness in her tone which struck me as curious. What could she, a girl living in a quiet country village in England, know about "the machinations of unscrupulous enemies?" She spoke as though well versed in the diplomatic plots of Paris, even as though she would corroborate what the Princess had alleged. It was odd, and caused me much reflection. What could she possibly know?

"It is only fair to me that you should warn me of the peril," I said at last.

"Hush!" she whispered, looking round the room in fear; "the very walls have ears. If it were believed that I had spoken to you of this, a catastrophe, terrible and complete, would ensue."

"Really, Edith," I said, "you speak in enigmas. I don't know what to believe."

"Believe in me," she answered in a deep, earnest voice. "Believe in my truth and purity as you did before, for I protest that never for a single instant have I forgotten the vows I made to you."

"Ah," I said very sadly, "if I could only believe that you really love me, how happy I should be! But as it is, I fear this to be quite impossible."

"No," she wailed, tears welling in her eyes. "Surely the sight of that man unknown to you has not destroyed all your belief in woman's honesty and affection? You must, deep down in your heart, see that I love you firmly and well. You cannot be so blind, Gerald, as to believe that here, to-day, I am playing you false! Ah! if you only knew!" she sighed. "If you only knew all that I am suffering, you would pity me, and you would take me in your embrace as once you used to do, and kiss me on the lips as a sign of your forgiveness. I can suffer," she went on brokenly—"I can endure the awful anxiety and tribulation for your sake; I can cheerfully bear the jeers of men and the insults of women, but I cannot bear your coldness to me, because I love you, and because you once declared that you were mine."

"This estrangement has arisen between us through your own fault," I answered.

Just at this moment my man rapped smartly at the door, and Edith rose quickly from her knees before he entered with the tea. The little silver service was a quaint relic of the Queen Anne period, which had long been in my family, and which was always admired by the brilliant Parisiennes who often did me the honour of taking a cup of English tea—not, of course, because they liked the beverage, but because to drink it is nowadays considered chic. My man told me that a messenger had called from the Embassy, and I left the room for a few moments to see him.

But Edith disregarded the fact that tea had been brought. The instant I returned and the door had closed again, she came across to me, saying:

"It was not my fault, Gerald; it was *his*. He compelled me to meet him."

"For what reason?"

"He wished me to render him a service."

"Of what character?"

"That I cannot explain."

"You of course acquiesced?"

"No, I refused."

"And yet the fact that you met him against your will shows in itself that you were in his power," I remarked. "How was it that you could refuse?"

She was silent a moment, standing before me wan and pale in her black dress, her gloved hands clasped before her.

"I defied him," she answered simply.

"Well?" I inquired.

"Well, that is the reason why I live in dread of a catastrophe."

"Answer me this question, Yes or No. Your mysterious visitor was a foreigner?"

I recollected what the innkeeper's wife had told me—namely, that the word "Firenze" was on the tabs of his boots.

"Yes," she answered in a half-whisper.

"An Italian?"

"How did you know that?" she gasped in quick surprise.

"From my own inquiries," I answered.

"But do take my advice," she cried earnestly, her hand upon my arm. "Make no further inquiries regarding him; otherwise I may be suspected and all my plans will be frustrated."

"What plans?"

"Plans I have made for our mutual protection," she whispered. "If you knew all the details you would not be surprised at my anxiety that you should remain inactive and leave all to me. I am but a woman; nevertheless, I am at least loyal to you, the man I love. Forgive me," she implored, raising her white, pained face to mine—"forgive me, Gerald, I beg and pray of you. Have confidence in me, and I will some day, ere long, prove to you that I am, after all, worthy of your love."

"Forgiveness is easy, but forgetfulness difficult," I said, taking her hand and looking straight into the dark splendour of those soft eyes.

After the shrill-tongued, voluble foreign women by whom I was ever surrounded, this sweet English girl breathed peace and paradise to my wearied heart.

"But you will forgive me?" she implored in deep earnestness. "Say that you will!"

Her attitude impressed upon me forcibly the conviction that, after all, she really loved me. Nevertheless, the whole affair seemed so mysterious and perplexing that I found it difficult to regard her motives with unquestioning faith. "Yes," I said at length, "I forgive you, Edith. But until you can explain all the mystery, I tell you frankly that I cannot entertain full confidence in you."

"You will, however, leave me to carry out the plan I have formed?" she urged anxiously.

"If you wish."

"And if I am denounced by one or other of my enemies, you will not believe that denunciation before I am at liberty to expose to you the whole truth? Promise me that—do!"

"Very well," I responded, "it shall be as you wish."

Then as those words left my lips she sprang forward with a loud cry of joy, and, throwing her arms about my neck, kissed me wildly in joy, saying:

"You shall never regret this decision, Gerald, never—never!"

For fully an hour we sat together, our tea untouched, so preoccupied were we with the burden of our hearts; then, declaring that Aunt Hetty would miss her, she reluctantly rose. When I had put her cape round her shoulders, we went downstairs together, I having promised to accompany her in a fiacre as far as the Grand Hotel.

Just as we were about to step into the street, I encountered Kaye, who evidently wished to have a word with me. As he raised his hat, I noticed how intently he was examining my companion's face; then he passed us and entered the wide hall leading to the stairs. A moment later, however, he turned suddenly, and said:

"Excuse me, Mr Ingram, might I speak with you for one moment? I see you are going out."

"Certainly," I answered; and after excusing myself to Edith I moved off a few paces with him.

The words he uttered were spoken in a whisper. They startled me:

"Have a care, Mr Ingram," he said meaningly. "We know that woman!"

Chapter Twenty Nine
Kaye is Puzzled

Having seen Edith as far as the Grand Hotel, I re-entered the fiacre and at once drove back to my own rooms, where I found the chief of the secret service awaiting me.

"What do you mean by saying that you know that lady?" I inquired breathlessly.

"Simply that we know her, that's all," he replied, with an air of mystery.

"Look here, Kaye," I said, "just tell me plainly and straightforwardly what you know regarding her?"

"She's a person to be avoided, that's all."

"To be avoided!" I echoed. "Why, surely she has no connection with the persons you are watching? She lives in Norfolk, in a little country village, and scarcely ever comes abroad."

"I know it," he answered with his sphinx-like smile. "She lives at Great Ryburgh, near Fakenham, is in possession of a fair income, and has a maiden aunt as companion."

"How did you know that?" I demanded in surprise.

"It is our duty to know all who are the enemies of England."

"And is she an enemy?"

"Most certainly," he replied.

"I can't believe it, Kaye!" I cried, aghast. "I won't believe it! First you tell me that Yolande de Foville is a spy, and now you denounce Edith Austin."

"I only tell you the truth," he answered, leaning against the table and folding his arms.

"Then as you know so much about her, you probably know our relationship," I said, rather annoyed that this ubiquitous man, whose proclivities for fathoming a secret were prodigious, should have watched her.

"I am quite well aware of it, Mr Ingram," he responded; "and if I might be allowed to advise you, I should end it at once. It is dangerous."

"Why?"

"Because she is playing you false."

"How do you know that?"

"By the same means that I know she is working against us—and against you. If you knew the facts they would astound you. Even I, with all my experience of the ways of felons and spies, was dumbfounded when I learnt the truth."

"But can't you see that it's ridiculous to ask me to cast her aside without giving me any plain and ample reason?"

"The reason is certainly sufficient," he replied.

"What is it?"

"You visited her at Ryburgh some months ago, and suspected her of having a secret lover. Is not that so?"

"Extraordinary!" I gasped. "How did you know that? You set your spies upon me!" I added angrily.

"No, not upon you," he said. "She was already under observation."

"Why?"

"Because of some suspicion that had been aroused regarding the Ceuta incident."

"Nonsense!" I cried, unable to believe his allegation. "What possible connection could she have with that?"

"A rather intimate one, judging from the result of our inquiries."

"In what manner?"

"Well, as a secret agent."

"In the employ of whom?"

"Of France."

"Of France?" I echoed. "Impossible!"

"My dear Mr Ingram," he protested, "I'm not in the habit of misleading you or of making statements which I can't substantiate. I repeat that Miss Edith Austin, the lady who has been here with you this afternoon, is a French agent."

"I can't believe it!" I gasped, utterly staggered. "Why, she's a simple, charming English girl, leading a quiet life in that sleepy little village, and scarcely seeing anybody for weeks together."

"Exactly. I don't deny that. But as her affection for you is prompted by ulterior motives—pray pardon me for saying so—you should be forewarned; and this is the more desirable in view of the fact which you yourself discovered."

"What fact?"

"That she has a secret lover."

"Ah!" I cried eagerly. "Tell me, who is he?"

"An Italian named Bertini—Paolo Bertini."

"Bertini," I repeated, the name sounding somewhat familiar. "Surely I've heard that name before!"

"Of course. You remember, when you were in Brussels, the bold attempt he made one afternoon in your room at the Embassy?"

"Ah! I remember. Why, of course! And is he actually the same man?"

In an instant I recalled the face of Edith's midnight visitor, and recollected where I had seen it on a previous occasion.

Kaye's words brought back to me in that moment an incident which showed plainly the dastardly tricks of the foreign spies who constantly hover about every legation or embassy on the Continent. One afternoon, years ago, in Brussels, a well-dressed, gentlemanly man called to see His Excellency, and was shown into my room. Half an hour before, a Foreign Office messenger had arrived from London with despatches, and I was busily engaged in deciphering them when the servant showed in the stranger. The latter, who introduced himself as a shipowner of Antwerp, was seated near my table, and was talking to me about a complaint he had recently lodged against one of our consuls, when suddenly he stopped, turned pale, and fell back in a faint. I sprang up, and, rushing out of the room, went to get a glass of water. Fortunately I had on thin shoes, and the carpet in the corridor was so thick that my feet fell noiselessly. Judge of my surprise when, on my return, I saw my visitor standing in a perfect state of health with one of the deciphered despatches pinned against the wall and a camera in his hand! He had actually photographed it during my absence.

Without an instant's hesitation I sprang upon him from behind, wrenched the camera from his hand, shouted for help, and held him until some of the servants came, when he was taken in charge by the police. After a short trial, during which it was proved that he was one of the cleverest spies employed by France, he was sentenced to six months' imprisonment for attempted theft, while the camera, together with the photographic films, was returned to us. The latter, on being developed, proved extremely interesting and very valuable, for not only did we find the photograph of our own despatch, but those of three other secret documents taken in the Italian Embassy in Brussels.

And it was this artful adventurer who had become Edith's lover. She, young and inexperienced, had no doubt fallen his victim. She had become enmeshed in the net he had spread for her, and was the subordinate by means of whom he intended to operate further against us.

"What you tell me, Kaye, really staggers belief," I said after a pause. "That man is absolutely unscrupulous."

"He's one of the most ingenious of all the army of secret agents. Indeed, I have a suspicion that he is the chief of the French spies operating in England. His intimate acquaintance with your friend Miss Austin shows conclusively that he is contemplating a big coup."

Had this matter, I wondered, any connection with the gigantic conspiracy of which the Princess had told me? My promise of secrecy given to her prevented me from mentioning it to Kaye. Only a few weeks ago the *Figaro* had announced that Her Highness the Princess Léonie von Leutenberg had left the Château de Chantoiseau, and had returned to her mansion in the Frieung, in Vienna. She had left France without sending me a word.

"What connection had this man Bertini with the exposure of the Ceuta negotiations?" I inquired.

"He got to know of them by some means—how, I can't tell. It is an absolute enigma."

"And that despatch I brought from London, the exact contents of which were known a few hours after my return here, what of that?"

"Through him, I feel assured," answered the clever man before me. "I only returned from London three days ago. I went myself to make inquiries."

"And what did you find?"

"He carries on the business of a jeweller, and has a small shop half-way up the Edgware Road, one of those cheap Brummagem places that sell earrings and brooches for servant-girls. He poses as quite a respectable shopkeeper, and employs an Englishman as manager. The signor, it appears, has many friends in London, and when they call to see him they are always shown to his private room over the shop. I also learnt that your visitor of to-day has called upon him there."

"Are you sure?" I cried quickly. "Are you absolutely certain of that?"

"I gave her description and name to the manager, who said he recollected her calling there twice about three weeks ago. Once his master was not in, but on the second occasion she had an interview with him. It has more than once struck me as curious that this fellow Bertini should have been near you on the day of the mysterious theft of the contents of that despatch. You don't think that he followed you from Ryburgh to London?"

"I can't tell. If he did, I had no suspicion of it. And besides, not a soul except the Chief could have possibly obtained sight of that despatch. I saw it written, saw it sealed, and it never left my possession for a single instant."

"She did not accompany you to London?" he asked half-suspiciously.

"Certainly not," I said.

Then I told him all that occurred on that well-remembered night, and how I had wandered in the early morning over the country-side to the village inn where for a moment I saw the Italian.

"Then he evidently saw and recognised you there!" Kaye exclaimed quickly. "In all probability he followed you to London. That the copy of the despatch was transmitted to Paris by him is certain."

"And with regard to the Ceuta incident?"

"In that, I believe, he made Yolande de Foville his agent. Undoubtedly it was through her ingenuity that Lord Barmouth's instructions leaked out."

"But how could she possibly have known them?" I demanded. "Remember, you have denounced her as a spy, but as yet have given me no proof whatever."

"You have sufficient proof in the fact that she fled in alarm from Paris, I should think."

"But I understood from you that she was in the German service. If so, she would certainly never ally herself with Bertini!"

"He might, on the other hand, ally himself with her," remarked the secret agent shrewdly. "It would be distinctly to his advantage if he could obtain her aid, for by means of her he could ascertain various facts which might be considered extremely valuable at the Quai d'Orsay."

"It is all astounding!" I declared, puzzled. "Half the women one knows here seem to be secret agents. Paris is just now a veritable hotbed of diplomatic intrigue."

"I quite agree; and it all tends to show that never, in the history of Europe, has there been a blacker outlook than to-day."

I was silent. What he said was only too true; and, further, the mysterious exposure of the secret instructions contained in the despatch I had brought from London had thwarted English diplomacy throughout Europe, and tied the hands of all our ambassadors at the various Courts. Signs everywhere convinced me that the statement of the Princess was actually true, and that we were on the brink of a war in which the whole of Europe would be involved.

Russia alone remained inactive. It is the fashion of journalists who know nothing of the inner life of the diplomatic circle, and of alarmist writers who build up political theories for themselves, to abuse Russia and Russian methods. We have been told for the past half-century that Russia means to seize India, merely because she has taken steps to colonise her enormous Asiatic possessions. Why, a Russian ambassador in any one of the capitals may hardly pare his nails without a sensational article in the Press appearing next day. All this is very amusing; for the truth is, Russia does not intend to be aggressive, nor does she want war. Peaceful expansion of her commerce and the development of Siberia are her aims; and if certain journalists insist on exhibiting to us the war bogey, it is because they have never been in Russia, and know absolutely nothing of the conduct of Muscovite diplomacy. This, it must be confessed, is, next to that of the Vatican, the second best in the world; but it is never aggressive; as every genuine diplomatist will hasten to admit. Indeed, if the truth were told, there have been times in recent years when only the firmness of Russia and the peaceful policy of the Czar have averted war!

It is the journalist, nearly always the journalist, who creates the European scares! Because of this state of affairs, we at the embassies are compelled to be always on our guard against those ubiquitous writers who vie with one another in obtaining interviews.

The present situation was, however, no journalistic canard, but a stern and perilous reality. The tension of the acute crisis, which had been increasing ever since the Ceuta incident, was terrible. Everywhere in diplomacy there was a spirit of reserve, which showed that the amity of nations was strained to its utmost limit. War might be declared upon England at any moment.

Chapter Thirty
Knights of Industry

After Kaye had left, I sat for a long time pondering over his words. The assertion that Edith was a spy helping Paolo Bertini staggered me. At first I could not believe it, but what he had told me left no room for doubt. I recalled the man's face as he had passed down the inn passage and out into the village street, and with the clue that Kaye had furnished recognised him. Without doubt all that the chief of the secret service had told me was true, for had not Edith herself refused to disclose the man's name or the character of their friendship? Had she not at the same time acknowledged that he held power over her, invisible but complete, and that the betrayal of her secret would mean her ruin—perhaps even her death?

I saw it all now, as I sat deep in doubt and perplexity. Edith was staying at the Grand. Should I call upon her aunt, and dine with them? My first impulse was to do this, for I felt anxious to obtain from her some further proof of her actual association with this adventurer; but, on reflection, I saw that such a course was not commendable, inasmuch as by calling I should perhaps arouse Aunt Hetty's suspicion that her niece had visited me. Therefore, I resolved to send a petit bleu to Miss Foskett, stating that I had seen her name in the visitors' list and hoped to do myself the pleasure of calling on the following day after déjeuner. This formality, which I at once proceeded to put in operation, would, I knew, greatly please the punctilious old spinster.

That evening I dined at the Brasserie Nationale, in the Avenue de l'Opéra, an establishment German in style, but one widely patronised of late. Among other things, it is famous for its wonderful hors d'oeuvres; the wines, too, are always excellent and the cuisine not expensive. Below is a beer-hall, always crowded during afternoon and evening; but above, in a salon decorated in the ancient German style, one finds a crowd of gaily dressed diners, Parisian in all respects. The foreign tourist happily never goes there, for he patronises the Gazal, a little farther along the avenue, where the dinner is prix-fixe, "two francs fifty, vin compris."

At the tables sat several persons whom I knew, for it chanced to be a première at the Opéra, and all Paris was dining in the vicinity.

Mariani, a well-known journalist on the staff of the *Figaro*, lounged in and took a seat with me. He was a thin-faced, middle-aged man of typical Parisian appearance. He had only that afternoon returned from Brussels, and presently, when we began to speak of the political situation, he paused with his wine-glass in his hand, saying, in that precise manner which was his chief characteristic:

"The *Patrie*, the *Libre Parole*, the *Gaulois*, the *Petit Journal*, and the *Autorité* repeat that war with England is inevitable; that it is always there, ready to break out at any hour of any day. Their object is clear: it is revenge for the High Court trials. They have realised that, despite all its efforts, they cannot overthrow the Republic in times of peace. They must, then, have war. And these misérables are preparing it in order to overthrow the Republic! They prepare war with England not only because they hate England, as a free country, but because they know that war with England would be a naval Sedan. Unless the Republicans abandon their blindness and their torpor, they will let the Republic and France be lost by means of these misérables."

I agreed with him, but breathed a trifle more freely, for the *Figaro* was the organ of the French Government, and he was always well-informed. Nevertheless, it appeared that he had no idea of the exact direction of the political wind.

Near midnight, having attended a reception given by a smart Englishwoman, the wife of a peer resident in Paris, I was strolling along the Avenue de Neuilly on my way home. The night was cold but bright, and there were many people still about. A garde-de-ville, in his short cape, stood like a statue on the kerb at the Porte Maillott; the electric globes illuminated the Rond Point brightly, and a couple of harmless roysterers of the lower class lurched past me, singing the latest patriotic jingle of the cafés, a song inspired by the prevalent Anglophobia in Paris. They were singing the last verse:

Sous les éclats de la foudre
On vit tomber, noir de poudre,
Le dernier de ces vaillants,
Il cria: Vive la France!
Et l'écho répondit: France!...
En avant!... Serrez vos rangs!...

I paused for a moment to glance at them. Truly the public spirit in Paris was everywhere anti-English. Fashoda had never been forgotten, and out of our difficulties with the Transvaal much capital was being made by the rabid organs of the Press.

Then I walked on until, at the corner of the Avenue de la Grande Armée and the Rue des Acacias, I suddenly became aware of two men walking slowly in front of me in earnest conversation. They were speaking in Italian, a language which I knew well, and it was a sentence I overheard which attracted my attention and caused me to glance at them.

Both were shabbily attired, and presented the signs of those hungry night-birds who creep forth at set of sun and slink about the boulevards. One wore a grey, soft felt hat stuck a trifle askew, as if its owner aimed at a rakish appearance, while the other wore a crumpled silk hat with a flat brim, the headgear typically Parisian.

Together, walking arm-in-arm, absorbed in their conversation, they passed beneath the big electric lamp which lit the street-refuge, and as the light fell upon them I drew back quickly in order to escape observation.

Those words in Italian had attracted me, and I now saw in front of me the two men whom I most desired to meet. The man who wore the high silk hat was none other than Rodolphe Wolf, while the other was that ingenious adventurer whom I had discovered at Ryburgh, Paolo Bertini.

They strolled along in a casual manner, as though well aware that out of doors they could talk freely. The fact that they spoke in Italian proved their desire to escape eavesdroppers. At the moment of recognition I had drawn back and allowed them to advance some distance in front; then, lounging along slowly, I followed them across the Avenue des Termes, up the narrow Rue Poncelet, and, traversing the Avenue Wagram, passed through a number of small streets until they suddenly halted before a small and uninviting-looking little café in the Rue Legendre, a few doors from the Mairie of Batignolles.

I was surprised to discover that Wolf was actually in Paris, while the presence of Bertini seemed to bear out all that Kaye had told me earlier in the evening. During the walk the Italian had pulled from his pocket a paper, which he handed to his companion, who stood for a moment beneath a street lamp reading it. Then he laughed lightly, folded it, and handed it back with an air of satisfaction. As neither of the interesting pair had once turned back, I had followed them entirely unnoticed.

Fortunately for me I was wearing a new overcoat, the astrakhan collar of which was turned up, the wind being chilly, so that my features were half-concealed. But the shabby appearance of the pair was in itself suspicious.

Wolf had always been something of a fop, and it was scarcely possible that if he were a secret agent he could have fallen upon evil days.

I glanced at their boots. Those worn by Bertini were good ones of russet leather, while those of his companion were a smart pair of "patents." This fact told me that for some unknown reason they had assumed the garb of loungers rapidly, and had not had time to change their boots. They had been, or were going, to some place where to be dressed well would arouse undue attention. That seemed certain.

I was standing back in the shadow of a doorway watching them, when suddenly, after some consultation, as it seemed, they entered the little café.

It was a frowsy, dirty place, at the window of which hung faded red blinds, much stained and fly-blown. From where I stood I could see that the ceiling, once white, was brown and discoloured by the gas, and the gilt decorations blackened and smoke-begrimed. It was called the Café de l'Étoile.

Dare I enter and risk detection?

Now that I had discovered them I intended to watch and find out where they were staying, so that Kaye and his staff might keep them under observation. The reason for their presence in Paris was without doubt a sinister one. Of all the men in the whole world who were my enemies the man Wolf was the bitterest; and next to him was this dark-faced Italian, with whom he had been walking so confidentially arm-in-arm.

As I stood in hesitation, an ill-dressed, unkempt fellow reeled out of the café, singing in a husky voice a vagabond song. His hat was askew, and he beat time with his finger:

> Qu' ça peut vous faire où qu' nous allons?
> Ça vous r'garde pas, que j' suppose.
> D'abord, j'allons où qu' nous voulons...
> ... Où qu' vous voulez... c'est la mêm' chose.
> Vous êtes d' ceux qu'ont des états?
> Ben! qué qu' vous voulez qu' ça nous foute?
> Des états!... j'en connaissons pas...
> Nous, not' métier, c'ést d'marcher su' la route.

I strolled past the place and peered inside. A quick scrutiny sufficed to show that the two men were not visible; therefore, I concluded that they were at a table close behind the door. Thrice I passed and repassed, until I became convinced of the fact. The red blinds were drawn, and, although the door was half open, I could not, from the pavement, see who was sitting at the table behind it. In Paris, however, it is often a trick of those who lounge in cafés and desire to pass unnoticed to sit close behind the door with their backs to it, thus occupying a position which does not in the least expose them to passers-by.

Presently, emboldened by the fact that the little place seemed sleepy and half-deserted, I lit a cigarette, and, slipping into the doorway, stood with my ears open to catch every sound. Yes, they were there, as I had supposed. I heard words in Italian spoken rather low and confidentially. I distinctly heard my own name mentioned, together with that of the Princess von Leutenberg. Wolf it was who spoke of her sneeringly.

"I've seen her of late in Vienna," he laughed. "Retirement at Rudolstadt did not suit her."

"Is there any truth in what is said regarding the reason of her stay at Chantoiseau?"

"Certainly," replied Wolf.

"Serious for her—eh?" remarked his companion.

"Very. She will be taught a lesson," was the response.

"And at the British Embassy, what do they know?" asked Bertini.

"They are, as usual, utterly unsuspecting, and will remain so until the mine explodes. We have laid it cleverly this time, and it cannot fail."

"I wonder whether the Princess told Ingram anything while he was a guest at Chantoiseau?" asked Bertini.

"She dare not. But what of the English girl? It is said she loves him."

"No," replied the Italian quickly, "I have her completely in my power. She cannot utter a word."

"She's a useful agent, I suppose?"

"Yes, at times. A girl of her character and appearance is never suspected."

"And of Yolande? She was in London a month ago assisting me. Where is she now?"

"In Rome, I think; but I am not certain," was the response. "Some little time ago I met Lord Barmouth's daughter, with a view to bringing them together as friends, for by so doing I saw that we might gain some valuable information," Wolf said. "The project, however, unfortunately failed, because of Ingram."

"May an accident occur to him!" exclaimed Bertini, using an Italian oath. "He stands in our way at all times. I have not forgotten how cleverly he tricked me in Brussels and obtained the negatives of half a dozen documents from other embassies."

"He is more dangerous to our plans than Kaye and the whole British secret service put together," Wolf remarked. I could hear that, by way of emphasis, he struck the table heavily as he spoke these words. "If we could only contrive to suppress him!"

"Ah, but how?"

A silence fell between the pair.

"In some countries," remarked Wolf in a low voice, "he would die suddenly. Here, in Paris, it would be dangerous."

These men were actually plotting to take my life; I stood there motionless, my ears strained to catch every word, my feet rooted to the spot. "Why so dangerous?" asked the Italian.

"Because the English girl might betray us, or, failing her, there is the Princess."

"The Princess! Bah!" ejaculated Bertini.

"She would never utter a syllable. She has too much to gain by silence."

"But the girl Austin? What of her?"

"I admit that she might instantly give us away if one of these days her lover was found mysteriously dead. Nevertheless, if the situation becomes acute, well, we must resort to a desperate remedy, that's all."

I smiled within myself. Happily I had overheard this extremely interesting conversation, and should now be on my guard against both spies and assassins. It was lucky for me that they feared Edith; otherwise murder would have been a mere nothing to them. That they were not discussing an impossibility I well knew, for during my career as a diplomatist I had known of at least half a dozen cases where persons had been found dead under mysterious circumstances; and also that the crime of murder had actually been brought home to the members of the secret service of the various Powers. They are unscrupulous gentlemen, these spies, and hesitate at nothing in their feverish desire to do the bidding of their masters and obtain the rewards so temptingly offered to them.

The men dropped their voices so low that for a few minutes I could distinguish nothing, while another vulgar-looking, ruffianly fellow opened the door suddenly and emerged. As long as I heard their voices in consultation I felt secure from discovery. I determined to remain there in the doorway calmly smoking, as though awaiting the arrival of a friend.

"And how is everything at Feltham?" I heard Wolf inquire presently.

"All works splendidly. Everything is complete." To what did they refer? I wondered. Where was Feltham? and what were the arrangements which worked so satisfactorily?

Again the Italian spoke, laughing low and contentedly, but I could not catch what he said, for my attention at that moment was distracted by the approach of a fiacre, which pulled up before the door of the café. The hood was up, and within the vehicle I saw the figure of a woman, who at once descended, and, as I moved into the shadow, walked straight into the place with the air of one who had entered there before. She was well-dressed in a dark tailor-made gown, and wore a close-fitting hat with a veil. She passed me by within a few feet, but, standing as I was in the deep shadow beyond the lamps of the cab, which, no doubt, dazzled her, she did not recognise me. But no second glance was necessary to tell me that the woman who had come there at midnight to meet the two spies was their associate and assistant, Edith Austin.

Chapter Thirty One
The Red Ass

When the woman who had declared her love for me had entered the uninviting-looking place I slipped back to my old position, but was prevented from listening too openly for fear of awakening the curiosity of the cocher who was awaiting her. I heard them greet her in English; then both rose, and all three passed through the café to a room beyond, apparently the apartment of the proprietor. Hence I was unable to discover the reason of her visit there.

As no purpose could be served by remaining longer in the doorway, I lit another cigarette with an appearance of carelessness and strolled away down the narrow street as far as the Avenue de Clichy, returning presently on the opposite side of the roadway, and waiting in patience for the conspirators to leave the café.

I congratulated myself upon my good-fortune in not being detected, and was resolved to watch further the doings of the spies. I only wished that Kaye or Grew were with me, in order to follow up at once the clue I had thus obtained.

The word "Feltham" was to me extremely puzzling. That chance remark doubtless referred to a matter brimming over with interest. What were the "arrangements" that worked so well and were so complete?

Truly, the conspiracy of the Powers against Great Britain, alleged by Léonie, was a gigantic one. Each hour brought home to me more forcibly the terrible truth that we were living upon the very edge of a volcano, whose eruption might be expected at any moment.

For fully half an hour I strolled up and down, always keeping a careful watch upon the café with the faded blinds, until suddenly Edith emerged, followed by her two companions. Bertini handed her into her cab, and I heard him order the cocher to drive to the Grand Hotel. Then, as they stood on the kerb, with their hats in their hands, she bowed and was driven rapidly off, while they turned and walked together in the opposite direction, passing down the avenue to the Boulevard de Clichy, and thence along to the Place Blanche, past that paradise of the British tourist, the Moulin Rouge.

The four illuminated arms of the Red Windmill were still revolving, and the night-birds of Paris in their gay plumage were entering and leaving, for the so-called "life" at that haunt of Terpsichore modernised and debased does not begin until long after midnight. I never glance in at those open doors without sighing for my compatriots; and usually fall to reflecting upon the reason why so many English fathers of families, who at home would not dream of going to a music-hall, so frequently drift there with their wives, and often with their daughters. It is a curious feature of Paris life, absurdly artificial, and almost entirely supported by my unthinking compatriots, who go there because to have been there is synonymous with having seen the gay life of the French capital. Alas! that the British tourist is so gullible, for the students who dance there in velvet berets and paint-besmirched coats are no students at all, while the pretty grisette, his companion, is merely a dancing-girl, in a befitting frock, paid by the management to pose as a mock Bohémienne. The Moulin Rouge is no more the centre of gay Paris than is Maskelyne's entertainment the centre of gay London.

Presently, having gained the Rue de Maubeuge, the spies entered that Bohemian café, where a charming air of chez soi and good-fellowship always pervades—the Café of the Red Ass. It has a small and unassuming front, except that the windows are profusely decorated with painted flowers and figures, while a red ass looks down from over the narrow door. It is furnished more like an old curiosity-shop than a café, and has its particular clientèle of Bohemians, who come to puff their long pipes, that hang in racks, and recount their hopes, aspirations, achievements, and failures, when not shouting some rollicking chorus. The place was filled with littérateurs of the Quarter, and a célébration was in progress, one of their number having succeeded in finding a publisher for a volume of his poetry.

Hence I was enabled to follow the pair unnoticed. They had, I found, seated themselves at a table with two rather small, ferret-eyed men, who had apparently been awaiting them. Then all four entered into an earnest discussion over their bocks, while I sat on the opposite side of the place, pretending to be interested in the Soir, but watching them as a cat a mouse.

The nature of their conversation was manifestly secret, for all four looked round furtively from time to time, as though suspicious lest someone should overhear. Wolf was relating some fact which apparently created a great impression upon the men whom he and Bertini had met. Whatever it was he told them, it created evident surprise.

Bertini rolled a cigarette in silence, lit it slowly, and sat back, blowing clouds of smoke into the air. Loud chatter and laughter and the rattle of saucers upon the tables sounded everywhere, mingled with the constant click of shuffled dominoes and the shouts of the rushing waiters calling their orders. The Red Ass always awakens from its lethargy at midnight, just as do the Café Américain and the showy establishments on the Boulevard des Italiens.

The short, middle-aged Frenchman who had been speaking pulled a blue paper from his pocket, and gave it to Wolf for examination. From its folding and size I perceived that it was a telegram. All this time the attitude of the Italian was that of a man who wished to affect an air of supreme carelessness.

More bocks were ordered, pen and paper were brought by the waiter, and a reply to the telegraphic message was written by the Frenchman, not, however, without some discussion, in which Bertini took part. The actions of these men showed that some further conspiracy was in progress, but what it was I was naturally unable to guess. I only knew that the two men whom I had followed were the most desperate, ingenious, and unscrupulous spies in Europe.

After nearly an hour, during which time I exhausted all the periodical literature provided by the management of the establishment, all four rose and went out. The two Frenchmen made their adieux, and the pair whose movements had so interested me walked slowly down to the Place de l'Opéra until they gained the narrow Rue des Petits Champs, a thoroughfare that intersects the Rue de la Paix and the Avenue de l'Opéra. At the end of this, not far from the Palais Royal, they turned suddenly into a dark alley, which led into a large courtyard, in which I soon discovered a small, fifth-rate hotel, evidently their temporary quarters.

I waited in the vicinity for nearly half an hour, until the concierge put out the lights and bolted the door; then I returned to the avenue, hailed a fiacre, and drove home just as the clocks were chiming three.

My vigil had been a long and tedious one, and when I entered my rooms I sank into a chair utterly worn out. I had, however, learnt several facts of supreme interest, not the least being the discovery of Wolf's headquarters. I got my man to ring up Kaye on the telephone, and presently gave him the information, suggesting that he should send one of his assistants to the Rue des Petits Champs to keep the spies under observation.

My statement filled him with feverish activity, for within half an hour he was seated with me in my room, and I was explaining all that had come to pass.

"Excellent!" he exclaimed. "They will not evade us now we know where they are. There is something fresh in the wind, without a doubt. We must discover what it is."

Then he went to the telephone, rang up one of his assistants who lived out at Passy, and gave him some instructions, together with the address of the obscure hotel to which I had followed the pair of rogues.

Far into the night we sat discussing the situation. As far as he knew, the Ceuta negotiations were at a standstill. All that was known in Madrid was that the Spanish Government had offered to sell that strategic position to France, and that the latter had accepted. Beyond this we had no further information, save that a complete tracing of the plans for the fortification of the place, which had been prepared in the French War Office, had found its way into our Embassy, where, as may be imagined, it had a cordial welcome. It had been purchased by Kaye from one of the draughtsmen, and showed plainly with what thoroughness it was proposed to fortify the place in opposition to our defences at Gibraltar. With its usual ingenuity the French Government, through its mouthpiece, the *Figaro*, had inspired an article alleging that Ceuta was about to be bought by Russia, in order, of course, to create alarm in England, where the periodical Russian bogey would at once be brought forward. But to us at the Embassy, who knew the truth, the *Figaro* article proved farcical reading.

During the past two or three days cipher télégraphie despatches had been constantly exchanged between the Quai d'Orsay and the various European embassies, and there had been many other signs of unusual diplomatic activity on the part of the Republic.

At last the chief of the secret service drained his glass, and, rising, left me to snatch a couple of hours' sleep before my next day's duties at the Embassy.

When I arose next morning I had occasion to go to the small writing-table in my sitting-room to obtain some note-paper, but was surprised to find the contents of the drawer in great disorder, as though they had been hastily overturned.

I called my man and questioned him, but he declared he knew nothing of it and that no one had entered my room. I frequently left the key in the drawer, as I had done when last I unlocked it. Whoever had searched that drawer had evidently looked for some private papers. I at once hastily set to work to rearrange them and find out whether any were missing.

Before five minutes had passed the truth became plain. A sealed envelope, in which I had placed the letter the Princess had written me offering her secret in exchange for my love, had been stolen. In an instant it flashed upon me that I had spoken of it to her as being destroyed. But it had now passed into the hands of our enemies!

Dark and mysterious are the ways of modern diplomacy as practised in the capitals of Europe, but this dastardly theft was not far from being the most daring and mysterious of any I had known.

Carefully I examined each of the papers. As far as I could discover, the only one missing was the letter of the Princess. Who could have stolen it? The only stranger who had entered the room was Edith, and I remembered that on the previous afternoon she had waited there alone before my arrival.

It was a strange thought, but it impressed itself upon me as a key to the truth. Surely she had not visited me for the sole purpose of stealing the letter which Léonie had sent to my room on that well-remembered night at Chantoiseau? I could not believe her capable of such duplicity, unless perchance it were prompted by jealousy. She might have heard of our acquaintance through one or other of those spies, her associates, and forthwith resolved on revenge. In any case the loss of the letter placed the Princess in an exceedingly serious position, and compromised her honour.

When I entered my room at the Embassy I found Lord Barmouth and Sibyl together. She was persuading him to allow her to accept an invitation to visit some relatives in the north of England, for she was tired of Paris, she declared. When I entered he dismissed her, saying that he wished to talk with me privately.

"Ingram, something extremely serious is in the wind," he said, when the door had closed and we were alone. His face was pale and showed traces of sleeplessness. "I was at de Wolkenstein's reception last night, and overheard a conversation between Berchtold and de Hindenburg. There is a conspiracy against us!"

"In what manner?" I asked, surprised that he should have become aware of it.

"The intercepting of those secret instructions which you brought from London some months ago is part of it; the Ceuta affair is another portion; and it appears, as far as I can gather, that the Powers, with the exception of Russia and Italy, have formed a gigantic plot against us to provoke war."

"To provoke war!" I echoed. "What details do you know?"

"Olsoufieff, who, as you know, is my personal friend, dropped a hint which we may take as a warning. He told me he had reason to believe that the secret service of both France and Germany had of late made several successful coups against us, and that the interests of those two nations had been considerably promoted thereby."

"He told you nothing further?"

"He could not be more explicit," replied His Excellency. "Russia, who, according to the Press, is our hereditary enemy, is in reality our friend. If every monarch loved unity and concord as well as the Czar, the peace of Europe would to-morrow be assured. Yet diplomatic usages prevented Olsoufieff from betraying his confrères in their diplomacy, even though he is my intimate friend."

"And how are we to act?" I asked. "The theft of the contents of that despatch was certainly most astonishing. How it was accomplished is an inscrutable mystery."

"Sibyl has been endeavouring to assist us," answered the Ambassador. "She, too, was at the reception last night, and kept eyes and ears open. She heard that both Wolf and that scoundrel Bertini are in Paris in company. Surely that bodes no good!"

"I was watching the pair until nearly three o'clock this morning," I explained. "At present Kaye has the matter in hand;" and then I proceeded to explain all the occurrences of the previous night and those that befell in the early hours of the morning. I told him of Edith, of my visit to her at Ryburgh, of her call upon me, and of my subsequent discovery of her at that low café near the station of Batignolles.

"Extraordinary!" he exclaimed in wonder, when I had finished. "Then this woman who declared that she loved you is, although an English girl living in a rural Norfolk village, actually a French spy? The ramifications of the secret service of our enemies are indeed amazing. The plot which has for its object the downfall of England is the most gigantic and at the same time the most ingenious and carefully planned of any known in modern history. Save for the little rift in the veil of secrecy, through which we have fortunately detected the danger, it is absolutely perfect."

Chapter Thirty Two
Betrayal

Winter came, grey, cold, and cheerless, in Paris. The war that had broken out in the Transvaal dragged on, and the European outlook grew daily darker and more lowering.

Occasionally I had received letters from Edith in Bordighera, telling me how pleasant life was there amid the sunshine and the palms after the leafless dreariness of an English winter. She, however, never once mentioned the man Bertini. Her letters were still affectionate, despite the fact that my replies were very cold and distant.

I entertained a distinct suspicion that she it was who had stolen the compromising letter of the Princess. In addition to this, her midnight visit to that pair of adventurers in the café had incensed me. For this reason her letters to me were unwelcome, and I answered them in quite an indifferent spirit. There was a wound in my heart that never could be healed. Edith Austin, it was proved, was the associate of two of the most unscrupulous adventurers in Europe.

In Paris matters were extremely critical. Lord Barmouth had been to Downing Street to have an interview with the Marquess, the latter refusing further to trust his secret instructions to any messenger; yet though not a word had been written and though the interview had taken place in the Foreign Secretary's private room, where the doors are double, thus preventing any sound from reaching the corridor, the exact nature of His Excellency's instructions was actually known at the Quai d'Orsay. The thing was incomprehensible; it rendered our diplomacy utterly powerless, forewarning the French of our policy and giving them a weapon to use against us. The mystery was impenetrable. Yet the truth was only too evident. Within four days of the interview taking place in London, Kaye brought to the Embassy a copy of a cipher telegram handed in at the Waterloo Station Telegraph-office, and received by the French Foreign Office, giving practically every detail of the verbal instructions received by the Ambassador. The way in which the truth had leaked out staggered belief.

The Marquess, on receiving the despatch from our Embassy, was at first disinclined to believe that such a thing could be possible, but I myself next day carried the copy of the spy's telegram to London and placed it in his hands. It was in mid-February, and the Channel passage had been about as bad as it possibly could be. He read the telegram with its decipher, and stood utterly bewildered.

"Absolutely nothing seems safe from the scoundrels!" he cried angrily. "How they have obtained this is a complete mystery. No one was present, for I myself took every precaution. While this goes on we are powerless—utterly powerless. In order to render our diplomacy abortive the French are spreading the secret of our policy broadcast in every capital. The thing is monstrous, and can only be done with the object of creating war."

"Every negotiation which England has had with the Transvaal since the commencement of the war is known at the Quai d'Orsay, as you will have noticed from the reports we have sent from the Embassy," I said. "Indeed, the news of the declaration of war by President Kruger was known to the French Government within half an hour of its receipt by our Colonial Office."

"It may have been sent to Paris direct from Pretoria," answered the great statesman, frowning in his perplexity.

"But our reply was known in Paris hours before it was officially issued. The decision of our Cabinet was known at the Quai d'Orsay before the meeting actually broke up," I remarked.

"I know, Ingram—I know," answered the Marquess. "Unfortunately for us, this was indeed the case. The mystery of how they obtain their intelligence is absolutely inscrutable."

We sat together for a long time in deep discussion. From his agitated manner and the unusual greyness of his fine, intelligent face, I knew that this man, upon whose shoulders rested the responsibility for England's security at the most critical moment when the greater part of her Army was in South Africa, was in fear of some terrible disaster. That England, with her land forces in the Transvaal, was vulnerable was known not only to every diplomatist, but also to the man in the street in every foreign capital. Now that Lord Barmouth had discovered the existence of the great plot against us, of which the defiant attitude of the Transvaal was part, active inquiries had been made all over the Continent to discover its character, and it had been ascertained that it was the intention of certain Powers to intervene in favour of the Boers, and thus cause a general rupture with Great Britain.

The plans had been carefully laid. The Boers, backed by France, Austria, and Germany, had fought well, but British pertinacity and pluck, under Lord Roberts, had won their way to the relief of Ladysmith and the occupation of Bloemfontein. With Joubert dead, with Cronje captured at Paardeberg, the Majuba stigma had been wiped out. Besides, Pretoria had been occupied. Now the Continental Powers, having planned to league themselves against us, were awaiting their opportunity to intervene, cause a rupture, and declare war against us on the slightest pretext.

It was this matter that we were discussing.

"The plan has been fostered for two years past," the Marquess declared. "The hostility of the French Press was part of the programme; the disgusting caricatures in the *Rire* inflamed the Anglophobes against us, and this—" and he took up a copy of the *Monde Illustré*, consisting wholly of a lurid forecast of the "Downfall of England" profusely illustrated,—"this, coming at such a moment, is more than mischievous. It will fan the too vigorous flames of French detestation of England, and increase the craving in France for war. I have read it, and it is apparently written to show how vulnerable our country is at this moment. I am not one who fears the downfall of our country; but should a war unhappily result, it would be a great calamity for Europe, and for France and the Republic most of all."

"It is an odd thing," I remarked, "that just as this pleasing brochure appears France should decide to mobilise four army corps in the coming autumn. All these corps are to be assembled in the north-west, close to the sea, and ready for a move if an opportunity comes. This is, I grant, not the first time that such a step has been taken, but it certainly requires to be met by ample precaution."

"Yes," he answered gravely, beating a tattoo upon his writing-pad with his quill. "It is not pleasant to reflect that, owing to the savings on the shipbuilding vote during the past three years, our Navy is not in a condition to warrant a feeling of security. Battleships and destroyers are hopelessly in arrears. An addition to our destroyer fleet—the best preventive of invasion—should be made without delay, as a simple precaution; for the risks are great with our Army absent, as it will still be in August, in South Africa."

"In Paris," I said, "we have been asked by the representatives of the Powers to believe that we have nothing to fear from a deliberate war policy on the part of the Governments of Germany, France, and Austria. They are all engaged in enterprises of far-reaching importance, which would be injured almost beyond recovery by war. Germany, de Hindenburg has pointed out, has entered with an unparalleled degree of enthusiasm into the struggle for industrial supremacy, with America and Great Britain as her only dangerous rivals."

"To blind us to the truth," observed the great Minister, smiling. "The *Libre Parole* inadvertently exposed the French secret when two months ago it declared that the bogey of British power had been flaunted in the face of the civilised world once too often, and a small but resolute nation had accepted the challenge. England, that outspoken sheet declared, has claimed to be predominant everywhere. The nations are tired of her pretensions, it insisted, and as soon as diplomacy has been forced to act in accordance with public opinion, there will be an end to this tyranny of the seas. The French forget," he added, "that it is not always safe to try to take advantage of a nation hardened by recent warfare. A country is sometimes more remarkable for military power at the end than at the beginning of a campaign."

"It appears to me," I remarked, "that Kruger demands peace upon impossible conditions, in order to be able to say that England has refused to discuss peace, that she is quite intractable, and that she is, therefore, responsible for the bloodshed which will continue."

"Most certainly Kruger's peace proposals are part of the Continental plot. He knows well enough how to play upon human simplicity and at the same time to assist his friends," observed the great statesman who controlled England's destinies. "But," he urged, "we must do one thing, Ingram. We must stop our policy leaking out as it does. This has already nearly landed us into war over the Ceuta incident, and must be a constant menace to us. Kaye, who was over a few days ago, told me that you had discovered certain persons who were evidently spies. What do you know of them?"

I told him all that I had discovered, omitting of course all reference to Edith and my love for her, as well as the fact that the Princess had offered me details of the plot upon terms which I had been unable to accept.

"Strive to keep them well under observation and discover the source of their information," he said. "By doing this you will in a great measure frustrate the plans of our enemies, and afterwards our diplomacy can checkmate them. But while all our intentions are known our diplomacy must of necessity be rendered futile. You know these people, Ingram, and with you rests a very great responsibility."

"I have all along striven to do my duty," I answered. "I have made effort after effort in order to obtain the truth, but up to the present all has been in vain."

"Continue," he urged, looking at me with those grave, serious eyes, beneath the calm gaze of which many a foreign diplomatist at the Court of St. James had trembled. "By perseverance and with the help of the secret service you may one day be successful. Then we will unite all the peaceful forces of England in order to break up this dastardly conspiracy. It shall be done!" he cried angrily, striking the table with his clenched fist. "My country shall never fall a victim to this cunningly devised plot of Messieurs les Anglophobes—never!"

The very thought had set fire to his indignation, he rose, and paced the room with a flush upon his ashen checks.

"I trust you, Ingram, just as I have always trusted you in the past," he said, turning suddenly on his heel towards me. "You have a clever and trustworthy chief in Lord Barmouth, a man fully fitted to occupy the place I hold in the British Government; therefore, strain every nerve to thwart the machinations of our enemies. Otherwise there must be war before the year is out—*there must be!*"

"I shall do my utmost, rely upon me," I answered. "It shall not be because of my want of enterprise that this base system of espionage is allowed to continue."

"Good," he said, offering me his hand. "Return to Paris to-night, resume your inquiries, and remember that in this affair you may be the means of saving your country from a war long and disastrous. There is a conspiracy against our beloved lady the Queen. That in itself is sufficient incentive to arouse to action any man in the Foreign Office. Remember it always while working at this inscrutable mystery."

I took his thin, bony hand, and he gripped mine warmly. The secret of the great statesman's popularity with all his staff, from ambassador down to fourth-grade clerk, was his personal contact with them, his readiness to consult and advise, and his unfailing friendship and courtesy.

I promised him that I would continue to do my utmost to discover the truth. Then, taking my leave, I went out and down the great staircase into Downing Street, where the dark afternoon was rendered the more cheerless by the rain falling heavily; and the solitary policeman in his dripping cape touched his hat respectfully as I passed. The outlook in every way was certainly a most dismal and oppressive one.

In obedience to the Marquess' command, I returned to Paris by the night mail from Charing Cross. During that journey I reflected deeply upon the best course to pursue in solving the problem. But the enigma was difficult, and its solution beyond the efforts even of the ubiquitous Kaye and his associates. If I obtained leave of absence, and went down to the Riviera, was it at all probable that I could learn some clue from Edith? I was doubtful.

Ever since that night, three months ago, when I had followed the spies to that obscure hotel in the Rue des Petits Champs, they had been shadowed, and their doings reported. Wolf had been to Brussels and to Berlin, while Bertini had returned to London; but their actions, although sometimes suspicious, had never supplied us with the clue we wanted.

Bertini was at that moment, according to the reports of the special section at Scotland Yard, whose speciality it is to watch suspected secret agents in England, living in comfort at the Midland Hotel at St. Pancras Station. He usually passed his evenings with a few of his compatriots, playing dominoes at the Café Royal or the Café Monaco. Wolf, on the other hand, was travelling hither and thither visiting various people, all of whom were noted in the elaborate system of espionage which was now being exercised upon them.

After a week in Paris I consulted Lord Barmouth, and he agreed that it would be wise for me to travel to Bordighera and make a final attempt to obtain some fact from the woman whom I had once hoped to make my wife. Truth to tell, I made up my mind to travel South with great reluctance, for so false and untrue had she been that I had long ago resolved within myself never again to see her. But it was a matter of necessity that we should no longer remain in ignorance of the source of the information which constantly leaked out to our enemies; hence, one evening I busied myself in assisting Mackenzie to pack my bag. While doing so the electric bell rang suddenly, and when my servant returned from answering the summons, he announced a visitor, saying:

"A lady has called to see you, sir—the Princess von Leutenberg."

"The Princess!" I gasped in surprise.

Then, wondering what could be the nature of her business with me at that hour, I smoothed down my hair before the glass, drew a long breath (for I expected a scene), and entered the room into which she had been shown.

"Léonie—you!" I cried in surprise.

Her rich sables were unclasped at the throat, and when she rose quickly they fell from her, displaying her finely moulded white neck and arms, shining like alabaster in contrast to her low-cut corsage of black chiffon.

Her face was blanched to the lips, the slim, gloved hand she gave me trembled, and her beautiful eyes, usually so brilliant and sparkling, had a look of haunting fear in them.

"Gerald!" she whispered hoarsely, as if fearful lest she might be overheard, "my secret is out! I am ruined—*ruined*! And through you! You have betrayed me to my enemies—you, the man I love!"

Chapter Thirty Three
Which Contains a Surprise

"Betrayed you, Léonie!" I echoed. "I have not betrayed you!"

"But you have!" she declared angrily, her eyes flashing upon me. "You have broken your oath to me."

"I have broken no oath," I answered calmly; adding, "Let us sit down and talk quietly."

"Talk quietly!" she cried, speaking rapidly in French. "Do you think I can talk quietly with ruin staring me in the face?"

"In what manner does ruin threaten you?" I inquired, placing my hand upon her arm in an effort to calm her.

She was terribly agitated, I could see, and her anger knew no bounds, although she was striving strenuously to suppress it.

"You have betrayed my secret—the secret of my love for you!" she cried. "That letter which you promised me to destroy is in the hands of my bitterest enemy."

"Forgive me, Léonie," I cried quickly. "The letter was mysteriously stolen from that writing-table there. How, I know not."

"Cannot you even guess who is the thief?"

I hesitated. The only person I suspected was Edith, who had been the solitary occupant of that room while she waited for me. It was after her departure that I found the drawer in confusion and the letter missing.

"I have suspicion," I replied with some hesitation, "yet I feel assured it is unfounded."

"Of whom?"

"Of a friend."

"A friend of yours?" she exclaimed quickly. "Therefore, an enemy of mine. It is a woman. Come, admit it."

"I admit nothing," I answered with a forced smile, my diplomatic instinct instantly asserting itself.

"Is it a woman, or is it not?" she demanded.

"I am not compelled to answer that question, Léonie," I remarked in a quiet voice.

"But having betrayed me—or rather having allowed me to be betrayed—it is surely only manly of you to endeavour to make amends!" she cried reproachfully. "Even if you do not love me sufficiently to make me your wife, that is hardly a reason why you should expose me to my enemies."

"I have not done so wilfully," I declared. "As the letter has been stolen by an enemy, I feel sure that the suspicion resting upon my friend is unfounded."

"But if the thief is a woman and she loves you, she would naturally be my enemy, and seek to overthrow me," argued the Princess logically.

"It is my fault," I said. "I regret the incident, and seek your forgiveness, Léonie. I had no idea that spies and thieves surrounded me, as apparently they do, or I would have destroyed it instead of keeping it as a cherished relic of one of the few romantic incidents of my life."

"You w'ere very foolish to keep it, just as it was foolish of me to have written it," she observed. "Cannot you see how compromised I am by it? I have offered to betray to you a secret of State, a secret known only to kings, emperors, and their immediate advisers, in return for your love. I am self-condemned," she added wildly.

"But into whose hands has the letter passed?" I inquired, now quite convinced of the extreme gravity of the situation.

"Into the possession of a man who is my most bitter enemy in all the world. Ah, you don't know, Gerald, how I am suffering!"

She placed her hand upon her brow, and stood rigid and motionless.

"Why?"

"Because this man, with the evidence of my treason in his possession, is endeavouring to force me into a hateful bondage. To save myself," she added hoarsely, "I must obey, or else—"

"Or else what?" I inquired, looking at her in astonishment.

"Or else escape exposure and ruin by another method, more swift and more to be trusted."

"I don't understand you. What do you mean?"

"Suicide," she answered in a low, hard voice, regarding me coldly, with a truly desperate look in her eyes.

"Come, come, Léonie," I said quickly, "to talk like that is absurd."

"No, it is not in the least absurd," she protested, a heavy, serious look upon her face. "Like yourself, I am the victim of a vile conspiracy. This man has long sought to entrap me, and has, alas! now succeeded."

"For what reason?"

She remained silent, as though doubting whether to tell me the whole truth. In a few moments, however, she made a sudden resolve.

"Because he wishes to marry me," she answered briefly.

"And by holding this letter as a menace he now seeks to force you into a marriage that is distasteful?"

"Distasteful!" she echoed. "I hate and detest him! Rather than marry him I would prefer suicide."

"Why?"

"Because if I do not accept his conditions for the return of that letter he will expose me," she answered in despair.

"Has he threatened this?"

"Yes."

"And what is your response?"

"I have refused, Gerald. Even though he were not so hateful I could not marry him, because I love you."

She was trembling with agitation, and tears stood in her fine eyes.

"Love for me is out of the question, Léonie," I answered kindly, yet firmly. "Now that you find yourself in this critical situation it is for us both to strive to frustrate this enemy of yours. It is my duty to assist you."

"Ah, you cannot!" she said in a tone of utter despair. "The power he holds over me by possessing the written evidence of my treason—my offer to betray to you the secret of my Emperor—is complete, and he is well aware of it. He demands marriage with me, or he will ruin me, and brand me as a traitress to my country and my Emperor."

"This man is, of course, now aware of what passed between us during my visit at Chantoiseau?" I said.

"He knows everything," she answered. "I was living quietly at Rudolstadt, and endeavouring to forget you, when of a sudden, a fortnight ago, there came to the castle a stranger, who sent in his card sealed in an envelope. My servants regarded him with some suspicion, and well they might, for when I opened the envelope and took out the card I knew that at last the blow had fallen. He had dared to come and seek me there."

"You saw him?"

"Yes, he demanded an interview. We had not met for nearly two years, yet he approached me with a declaration of love upon his lips. I laughed at him, but presently he held me dumb by producing from his pocket the compromising letter. He began by pointing out how easily he could ruin me socially, and prove me to be a traitress. He made an end by offering to place the letter unreservedly in my hands on the day I became his wife."

"He had declared his love to you before?"

"Yes, two years ago. But I knew him too well, and hated him too thoroughly, to take a favourable view of his ridiculous declaration."

"And this man?" I asked. "Who is he?"

"He was once in the employ of my father, Prince Kinsky von Wchinitz, and was administrator of the estates at Wchinitz and Tettau, in Bohemia. Immediately my husband died and the feudal estates of Schwazbourg passed into my possession, as well as those of my late father, this man pressed his claim. He first endeavoured to pay court to me; then, on finding I was cold to his attentions, he became threatening, and I was compelled to discharge him. Afterwards he drifted away, became a chevalier d'industrie, and at last, because of my refusal to hear his repeated declarations of affection, he made a dastardly attempt upon my life."

"He tried to kill you?" I exclaimed incredulously.

"Yes," she responded. "Had it not been for the timely intervention of a stranger—a person whom I did not see—he would have murdered me."

"Through jealousy?"

"Yes, through jealousy."

"And this fellow's name?" I asked, my anger rising at the thought of a discharged employé thus holding Léonie in his power, and, despite the fact that he had made an attempt upon her life, badgering her to marry him. "Is there any reason why I should not know it?"

There was a brief silence. She hesitated to tell me, and not until I had pressed her several times to disclose to me his name would she answer.

"The man who is seeking to drive me to destruction and to suicide is," she replied reluctantly, "an adventurer of the worst type—a man who is seeking to make a wealthy marriage at the expense of a woman whom he holds in his power, and whom he can ruin at any moment if he chooses."

"His name? Tell me."

"His name is Count Rodolphe d'Egloffstein-Wolfsburg."

I held my breath, utterly amazed by this disclosure.

"The man known as Rodolphe Wolf?" I cried—"the adventurer who fell into the hands of the police at St. Petersburg, and served nine months' imprisonment as a rogue and vagabond?"

"What! you know him?" she demanded in surprise. "Is he a friend of yours?"

"A friend!" I echoed. "No, not a friend by any means. An enemy, and a bitter one."

"Then he is mutually our enemy?" she declared.

"Most certainly," I answered, adding, "What you have just told me, Léonie, reveals to me the truth regarding several incidents which have been hitherto unaccountable. Was Wolf actually in your father's employ?"

"Yes, for years. He was the younger son of old Count Leopold d'Egloffstein-Wolfsburg, whose small estate joined that of Tettau, and, after a wild career in Vienna and Paris, returned home a ne'er-do-well. My father, in order to give him another chance in life, gave him control of a portion of the estates, and, finding him shrewd and clever at management, ultimately made him administrator of the whole, which position he filled up to the time when, after my husband's death, I discharged him on account of dishonesty and of the constant annoyance to which I was subjected by him. When he left me he vowed that one day I should become his wife, and it seems that in order to gain that end he has been scheming ever since."

"He is a spy in the French secret service," I observed thoughtfully, for strange reflections were running through my mind at that instant.

"I have heard so," she answered. "But that is not actually proved, is it?"

"Absolutely."

"Is it possible that he himself stole the letter from your desk there? Has he ever been here?"

"Never, to my knowledge. He would never dare to enter here," I replied. "No, that letter was stolen by one of his accomplices."

"A woman?"

"Yes, I think it was a woman."

"A woman whom you love, or have loved, Gerald? Come now, be perfectly frank with me."

"You guess aright," I answered, remembering that as far as I was aware she knew nothing of the existence of Edith Austin.

A dark look crossed her features.

"Then if that woman knew the contents of the letter she had a motive of jealousy," argued the Princess.

"She may have had. At any rate I have suspicion that, acting under Wolf's instructions, she abstracted the letter and handed it to him without previous knowledge of what it contained."

"No, I scarcely think that. Wolf would tell her that I loved you and was her rival in your affections, in order to incense her against me. What is her name?"

I kept silence for a moment, reflecting upon the wisdom of telling her the truth at that juncture. At last I resolved that, as our interests were mutual, there should be no secrets between us.

"She is English, and her name is Austin—Edith Austin."

"Edith Austin!" she cried in dismay. "And you love her?—you love *that woman*?"

"Why do you speak of her in that manner?" I demanded.

"Austin—Austin?" she repeated. "It is certainly not the first time I have heard that name. Certainly her reputation is not above suspicion. And you actually love her, Gerald?" she added in a blank tone of reproach. "Is it really possible that you love her?"

"Why?"

"Because Bertini—who was once in the Austrian service, and is now a secret agent of the French—told me in Vienna not long ago that one of the most successful French agents in England was a young girl named Edith Austin. She must be the same. I know Bertini well, although he is not at all a desirable acquaintance. And you love this girl—you, in your responsible position at the Embassy? Is it not extremely dangerous?"

I admitted that it was, but expressed disinclination to discuss the matter further, feeling that the more we talked of it the deeper would be the pain I caused to the handsome and desperate woman before me.

"You told me just now that Wolf once made an attempt upon your life," I said presently. "These words of yours have given me a clue to an incident which has to me long been a mystery."

"How?"

"Listen, and I'll tell you. One day in late autumn two years ago I alighted at the little station of Montigny, on the line to Montargis, in order to ride through the forest of Fontainebleau to Bois-le-Roi, and return thence to Paris by rail. I am fond of the forest, and when I can snatch a day, sometimes go for a healthy spin through it, either riding, cycling, or on foot. Having lunched at the little inn at Marlotte, where my mare was stabled, I started off on the road which, as you know well, leads through the wild rocks of the Gorge aux Loups to the Carrefour de la Croix du Grand Maître in the heart of the forest, and thence away to the town of Fontainebleau. The afternoon was gloomy and lowering, and darkness crept on much more quickly than I had anticipated. It had rained earlier in the day, and the roads were wet and muddy, while the wind that had sprung up moaned dismally through the half-bare trees, rendering the ride anything but a cheerful one.

"By six o'clock it was already quite dark, and I was still in the centre of the forest, galloping along a narrow by-way which I knew would bring me out upon the main road to Paris. The mare's hoofs were falling softly upon the carpet of rain-sodden leaves when of a sudden I heard a woman's cry of distress in the darkness close to me. A man's voice sounded, speaking in German, and next instant there was the flash of a revolver and a loud report. The light gave me a clue, and, pulling up, I swung myself from my saddle and without hesitation rushed to the woman's assistance. I slipped my own revolver from my pocket and sprang upon the man who had fired, while at the same instant the woman wrested herself from the assassin's grasp. By means of the white shawl she wore about her head I saw her disappearing quickly through the undergrowth. With a fierce oath the man turned upon me, and, as we struggled, endeavoured to get the muzzle of his weapon beneath my chin. I felt the cold steel against my jaw, and next instant he pulled the trigger. My face was scorched by the flash, but happily the bullet went harmlessly past my cheek. I had dropped my own weapon early in the encounter, and now saw that the only way in which I could save my life was to beat the fellow's head against a tree until he became insensible. This I succeeded in doing, tripping him suddenly, forcing him down, and beating his skull against a tree-stump until he lay there motionless as a log. Then I took his weapon from him, and, striking a match, bent down to see his face. To my astonishment I found that he was a man I had known slightly several years before—the man who holds you within his power—Rodolphe Wolf."

"And the woman who so narrowly escaped death—indeed, whose life was saved by your timely aid—is the woman who loves you—myself!" she cried.

"I never dreamed, until your words just now gave me a clue to the truth, that you were actually the unknown woman who escaped from the hands of the assassin," I said.

For answer she grasped my hand warmly and looked straight into my eyes, though she did not utter a single word.

Chapter Thirty Four
At Bordighera

Bordighera, that charming, well-sheltered little town which, lying well back in its picturesque bay on the Italian Riviera, has during the past year or so come quickly into fashionable prominence, is at its best towards the end of February. It is not by any means a large place. The quaint old town is perched upon a conical hill with queer ladder-like streets, so narrow that no vehicles can pass up them. There are strong stone arches to support the houses against possible earthquakes. The streets are dark, sometimes mere tunnels, as is so frequent in those neighbouring rock villages, Sasso, Dolceacqua, Apricale, and the rest, the reason being that they were built in the days when the Moorish pirates made constant raids along that coast, and the houses were clustered together for mutual protection against those dreaded raiders.

But below the ancient town, Bordighera has spread along the seashore and into the olive-woods. In February, when in England all is bare and cheerless, the gardens of the handsome hotels and the big white villas on the hillsides are ablaze with flowers, the air is heavy with the perfume of the heliotrope, growing in great bushes, and the sweet scent of the carnations, grown in fields for Covent Garden and the flower-market outside the Madeleine.

The tourist in knickerbockers, with his camera over his shoulder, never goes to Bordighera, for to the uninitiated it is far too dull. There is no casino, as at Nice, no jetty, no cafés with al-fresco music, no tables out upon the pavement; and, truth to tell, such attractions are not required. The people who winter at Bordighera represent the most distinguished coterie in Europe. They are not of the snobbish crowd who frequent San Remo, and they do their best to avoid attracting into their midst the undesirable crowd from Monte Carlo, or the Cookites from Nice. Life in Bordighera from November until the end of April is essentially charming. The people who winter there regularly—English, Germans, Russians, Belgians, and Italians—all know each other, and nearly every evening there are brilliant entertainments, at which princes, dukes, marquesses, and counts attend as thickly as blackberries grace the hedgeside in autumn. The big hotels give dances weekly, to which everyone in Society is welcome. In fact, life in Bordighera is very similar to that in a pleasant country town in England, but with the difference that it is purely cosmopolitan, without any distinction of caste. Emperors, kings, grand-dukes, and reigning princes are all patrons of the place, and it certainly stands unique in the whole world both for its natural beauties and for its unpretentiousness. There is no artificial charm, as at Nice, San Remo, Monte Carlo, or Cannes. The easy-going people of Bordighera are well aware that the charm of their clean, white little town lies in its natural beauty and quaint old-world picturesqueness; hence, although the health and comfort of their foreign visitors are studied, no attempt is made to give it a false air of garishness and gaiety.

When at noon, two days after the Princess's visit to me, I stepped from the sleeping-car that had brought me down from Paris, and, entering a fiacre, drove up to the Hôtel Angst, I turned back and saw before me a sunny panorama of turquoise sea and purple mountains, which compelled me to pause in rapt admiration. The grey-green of the olives, the brighter foliage of the oranges with the yellow fruit gleaming in the green, the high feathery palms waving in the zephyr, the flowers of every hue, the dazzlingly white town, and its background of grey inaccessible crags, snow-tipped here and there, behind Apricale, combined to make up a picture unique and superb.

I had been in Bordighera once before, but this second impression in no way destroyed the former. On several previous occasions I had spent a month or so in the South at Monte Carlo, Mentone, and Nice, but I must admit that I preferred King's Road at Brighton to the Promenade des Anglais at Nice. Mentone I disliked because of its bath-chair invalids, San Remo because of its snobbery; and Monte Carlo, with all its jargon of the play, the eternal Casino, the band outside the Café de Paris, the clatter at Ciro's, and the various pasteboard attractions, was to me only tolerable for a week. Bordighera, with better climate and a native population exceedingly well-disposed towards the English, possesses distinct advantages over them all, although it never advertises itself on railway-station hoardings, like Nice or San Remo, by means of posters in which the sea is the colour of washing-blue.

As I had not advised Edith of my coming, it being my intention to surprise her, it was not until after the dressing-bell had rung for dinner that evening that I went below. I watched her descend the staircase, a neat figure in cream, with corsage slightly décolleté, and with pink carnations in her hair. Then I approached her in the great hall and held out my hand.

She drew back in amazement. The next moment she welcomed me warmly, evidently under the impression that I had come there in order to forgive.

Aunt Hetty, looking quite spruce in black satin, and wearing a gay cap and an emerald brooch, came downstairs a few minutes later, and, after a brief explanation, we followed the others in to the table-d'hôte. As early arrivals, they had places near the head of the table, while mine was far down, near the end. Therefore, not until the meal was over, and we sat in rocking-chairs in the hall listening to the music, was I able to chat to her, and then nothing confidential could pass between us because of the other guests seated around, the men smoking and gossiping, and the women enjoying the lazy post-prandial hour before the arrival of the English mail with the two-days-old letters and newspapers.

After a long talk with her, mostly upon trivialities, I retired that night with a distinct impression that somehow my presence there was unwelcome. She had told me that they did not intend to remain much longer in Bordighera, and that they would either go on to Rome or back to England. I felt convinced that this decision had been suddenly arrived at since my advent.

On the following morning, after my coffee, I went forth for a stroll into the long high-street of the town, where, in the window of the British Vice-Consulate, was placed a board bearing a number of telegrams. I paused, finding that they gave the latest news of the war in the Transvaal, which was telegraphed from London twice daily. As I did so, another passer-by paused and eagerly peered into the window beside me.

He was a shabbily dressed Italian, smoking a long, rank Toscano, and as I turned away from the board my eyes fell suddenly upon his face.

It was Paolo Bertini.

Our recognition was mutual, and I saw in an instant that he became confused. He moved away, but I walked beside him.

"Why are you here?" I inquired in French with some warmth.

"I may put to you the same question," he answered defiantly, his dark eyes flashing upon me with an evil gleam.

"Remember," I said, "you have been already condemned as a French spy, although you are an Italian. They are not fond of French spies here, on the frontier."

"What do you mean?" he cried, turning upon me quickly. "Is that a threat?"

"It is," I answered boldly. "We have met now, and you must answer to me for several things."

"For what?"

"For your recent actions as a spy."

"You are extremely polite—like all the English," he said sneeringly.

We had turned back and were walking in the direction of the hotel again.

"In this matter politeness is not necessary—only plain speaking," I said. "First, I may tell you, for your own information, that I know well your methods and all about your assistance to your accomplice Wolf. Every action of yours during these past three months has been watched, and the truth is now known."

His face went pale, but his nerve never deserted him. Even though I myself had once given him into the hands of the police, he was still the same scheming, desperate spy as he had ever been.

"Well," he laughed, "if you know the truth I hope it interests you. You had best go back to Paris and not seek to interfere with me."

"I came here for a purpose," I told him plainly, "and that purpose was to find you and hand you over to the police as a French secret agent. In France you are secure, but here you will discover that your countrymen are not so well-disposed towards a traitor."

"I have no fear of arrest," he replied. "Do your worst, caro mio. You cannot harm me."

"Very well," I answered, "we shall see."

He glanced at me quickly with an evil look. If he had dared he would have struck me down with the poignard which he kept always concealed in his belt. But he was a coward, I knew; therefore, I felt safe while among the crowd of gaily dressed promenaders who were enjoying the morning sunshine. If he made an attempt upon me, it would be in secret, not in the open.

"Shall I tell you why you are here?" he asked. "You have come to Bordighera to follow Edith Austin—just as I did."

"And if so, what then?"

"Return to Paris. She is mine."

"She shall never be!" I cried furiously. "You, a spy, a coward, and a traitor, hold her within your power, and are forcing her to become your catspaw. I know it all. I saw you that night at Ryburgh. I followed you. I made inquiries of her, and learned the truth."

"What!" he cried, "she told you—she has dared to give me away?"

"I know all," I answered firmly, "and your doom is imprisonment on the Island of Gorgona for the remainder of your life."

"You exposed me once!" he cried in anger. "I have not forgotten it. We shall be quits one day."

"We shall be quits this very day," I asserted hotly.

"Ah!" he laughed defiantly, "that remains to be seen. You are jealous of Edith Austin," he added with a supercilious sneer.

"She is your victim!" I cried, "and I have resolved to rescue her."

"Because you think she is pure and honest, and that she loves you? But very soon you will discover your mistake."

"Do you make an imputation against her honour?" I demanded fiercely.

He shrugged his shoulders meaningly, his face broadening into an evil grin.

"You are a coward in addition to being a spy and a traitor!" I declared. "You would even endeavour to besmirch a woman's fair name."

"Fair name!" he laughed insultingly. "Love like yours, amico mio, is always blind. You English are always so amusingly simple."

"Come," I said, halting suddenly when we had arrived at the small garden in the centre of which the band-stand is placed. As we were some distance away from the promenaders, we could not be overheard. "Enough has passed between us. I tell you plainly that it is my intention to end all this and to apply for your arrest as a spy."

"And supposing I do not allow myself to be arrested? Suppose I cross the frontier at once?"

"A telegram to the police at Ventimiglia will prevent you," I answered quite calmly. "You see that city guard yonder?" I said, pointing to a man in uniform standing not far off upon the kerb. "I have only now to demand your arrest, and you will never again enjoy freedom your whole life long."

"But you don't think I should be such a fool as to allow myself to be taken, do you?" he said, his air of defiance still perfect.

He went on chewing the end of his Virginia. "Your description is too well known. You will not be at liberty a single hour after I make my statement to the Prefect." Then I paused, and, looking straight into his evil face, added, "There is, however, yet another way."

"How?"

"A way in which you may avoid arrest—the only way."

"Explain," he said. "This is very interesting."

"By being perfectly frank with me," I replied, "and by making explanation of your work of espionage in London."

"You will never know that," he replied quickly. "Cause my arrest if you wish, but upon the incidents of the past year my lips are sealed, because I know that you can never secure my conviction in Italy."

"Then you still defy me, and refuse to explain anything?"

It was my endeavour to obtain from him the secret of how despatches had so frequently been stolen.

"I will explain nothing," he declared firmly.

"You have no evidence upon which to convict me."

"Very well," I answered slowly and distinctly, "we shall see. You apparently forget that within your photographic camera, which so fortunately fell into my hands, was an undeveloped negative of an important diplomatic document having reference to Italy's position in regard to the Triple Alliance, which you photographed in the Italian Embassy in Brussels and intended to hand to your employers in Paris? I have a print of it here, in my pocket-book, and I think it will be of considerable interest both to the Italian police and the Italian Government."

His jaw dropped, and the light went out of his dark, sallow countenance. I saw that if ever the spirit of murder was in this scoundrel's heart it was there at that moment.

Chapter Thirty Five
In which Edith Speaks Plainly

After luncheon, when Miss Foskett, as was usual, ascended to her room to take her afternoon nap, Edith managed to escape and accompany me for a walk. The hotel was crowded with visitors, mostly English, who had come South in search of sunshine. The Battle of Flowers was to be fought that day. The little place was gay with flags, the pavements covered with confetti, and there was everywhere that air of gaiety and irresponsibility that Carnival lends to every Italian town. In Carnival Bordighera is at her best, and the fun of the festà is fast and furious, without the rough horseplay and pellets of lime indulged in at Nice.

Edith had, however, seen the Battle of Flowers at Nice in the previous week, having gone over there for the day. As this was so, we resolved to climb the hill behind the town and wander through the grey olive-woods, away from the boisterous merrymakers. Up a steep road on the outskirts of the town in the direction of sunny Ospedaletti we climbed, and thence by a mule-track we ascended zig-zag until we entered the beautiful olive-groves. Seen through the grey-green trees with their twisted trunks, the panorama spread before us was truly wonderful, the whole line of rugged coast being in view for miles on either hand, the brown, bare rocks standing out in sharp contrast to the deep sapphire of the glassy sea. Although February, it was like a May day in England, the air flower-scented and balmy, the sun so warm that to walk in overcoats or wraps was impossible.

"Well," I said at length, when we had halted a second time to turn back and admire the view, "you are displeased with me, Edith? Why am I so unwelcome?"

"You are not unwelcome," she declared quickly. "I am certainly not displeased."

"I begin to think that during the months you've been here you have forgotten those words you uttered to me in Paris, just as you forgot your vow made to me beneath the willows at Ryburgh."

"I have forgotten nothing," she protested. "This is cruel of you, Gerald, to reproach me thus."

"You told me then that you reciprocated my affection, yet you allow this man Bertini to follow you everywhere. He is here."

"Here?" she gasped in alarm, her face pale in an instant. "Are you certain?"

"I have seen and spoken with him this morning."

I did not tell her the nature of our conversation, or how I had given him twelve hours in which to decide whether he preferred to reveal the truth or take the consequences of arrest; neither did I tell her that I had called at the police-office and that the spy was already under close observation, the police believing him to be an undesirable visitor from Monte Carlo.

"You've spoken with him? What did he tell you?"

"Very little of consequence. I know that you are his victim, and I am seeking to release you from the thraldom," I answered gravely.

"Ah!" she cried wistfully, "if you only could! If you only could, then I should commence a new life and be happy! The awful suspense is killing me."

"Suspense of what?"

She was silent for a moment.

"I fear his threats," she faltered. "I know he would have no compunction whatever in causing my ruin when I am no longer of further use to him."

"Now, tell me plainly and honestly, Edith," I asked, looking straight into her white, anxious face. "Do you love him?"

"Love him!" she echoed wildly. "Why, I hate him! Have I not already told you so?"

"But he loves you."

"Of that I am not certain. If he does, it is through no fault whatever of mine. I detest and hate him!"

"Will you not tell me how he managed to obtain this irresistible power over you? Can you not help me in my search for the truth?"

"I must not speak; I dare not, Gerald," she answered in a hoarse whisper, as though the very thought of exposure filled her with alarm.

"You fear his revenge?"

She nodded, adding in a low tone, "He knows my secret."

"And I, your lover, do not," I observed reproachfully. "Well," I continued, "answer me truly one question. Tell me whether, when you called upon me on the last occasion in Paris, you stole a letter from my desk—a letter from the Princess von Leutenberg?"

"From the woman who loves you?" she cried huskily. "Yes, I did."

"And you stole it at Bertini's instigation? He told you where it would be found, the colour of the envelope, and the coronet and cipher upon it, did he not?"

She nodded in the affirmative.

"And that same night you met him in a small café at Batignolles, and handed him the letter? He was with his accomplice, Rodolphe Wolf."

"It is just as you say," she answered. "But how did you know this?"

"Because I myself watched you," I answered. "That letter was stolen to be used against the Princess."

"And if it is, what then? That woman who offered to betray her country in return for your love is my rival!" she cried fiercely.

"The theft of that letter was committed with quite another motive," I replied. "That adventurer Wolf desires to marry the Princess, and with his accomplice has made you his catspaw to obtain the letter, and thus compel her to marry him. If she refuses, he threatens to denounce her."

"Has he actually threatened this?" she cried in surprise. "I never dreamt that such was his motive."

"She is in Paris, suffering from this scoundrel's tyranny. As the man is an adventurer and spy, marriage between them is out of the question." She turned to me, and, looking into my eyes, earnestly demanded:

"Tell me, Gerald, do you love her, as they told me that you do? You visited her at Chantoiseau, and it is said that you often went long walks in the forest together. Besides, in Paris you met often at various receptions and dances."

"True," I admitted. "We met often, and I have more than once been her guest at the château; but as to loving her, such an idea has never entered my head. She is a smart and attractive woman, like many others in the circle in which I am compelled to move; but I swear to you, by all I hold most sacred, that I never loved her in the past, and that to-day is as yesterday."

"She loves you. That letter is sufficient proof of it."

"It was written in a moment of madness," I assured her. "She regretted it a few hours afterwards, and asked me to destroy it. The fault is entirely my own, for I neglected to carry out her wish. By my own culpable negligence she is placed in this position."

"Yes," she replied. "Forgive me, Gerald; I acted under compulsion, as I have always been compelled to act."

"Certainly I forgive," I answered. "But will it not be humane conduct on your part to rescue the Princess from this terrible doom? Wolf wishes to marry her for her money alone, and will force this step upon her if we can find no means to save her."

She paused. Hitherto she had been jealous of Léonie, but now, upon my assurance that I had no love for her, I saw that she inclined towards mercy.

"If I could," she said at last, "I would assist her. But I cannot see that it is possible."

"You can do so by explaining your own position to me," I said. "Despicable though it may seem, the ghastly truth is, that you are actually a spy in the service of France. If you do not seek to clear yourself now, you may be condemned with your accomplices Wolf, Bertini, and Yolande de Foville."

"That woman!" she cried quickly. "It was she who plotted against you."

"Then you have met her!" I exclaimed, surprised at this revelation.

I had never believed that they had met.

"Yes," Edith replied, "I met her in London; and while dining one night at the Carlton with Wolf and Bertini she told me how she had misled you into the belief that she loved you passionately, in order to obtain from you certain official information which had been of the greatest use to them at the Quai d'Orsay. She little dreamed that I knew you and loved you, and the three of them laughed heartily over what they called your gullibility."

I pursed my lips, for I now saw that woman's motive in responding to my declaration of love long ago. At the time I would not believe the whispered condemnation of the Countess and her daughter as secret agents, but of late the truth had been shown me all too plainly.

"And did she mention an incident last year in Paris as the result of which she nearly lost her life?" I inquired.

"Yes; she told us a long story of how a mysterious attempt had been made to poison her in her own apartment in Paris by some subtle poison being placed upon the gum of the envelopes in her escritoire. She wrote a letter, and licked the envelope in order to seal it, when she was seized suddenly by excruciating pains, followed by coma and a state so nearly resembling death that even the doctors were at first deceived. Only by an antidote administered by an English doctor—a friend of yours, I believe— was her life saved. Because of your efforts she had, she said, been seized by remorse, and ceased to mislead you further, because of the debt of gratitude she owed you."

"Very kind indeed of her," I laughed.

A silence fell between us. We were both looking seaward, far away over the great expanse of clear bright blue, to where a distant steamer was leaving a trail of smoke upon the horizon. Down in the carnation-gardens some girls were singing an old Italian folk-song while they cut and packed the flowers for the London market; at our feet were violets everywhere.

"Can you tell me absolutely nothing, in order to lead me to a knowledge of the truth, Edith?" I asked again. "Remember that our love and our future depend upon you alone. At present you are a spy, liable to arrest as a traitress."

"I know—I know!" she cried, bursting into a flood of tears. "It was not my fault. I could not help it. I was compelled—compelled!"

"You are aware of the channels through which knowledge of our diplomatic secrets have been obtained by our enemies. Will you not make amends by telling me the truth?" I asked in a low, persuasive, earnest tone, my arm about her slim waist.

"I dare not!" she sobbed—"I dare not! They would kill me, as they have sworn to do if I betrayed them!"

During the hour that followed, as we wandered together among the olives, I ascertained a few unimportant facts from her—facts which threw considerable light upon the ingenuity of the spies with whom she had been compelled to ally herself. But upon the secret of how their great coups had been accomplished her lips were sealed.

I gave her to understand that Bertini was now within an ace of arrest, and that in less than an hour he would, if I willed it, be inside the Prefecture, charged with treason against his own Government; but in such terror did she hold him that even my assertion that his power over her had ended did not induce her to disclose anything.

At first it had seemed to me almost impossible that she, living in the country with the strictly prim and proper Miss Foskett, could at the same time be a member of the secret service of our enemies. But I had witnessed her midnight meeting with Bertini, and that had convinced me.

"And if you cause his arrest," she exclaimed reflectively, as we descended the mule-path on our return, "what will be the result?"

"The only result will be, as far as I can tell at present, that his evil influence over you will be ended, and you will be free."

"No," she responded, sighing, "there are the others. His arrest would only bring their wrath upon me, for they would believe that I had betrayed them."

"They are spies and enemies of our country and our Queen, Edith," I urged. "To betray them is your duty as an Englishwoman."

"To disclose their secret would mean to me a swift and terrible death," she answered.

I saw that all my efforts at persuasion were unavailing. As we retraced our steps the silence between us was a sad and painful one.

"You do not love me sufficiently to sacrifice all for my sake, Edith," I said at last gravely; "otherwise you would help me to unravel the mystery." We were just descending a narrow winding path to the high road as I spoke, and she halted suddenly in indecision.

"I do love you, Gerald," she cried with sudden resolution. She flung her arms about my neck; she buried her face upon my shoulder; she burst again into tears. "I love you—I have never loved any man except yourself!" she declared passionately, lifting her face to me until our lips met.

"Then will you not make this sacrifice, if you really love me so well?" I asked. "Will you not tell me the truth, and allow me to be your champion?"

She hesitated, and I saw the terrible struggle going on within her.

"Yes," she cried hoarsely at last, "I will—I will! and if they kill me, you will at least know that I loved you, Gerald—that I loved you deeply and dearly!"

"I am convinced of that, darling," I said. "But in this affair your interests are my own. Tell me the truth, and give me freedom of action. If you will, we may yet overthrow our enemies."

For a few moments she did not speak, but sobbed convulsively upon my breast. Then, suddenly holding her breath, she raised her tear-stained face to mine. At last, her love for me conquering all else, she said in a low whisper, as though fearful lest someone should overhear:

"Go to the little village of Feltham, near London, the next station to Twickenham, and find Cypress Cottage. You will discover the secret there."

Feltham! It was the place mentioned by Wolf when I had listened to that conversation in the dingy little café at Batignolles.

"What is there?" I inquired quickly. "What secret does the cottage contain?"

"Have a care in approaching the place. Obtain the assistance of the police—surround it—search it—and see."

"Is there sufficient evidence there to justify the spy's arrest?"

"Certainly. Go and ascertain for yourself. I have betrayed their secret—that is enough. If their revenge falls upon me, then I am content to bear it, Gerald, for your sake. Tell me, however, that you have forgiven me all the past; that you will believe no word of any vile scandal that may be uttered against me by that pair of adventurers. Promise me," she cried in deep earnestness.

"I will believe nothing without proof," I answered, kissing her fondly. "I love you to-day, darling, just as passionately as I did when first we met long ago. I start for London by the Calais express at six to-night, and will at once follow your directions."

"And Bertini, what of him?" she asked in alarm. "He is here, in Bordighera, for an evil purpose, without a doubt. If he knows, I shall be in deadly peril."

"Have no fear," I assured her. "Before I leave he will be in the hands of the police. My plans are already matured." We walked back through the orange-grove down to the hotel hand-in-hand, both resolved to act firmly and fearlessly. As we walked along we seldom spoke with our lips; but our hearts discovered a beautiful language in the silence; and used it.

I loved her and she had proved her affection for me. The betrayal of their secret made it plain that after all she was really mine; for she had now defied her enemies and had placed her life in deadly jeopardy for my sake.

Chapter Thirty Six
The Secret

The village of Feltham is a sleepy little place standing in the centre of a bare, flat country half-way between Twickenham and Staines. It is still quite a rural spot, even though only a league outside the twelve-mile radius.

When I alighted from the train which had brought me down from Waterloo on the third day after leaving the sunshine of the Mediterranean, a cold cast wind was blowing, and the platform was covered with finely powdered snow. I had as companions three plain-clothes officers from Scotland Yard, one of whom was Inspector Chick of the special political branch of the Criminal Investigation Department. Application for assistance to the Commissioner had quickly been responded to, and outside the station we were met by the local plain-clothes constable of the T Division, who had been informed by telegraph of our advent. On my arrival in London that morning I had received a telegram from the police at Bordighera stating that Paolo Bertini was already under arrest.

We at once inquired the whereabouts of Cypress Cottage, and the local officer explained that it was a lonely house, situated nearly three miles away across the plain beyond Ashford, towards the valley of the Thames. We therefore obtained a wagonette at the station inn, and were very soon driving in company over the snow-covered road towards the spot indicated.

About a mile beyond Ashford village Chick, who directed the operations, ordered the coachman to stop, and he and I descended. In the distance we could see outlined against the gloomy, snow-laden sky a small, whitewashed cottage, standing where the road we were traversing made a junction with the high road between Staines and Kingston. This the local constable pointed out as our goal. It was a truly lonely place of residence, for there seemed no other house within a radius of several miles.

Chick, nimble of wit and resourceful, decided that we both should approach the place on foot, investigate, and endeavour to enter upon some pretext, while our three companions, at the moment of our entry, should drive up, leave the wagonette, and surround the place.

As soon as we had arranged our plan of operations, I buttoned my coat and strode on beside the inspector, who now took from his hip pocket a police-revolver and placed it in readiness in the outside pocket of his overcoat. With what resistance we might meet, or what was to be the nature of our discovery, we knew not. The revelation made by Edith was, to say the least of it, one of the strangest in my experience.

At last, after trudging through the snow, which lay thickly upon that road, we reached the cottage, a rather ill-kept place of about six rooms, and walked up the pathway to the door. That it was inhabited was shown by the smoke ascending from one of the chimneys and the stunted geraniums which screened the windows on the inside.

Chick knocked at the door, but for some anxious moments no response was made to his summons. Both of us listened attentively, and distinctly heard the shuffling of feet within, accompanied by an ominous whispering and the low growl of a dog, which was apparently being ordered to remain quiet.

"I hope these good people are not out," Chick exclaimed in a loud voice, with a meaning look. "It's evident we've lost our way."

His words were heard by those within, and apparently at once disarmed suspicion, for in a few seconds the door was thrown open, and a tall, bony-faced woman of middle age confronted us with a look of inquiry. She was grey-haired, with a face which bore evident signs of the burdens of life.

"I'm very sorry to trouble you," explained the inspector. "But we have unfortunately lost our way. We are strangers here. Could you direct us to the road to Littleton?"

"Certainly, gentlemen," she answered. "Take the road along here to the left, and the Littleton road is the first on the left again. You can't mistake it. There's a sign-post up."

Scarcely had the woman finished her sentence, however, before Chick pushed her aside and entered the place, I following close behind. The height of the woman was uncommon, and it occurred to me that she was the mysterious female who had watched me on the Calais boat some months before.

She gave a warning shout, and an ugly bulldog, released from the room beyond, came bounding fiercely upon us. Quick as thought Chick drew his revolver and shot the brute dead. The woman screamed "Murder!" So well-timed was our raid that at this very moment we heard outside the shouts of our companions, telling us that they had surrounded the place.

Those moments were full of wild excitement. From one room to another we dashed quickly, but discovered absolutely nothing to arouse any suspicions until we started to ascend the narrow flight of stairs, when, on doing so, we were suddenly confronted by the dark figure of a man standing at the head, with a revolver pointed straight at us. He spoke no word, but I was amazed to recognise him as the man who had once before made a dastardly attempt upon my life—Rodolphe Wolf! Then I knew that that cottage, as Edith had declared, contained the key to the mystery.

"If you attempt to come up here, I shall shoot!" cried the spy in English.

"I call upon you, in the name of the law, to surrender as my prisoner," responded Chick firmly in his loud, ringing voice. "I don't know your name, but I arrest you all the same."

"His name is Wolf," I explained breathlessly. "He is Rodolphe Wolf, the French spy!"

It seemed that then for the first time did the fellow recognise me, for, peering down, he cried: "It is you—you! Gerald Ingram!"

"Yes," I answered. "Your secret is out! We know the truth! Surrender!"

"Never!" he shouted, standing at bay. "Advance a step, and I'll shoot you both dead."

"The place is surrounded. You cannot escape," Chick replied. "I am an officer of Metropolitan Police, and command you to lay down your weapon."

But he refused, and we both saw that to ascend that narrow staircase in face of his revolver was a very risky proceeding. A dozen times Chick repeated the demand, but the adventurer was nothing daunted. The secret, if anywhere, was in that room, and he was evidently determined to guard it with his life.

Of a sudden the inspector, handing me the revolver, whispered to me to remain there, covering Wolf so as to prevent his escape, and assured me that he would return instantly. He rushed outside, but returned to my side in a few moments.

The vituperation which Rodolphe Wolf heaped upon me I need not repeat. Suffice it to say that during the few minutes which elapsed while we faced one another in that narrow way, each unable to move, he invoked upon my head all the curses of the evil one, vowing a revenge swift and terrible, not only upon myself, but also upon Léonie and Edith.

With a suddenness that startled all of us, however, there was a loud crashing of glass in the room behind him, and, thus taken by surprise, he turned to see how it had been caused.

In an instant Chick had sprung up the stairs, and we were both upon him. The spy fired his revolver, but at random, and the bullet pierced the ceiling. The inspector closed with him in deadly embrace, and a second later was assisted by one of the detectives, who had broken the window and entered the room by a ladder.

The fellow still held his weapon in a desperate grasp, and, having succeeded in pinning Chick against the wall, raised the revolver to his face. At that instant the other officer threw himself upon the pair. Wolf's revolver exploded, but the bullet, instead of entering Chick's head, penetrated the spy's own neck, close behind the ear.

"Dieu!" he shrieked, "I'm shot! I've shot myself!" and as his grip relaxed, the two detectives allowed him to stagger and fall back upon the ground.

In endeavouring to murder the inspector he had inflicted a fatal wound upon himself.

Chick, who had had such a narrow escape from death, only brushed his clothes here and there, and remarked with a smile:

"That was pretty tough, sir, wasn't it?"

Then, ordering his assistant to look after the wounded prisoner, we both searched the room. At first we saw nothing to account for Wolf resisting our progress so desperately. It was a bare place, with a couple of tables, a chair or two, and a few papers that had been strewn about in the struggle. I picked up some. They were copies of the *Figaro*, the *Libre Parole*, and the *Petit Journal*.

But in a corner by the fireplace, I saw a twisted heap of pale-green paper, like ribbon, and a moment later found beneath the table a broken telegraph-receiver. On taking it up I saw upon the small brass plate the words "General Post Office," while near it lay the other portions of the apparatus, which was one of those which print upon the paper ribbon, and are worked by clockwork.

"Hulloa!" cried Chick, crossing the room and bending over the instrument, "what's that?"

"A telegraph-receiver," I replied, at the same moment examining the ceiling of the room and at once discovering two loose ends of wires suspended from a corner.

The instrument had evidently been torn hurriedly from the wires, and an unsuccessful effort made to destroy it and remove all traces of its existence. Wolf, however, had not had time to accomplish his object.

While the wounded man lay groaning, we all proceeded to make further search, and the result of our investigations proved startling indeed. We found that from the room there ran two wires outside, which, after being buried in the garden and along a field on the left, emerged beside one of the telegraph-posts on the main road, and joined one of the lines running to London.

At first we did not realise the extreme importance of our discovery, but from the telegraph-tape found in the room and the deciphers of official despatches which we discovered locked in a cupboard, the amazing truth was disclosed.

The wire so ingeniously tapped was the Queen's private wire, which ran from Windsor Castle, along the road through Staines and Kingston, to the Foreign Office, and over which Her Majesty constantly exchanged views and gave instructions to the Secretary of State for Foreign Affairs and others of her Ministers.

In that comfortless room we found transcripts of all kinds of official despatches and confidential messages, which, although sent in cipher over the wire, had been deciphered by the spies, who had unfortunately also obtained a copy of the secret code in use. The interchanges of views included much that concerned England's attitude in the Boer war, then still in progress, and had without doubt been communicated to the Boers through their Continental agents. Not a single secret of State was safe from those emissaries of our enemies. Thus it was that before the suggestions or instructions of our Sovereign reached Downing Street, they were in the possession of those who aimed at our downfall, for every message transmitted between Windsor and Downing Street, every decision of the Sovereign or of the Cabinet, passed through that inoffensive-looking little instrument, and was registered upon the pale-green snake-like tape before it reached its destination.

A thorough search of the place revealed a perfect system of receiving and deciphering the despatches, all of which had been carefully registered by number in a book and the copies sent to the Quai d'Orsay. Hence it was, of course, that the knowledge of England's decision regarding the attitude to be adopted towards the Transvaal and of our policy in reference to Ceuta, had been obtained before the Marquess had even written his despatch; while the secret instructions which I myself had carried from Downing Street to Paris had actually been known to the spies before the Chief had put his pen to paper. They did not seek to secure the despatches, because they were always in possession of the decisions and line of our diplomacy beforehand.

Having taken possession of the whole of the papers, some of which I was amazed to discover were in Edith's handwriting, we removed the whole into the wagonette, placed a constable in charge of the cottage, and ordered the wounded man's removal to the Cottage Hospital at Staines, as being the nearest institution where he could be treated.

That same evening I had a long interview with the Marquess at his private house, and, assisted by Chick, showed him the papers secured as the result of our investigations. Afterwards, when he had gone through them, I related to him the whole story, concealing nothing. While I sat recounting the incidents a telegram arrived for the inspector, to whom it had been forwarded from Scotland Yard. It was an official police message stating that the prisoner Wolf had died in the hospital at half-past six, having made no statement.

Her Majesty's Minister heard me through, listening with breathless interest, and when I had concluded bestowed upon both of us many complimentary words.

"Both your Queen and your country owe a debt of gratitude to you, Ingram; for by dint of care and perseverance you have rescued us from our secret enemies," he said. "Rest assured that your claim to distinction as an Englishman will not be forgotten."

That night I sent a telegram from Charing Cross announcing to Léonie the death of the spy, which to her meant freedom. The same wire also carried a second message of comfort to Edith, with the promise that I would leave London for Bordighera on the following morning. Then, entering the telephone-box, I had a long conversation with Lord Barmouth, explaining to him the truth, and receiving his heartiest congratulations and best wishes for my happiness on my marriage with Edith Austin, who, he declared, had saved England's prestige.

Chapter Thirty Seven
Conclusion

Two days later I was again seated with Edith under the olives on the sunny hillside behind Bordighera.

I had told her all that had happened, explained what we had discovered in that upper room at Cypress Cottage, and demanded to know the reason why some of the copies of those messages were in her own handwriting. Our hands were clasped in fervent affection, and now, fearing not the revenge of either Wolf or Bertini, she revealed to me the plain and ghastly truth in regard to her connection with that band of unscrupulous spies who had sought to bring about England's downfall.

"I first knew Paolo Bertini when I was at school at St. Leonards, six years ago. He was then our Italian master, and we girls admired him, and were one and all enamoured of our teacher, as school-girls so often are. He and I became good friends, and one day he urged me to steal from another girl's locker a letter addressed to her by her father, a high official at the War Office. He wished to see it, and I gave it to him in ignorance that the real reason was that he desired the signature for purposes of forgery. I knew it afterwards, but he threatened if I exposed him that he would denounce me as a thief. From that moment he held me in his power, gradually drawing me into the net he so carefully spread in order to secure my assistance in his nefarious schemes of espionage in conjunction with Rodolphe Wolf. Although she knew that upon leaving school I should be comparatively wealthy, my aunt, who, as you know, is eccentric, insisted that I should be taught some means of earning my own livelihood. At Bertini's demand I chose telegraphy, and when I became proficient the wires from Windsor were tapped, and I was compelled to act as telegraphist in that lonely, unsuspicious-looking cottage, which became the headquarters of French spies in England. My many compulsory visits to London often aroused my aunt's suspicion, but I always managed to receive convenient invitations from relatives or old schoolfellows, until at last I succeeded in convincing her that all was well. Ah!" she added, her bright, honest eyes turned away over the broad Mediterranean, where the sun was going down in golden glory behind the dark purple rock of Ventimiglia, "I have suffered, Gerald, quite as bitterly as yourself. I was held in that man's power irrevocably, unable to extricate myself from the bond, unable to give you the least intimation of the evil influences always working against you, unable to accept your love. From the moment when, as a school-girl, I stole that letter, until to-day, my enemies implicated me more and more deeply, until to draw back became utterly impossible. I was their catspaw—held to them by fear of exposure and imprisonment, or even of death, if I disclosed their secret."

"I understand it all now, darling. All is plain, and our estrangement has only rendered our love the more perfect."

"You are generous to forgive, Gerald," she answered in a low, faltering tone. "But I swear it was not my fault. In my ignorance of the world and its ways I took one false step long ago while still at school, and then could not draw back. I became a traitress and a spy!"

"And what of Yolande de Foville?" I inquired. "She was one of us, and in the service of France," my love replied. "Like myself, she also was held in bondage. She wished to marry the young Count de Hochberg, an aide-de-camp of the Emperor William; but Bertini, who was in love with her, refused to allow her. It was because of jealousy that he made the ingenious attempt upon her life by the same means that he did later upon an Englishman in Paris, named Payne, who recognised him and suspected him of espionage. He is in possession of the knowledge of some subtle alkaloid poison, which he once boasted in my hearing to be even more deadly than the Indian Bikh poison, and unknown in the science of toxicology."

"And where is Yolande now?"

"In Rome. Having obtained some secret of Bertini's past, and a knowledge of his attempt upon her life, she defied him, and, freeing herself from the secret service, married de Hochberg only a fortnight ago. She is spending her honeymoon in southern Italy."

"She is married!" I exclaimed, surprised.

"Yes. Her declarations of love for you were all false, made at the instigation of those schemers, Wolf and Bertini, who intended that she should worm from you certain diplomatic secrets. She hated her position, but, like myself, was powerless and compelled to submit."

"To you alone, my love, is due the breaking-up of this ingenious band of spies, and the frustrating of the great conspiracy against England, which has, it seems, been fostered and aided by certain of the Powers."

"And have you really perfect confidence in my honour and purity, Gerald?" she asked again, looking at me dubiously.

"I love you, darling," I answered, bending down once more to kiss her beautiful mouth; "and that my confidence in you remains unshaken and is the same to-day as it was long ago in Scotland when I first declared my love, will be shown by our marriage, which nothing can now prevent. We are about to come into our kingdom."

"But that letter," she faltered, still dubious—"that letter of the Princess!"

"I do not love her, dearest. I have never loved her," I declared earnestly. "I am yours, and yours alone."

She turned quickly, kissing me fondly, and shedding tears of joy. We were both free at last, and that peaceful hour of our new-found happiness was full of that ecstasy which comes to man and woman only once in a lifetime, at the moment when two hearts first beat in unison.

But why need I dwell upon the supreme happiness of that calm and glorious evening high up above the tideless sea, except to say that it was then each read the other's heart openly and truly; then that we discovered how best to interchange a perfect and fadeless affection.

And you ask how this strange romance of an Englishman in his Sovereign's service ended? Well, Edith became my own queen within two months. We were married in London, and since my promotion and transfer to the Embassy at St. Petersburg our lives have been idyllic in their happiness. Edith likes the Russian capital, where everyone is so hospitable and the fêtes are never-ending. I also prefer it to the artificiality and glare of Paris which is to me a city of bitter memories.

As for the Princess, she is one of Edith's warmest friends. She was married four months ago to Prince Stroganoff, a charming Russian whom everyone knows in Moscow and the capital, and who lives at the great Stroganoff Palace in St. Petersburg, where we are frequent visitors Lord Barmouth's failing health compelled him to retire from the Diplomatic Service after the lamented death of Her Majesty, and he is now living in London once more, after so many years of compulsory exile; while the World, a few weeks ago, announced Sibyl's engagement to the Hon. Jack Willoughby, who is well known as a rising politician and Member for one of the Metropolitan Boroughs. Her ladyship has written to me, declaring it to be a most excellent match.

Bertini, the spy and traitor, having been condemned by the military court in Milan to imprisonment for life, is at this moment languishing in the convict prison at Orbetello. Assuredly Europe is well rid of such an ingenious and unscrupulous scoundrel.

Nothing appeared in the English newspapers regarding Wolf's death, beyond the statement that he had committed suicide rather than suffer arrest. For what reason the police raided Cypress Cottage never leaked out. It was kept a close secret, in order that the discovery of the headquarters of the French spies should not create undue public alarm. Hence all of the foregoing incidents long remained a secret chapter of England's history; and the gigantic conspiracy on the part of our nation's enemies is here related for the first time by one who was himself a principal actor in the stirring drama of diplomacy, and who has been fortunate enough to secure peace, happiness, and the love of a gentle and happy woman.